Facing the Challenge

*Responses to the Report of
the South Commission*

The South Centre

The South Centre publishes, and distributes to South countries, information, strategic analyses and recommendations on international economic, social and political matters.

The independence and "South" perspectives of the Centre have led to its work being taken into consideration by governments and organizations of the developing countries. Indeed the South Centre, like its predecessor the South Commission, enjoys support and co-operation from governments of South countries and is in regular working contact with the Non-Aligned Movement, the Group of 77 and the Group of 15.

The South Centre's base in Geneva has a very small staff and its studies and position papers are prepared by drawing on the technical and intellectual capacities that exist both within the governments and institutions and among the individuals of the South. Through working group sessions and wide consultations which involve experts from different parts of the South, and sometimes from the North, common problems of the South are studied and experience and knowledge are shared.

South Centre
Chemin du Champ d'Anier 17
Case Postale 228
1211 Geneva 19
Switzerland

THE SOUTH CENTRE

Facing the Challenge

Responses to the Report of

the South Commission

Foreword by Julius K. Nyerere

ZED BOOKS

London & New Jersey

in association with

Facing the Challenge was first published by
Zed Books Ltd, 57 Caledonian Road, London N1 9BU
and 165 First Avenue, Atlantic Highlands,
New Jersey 07716, USA in association with the
South Centre, Chemin du Champ d'Anier 17,
case postale 228, 1211 Geneva 19,
Switzerland, in 1993

Cover designed by Andrew Corbett

Printed and bound in the United Kingdom by
Biddles Ltd, Guildford and King's Lynn

A catalogue record for this book is available from
the British Library

US cataloging-in-publication data is available from the
Library of Congress

ISBN 1 85649 177 3 Hb
ISBN 1 85649 178 1 Pb

Contents

Note: The published contributions of the following persons are translations of the original submissions: Samir Amin, Ahmed Ben Salah, Christian Comeliau, Carlos Pérez del Castillo, Edgar Pisani and Alicia Puyana.

List of Acronyms

ACP	African, Caribbean and Pacific States
AIDS	Acquired Immune Deficiency Syndrome
APEC	Asia Pacific Economic Co-operation
ASEAN	Association of South East Asian Nations
BOOT	build-own-operate-transfer
CARDI	Caribbean Agricultural Research and Development Institute
CET	common external tariff
CFCs	chlorofluorocarbons
CGIAR	Consultative Group on International Agricultural Research
CIA	Central Intelligence Agency
CMEA	Council for Mutual Economic Assistance
DAC	Development Assistance Committee (of the OECD countries)
DAWN	Development Alternatives with Women for a New Era
EAI	Enterprise for the Americas Initiative
EBRD	European Bank for Reconstruction and Development
EC	European Community
ECA	Economic Commission for Africa
ECLAC	Economic Commission for Latin America and the Caribbean
ECOWAS	Economic Community of West African States
EEC	European Economic Community
FAO	Food and Agriculture Organization of the United Nations
FDI	foreign direct investment
Fonplata	River Plate Basin Development Fund
GATT	General Agreement on Tariffs and Trade
GDP	gross domestic product
GNP	gross national product
GSP	Generalized System of Preferences
GSTP	Global System of Trade Preferences

IBRD	International Bank for Reconstruction and Development
IDA	International Development Association
IIASA	International Institute for Applied Systems Analysis
ILO	International Labour Office
IMF	International Monetary Fund
IMR	infant mortality rate
LDCs	Least Developed Countries
LDR	Less Developed Region
Mercosur	Southern Cone Common Market (in Latin America)
MFA	Multi-fibre Agreement
NAFTA	North American Free Trade Agreement
NATO	North Atlantic Treaty Organization
NGO	non-governmental organization
NICs	newly industrialized countries
NIEO	New International Economic Order
NSC	National Security Council (USA)
NSD	North-South dialogue
NTBs	non-tariff barriers
ODA	official development assistance
ODI	Overseas Development Institute
OECD	Organization for Economic Co-operation and Development
OPEC	Organization of Petroleum Exporting Countries
R&D	research and development
RMDBs	regional multilateral development banks
S&T	science and technology
SAARC	South Asian Association for Regional Co-operation
SAL	structural adjustment lending
SDRs	Special Drawing Rights
SELA	Sistema Económico Latinoamericano (Latin American Economic System)
TNC	transnational corporation
TVET	technical/vocational education and training
UNCED	United Nations Conference on Environment and Development
UNCTAD	United Nations Conference on Trade and Development
UNESCO	United Nations Educational, Scientific and Cultural Organization
UNFPA	United Nations Population Fund
UNICEF	United Nations Children's Fund
UNIDO	United Nations Industrial Development Organization
UNU	United Nations University

The Contributors

The brief details given here about the various contributors refer to posts held or activities carried out at the time of writing.

Y. Seyyid Abdulai
   Director General of the OPEC Fund for International Development, Vienna, Austria.

Samir Amin
   Director, Third World Forum, Dakar, Senegal.

Ahmed Ben Salah
   International Foundation for Development Alternatives, Nyon, Switzerland.

Michel Camdessus
   Managing Director, International Monetary Fund, Washington, DC, USA.

Bernard Chidzero
   Senior Minister of Finance, Economic Planning and Development, Zimbabwe.

Noam Chomsky
   Professor of Linguistics and Philosophy, Massachusetts Institute of Technology, Cambridge, Massachusetts, USA.

Christian Comeliau
   Professor, Institut universitaire d'études du développement, Geneva, Switzerland.

Barber Conable
   President, World Bank, Washington, DC, USA.

K.K.S. Dadzie
   Secretary-General of the United Nations Conference on Trade and Development, Geneva, Switzerland.

John Kenneth Galbraith
   Professor of Economics, Harvard University, Cambridge, Massachusetts, USA.

Johan Galtung
   Olof Palme Peace Professor, Swedish Council for Research in the Humanities and Social Sciences, Stockholm, Sweden.

José Goldemberg
   Secretary of State for Science and Technology, Brazil.

Godfrey Gunatilleke
   Executive Vice-Chairman, Marga Institute, Colombo, Sri Lanka.

Nurul Islam
Senior Policy Advisor, International Food Policy Research Institute, Washington, DC, USA.

Abdul Aziz Jalloh
Senior Economist, Islamic Development Bank, Jeddah, Saudi Arabia.

Rajni Kothari
Professor, New Delhi University, New Delhi, India.

Percy S. Mistry
Senior Fellow, International Finance, University of Oxford, Oxford, United Kingdom.

Saburo Okita
Chairman, Institute for Domestic and International Policy Studies, Tokyo, Japan.

Carlos Pérez del Castillo
Permanent Secretary, Sistema Económico Latinoamericano, Caracas, Venezuela.

Hilkka Pietilä
Honorary President of the Finnish United Nations Association, Helsinki, Finland.

Edgar Pisani
President, Institut du Monde Arabe; Director, *L' Événement Européen*, Paris, France.

Alicia Puyana
Director, Centro Regional de Estudios del Tercer Mundo, Bogota, Colombia.

Delphin G. Rwegasira
Director, Development Research and Policy Department, African Development Bank, Abidjan, Côte d'Ivoire.

Arjun K. Sengupta
Ambassador of India to the European Economic Community, Brussels, Belgium.

John W. Sewell and Nicole Melcher
Overseas Development Council, Washington, DC, USA.

Maurice F. Strong
Secretary-General, United Nations Conference on Environment and Development, Geneva, Switzerland.

Tamas Szentes
Professor, Budapest University of Economic Science, Budapest, Hungary.

Immanuel Wallerstein,
Professor, State University of New York at Binghamton, New York, USA.

Foreword

When it was launched in August 1990, *The Challenge to the South* — the Report of the South Commission — offered a comprehensive analysis of the problems facing the countries of the South. On that basis it then advanced a framework for action to help these countries in their ambition to maintain their political and economic independence, and to improve the lives and living conditions of their peoples.

The Report was the result of three years' deliberations and work by a Commission composed of 28 individuals from different parts of the South. It was the first comprehensive study carried out by a group broadly representative of the spectrum of political views and development experience which exists in the South. The Report reflects the shared views of those who took part in the Commission's labours and is a collective statement.

The South Commission adopted an integrated approach to the challenges faced by the developing countries. Thus it took account of the interrelated nature of the problems which face them, linking together matters of national development, South-South co-operation, North-South relations, and the global system.

The Commission was aware that its Report would meet with criticism, in particular that its analysis had not dealt adequately with major global changes currently taking place in 1990. This was unavoidable; the Report had been largely completed by the end of 1989, and the Commission was no better than the rest of the world in anticipating the full extent of the far-ranging changes which began in that year.

Ironically, the public launch of *The Challenge to the South* in Caracas on 3 August 1990 coincided with the invasion of Kuwait.

At its last meeting in Arusha, in October 1990, the South Commission decided that a companion volume of commentaries on its Report should be prepared. By giving renowned individuals, experts and political figures concerned with development the opportunity to comment publicly on the Report, the Commission felt that its work could be supplemented and expanded. We hoped that the placing together of such comments in a single volume would also contribute to and encourage a continuing debate and action regarding its recommendations.

At the time of printing this volume, *The Challenge to the South* has been in circulation for three years. It will soon have been translated and published in 20 languages. When it was debated by governments in the United Nations Economic and Social Council in July 1991, the Report was also welcomed by the spokespersons from the North. This, however, was essentially because of its frank analysis of the situation within the developing countries and because of its stress on these countries' responsibility for their own development. Yet in the South Commission's view, the fact that it devoted primary attention to national development and South-South co-operation was in no way intended to diminish the importance of the other key areas of its analysis. These are North-South relations, the effects of the manner in which the so-called "international order" operates and the implications of the traditional development agenda.

In order to provide the reader with a useful frame of reference, this volume begins with an overview and summary of *The Challenge to the South*. This was initially prepared and published in 1990, as a pamphlet, for wider distribution to those who may not have had access to the Report.

The contributions to this volume were selected from among a large number of comments and reactions received by the South Centre. In publishing this volume we have three central aims in view. First, it is hoped that the contributions will encourage further consideration by people and governments, in both the South and the North, of the analyses and propositions contained in *The Challenge to the South*. It is also hoped that the analyses and reflections will further stimulate more sustained and strenuous efforts by different sectors in the South to develop "South" perspectives on national and international issues. But the final and more important wish must be that the countries of the South find the grounds for South-South co-operation sufficiently compelling as to strengthen their joint efforts to help resolve national, regional and international problems and conflicts.

Julius K. Nyerere
Dar-es-Salaam
March 1993

I. AN OVERVIEW AND SUMMARY OF THE SOUTH COMMISSION REPORT

1. THE SOUTH AND ITS TASKS

Three and a half billion people, three quarters of all humanity, live in the developing countries, the South. These countries vary greatly in size, in levels of development, in economic, social and political structures. Yet they share a fundamental trait: they exist on the periphery of the developed countries of the North. Most of their people are poor; their economies are mostly weak and defenceless; they are generally powerless in the world arena.

In the period following the end of the Second World war until the end of the 1970s, a great many of the countries of the South registered impressive social and economic gains. This gave rise to the expectation that the North-South divide in wealth and power could be bridged.

The 1980s belied that expectation. They have been rightly described as a lost decade for development. While the industrial countries recovered from the recession of the early 1980s and by 1990 had enjoyed seven years of uninterrupted growth, most countries of the South faced an acute and continuing development crisis. Per capita income and living standards were sharply squeezed. A large number of countries were driven to the edge of collapse. Their people's privations were acute and prolonged. Nations floundered in their efforts to struggle out of unprecedented difficulties. Hope gave way to despair, as confidence ebbed in the ability to recover their momentum of growth. Destabilizing and potentially explosive social and economic tensions rose.

The crisis was mainly the outcome of adverse turns in the world economy, which developing countries are powerless to control. Though it brought to light weaknesses in the economic structures and development strategies of countries of the South, the South's setbacks were largely the product of the contractionary policies followed by the industrial countries and the sudden drying-up of capital flows. The adjustment policies imposed on many developing countries by international financial institutions intensified deflationary pressures and added to the hardships. Yet the world community signally failed to take the enlightened measures that would have hastened an end to the predicament in which so many of the world's nations and people were trapped for so long.

The South Commission's task was to propose ways by which the South could surmount this crisis, resume growth and undertake a process of sustained development. We are convinced that the South can overcome its present malaise and reach out to a better future for its people. Our report is intended as a contribution to the South's endeavours to respond to this challenge.

We do not pretend that it will be easy. Success is not assured; it is conditional on what the countries of the South do, individually and together. But it is our view that the task of regenerating the South can be accomplished, given vision, determination and unrelenting effort.

The challenge to the nations of the South is to mobilize and deploy their resources more effectively – nationally and collectively – to energize their development, to draw strength from joint undertakings, to exploit global opportunities, and to make the international system more responsive to their interests.

Policies will need to be changed, institutions reformed and new mechanisms created. The tasks are formidable, but the South has to face them – or face further marginalization and greater impoverishment.

The World in the 1990s

In its new strategies, the South must take account of the unfavourable trends in the external economic environment:

- World commodity markets remain depressed, adversely affecting a large number of developing countries which derive a high proportion of their export earnings from commodities.

- Developing countries' exports continue to face formidable barriers in the markets of developed countries, including discriminatory protectionism in violation of internationally accepted principles.

- International efforts to deal with the debt overhang of the 1980s have met with refusal by the creditors to bear an equitable share of the burden; a revival of growth in the indebted countries is still a distant prospect.

- International interest rates remain unusually high, greatly adding to the cost of debt servicing for developing countries.

- Many developing countries – and the South as a whole – have become net exporters of capital to the rich countries of the North. Even the IMF and the World Bank are now net recipients of resources from the developing countries.

This sharp deterioration in the external environment has taken place in the context of radical readjustments and structural changes in the world economy, with far-reaching implications for global economic interdependence and for the position of the South. This transformation has involved essentially:

- The rapid expansion of transnational enterprises as the main producers of goods and services for world trade, with a growing proportion of international transactions taking place among branches of the same firm or among related firms.

- A related expansion of the role of private banks in creating international liquidity, which has become uncoupled from the growth of international trade in goods and services.

- A resulting excessive growth of indebtedness in both developed and developing economies, including the public and the private sectors, and domestic as well as foreign debt.

- Changes in the relative importance of factors of production which imply a move away from material/energy/labour-intensive products and processes and towards knowledge-intensive products and processes; this trend has meant a loss of comparative advantage for developing countries in a number of traditional export products.

- Related changes in the importance of sectors of production in the developed countries, implying a shift away from agriculture and industry and towards services, and rapidly expanding internationalization in the production of, and employment and trade in, services.

- Growing instability, unpredictability and fluctuation in the international economy, notably in interest and exchange rates, and growing uncertainty in capital markets.

- Significant institutional changes: at the national level, increasing deregulation, privatization and reliance on market forces; at the international level, the collapse of the Bretton Woods monetary system and the erosion of the multilateral trading system embodied in GATT.

These trends may not be transient. Indeed, unless the world community takes determined action, the international environment in the 1990s is likely to remain fundamentally hostile to the development prospects of developing countries in several respects.

Under such conditions, the South cannot prudently depend on the North to be an engine for its own growth, as it was able to do to some extent in earlier decades. Growth impulses from the North have become markedly weaker, and their transmission is obstructed by restrictive measures in the North. An improvement of the international environment through concerted intervention at the global level can undoubtedly be of major help. However, the South must recognize that even then its basic growth impulses must be found in its own economies, and that self-reliance, national and collective, is an imperative in the new global context.

Flaws in the Development Experience

While the South's misfortunes in the past decade were largely the outcome of hostile external factors, the lack of resilience shown by many economies points to defects in the patterns of development and policy frameworks in these countries. These have to be corrected as part of the difficult process of becoming more self-reliant.

With a few exceptions, post-1945 economic growth in the South did not lead to an adequate transformation and increased flexibility in economic structures, or to greater equity and social cohesion. It led more generally to greater inequalities, unplanned and usually chaotic urban-ization, the co-existence of small enclaves of modern industry and large semi-traditional sectors, continued rigidity in trade patterns, increased import demand combined with lagging export capacity, and much environmental damage. Most countries also failed to raise the social and economic status of women.

The declared aim of development was to combat poverty, ignorance and disease. Almost inevitably the countries of the South adopted as models the countries that seemed to have eradicated these evils – the developed countries. They overlooked the poverty, suffering and injustice that had accompanied the early economic advances in those countries, as well as the very different circumstances in which the South was having to work for its objectives. Placing too much confidence in the trickle-down effect of economic growth, the South took too little direct action to raise the income and productivity of the poor or to promote a fairer distribution of the benefits of growth. In particular, peasant agriculture was often neglected, with especially harmful results in the least developed countries.

Industrial development tended to meet the demands of the higher income groups. This led to greater dependence on imports, while export expansion and technical advance were neglected. The labour force swelled rapidly with population growth, but capital-intensive patterns of development and the use of inappropriate technologies created too few jobs. Environmental protection, particularly the need to conserve non-renewable resources, was also often neglected.

Scientific and technological dependence on the North became more pronounced since there was insufficient recognition of the role of science and technology in development and inadequate spending on research and development. The result was heightened vulnerability to external shocks. A lack of emphasis on self-reliance in many cases led to the ultimate unsustainability of the growth process.

Insufficient attention was paid to the cultural dimensions of development and to cultural enrichment through mass participation.

Uncritical imitation of Western models led to a failure to benefit from the South's reserves of traditional wisdom, creativity and enterprise.

Overcentralization in administration and planning was responsible for delays in decision-making and for inefficient management of public enterprises, and inhibited popular participation in development. Lack of democracy, corruption, and militarization further eroded the economic and political bases for development.

It is also now clear that inherent in the pattern of development generally adopted was a strong tendency towards the aggravation of inequality, despite the emergence of a middle class in several countries. The retrenchment forced on many countries in the 1980s aggravated the injustices arising from the attempt to develop along an inappropriate path, often creating explosive social conditions. The worst sufferers – and almost invariably the least able to protest or protect their interests – were usually the most vulnerable of the poor: women, children and other socially disadvantaged groups.

Grounds for Confidence

The setbacks of the past decade were severe and affected the large majority of the countries of the South. They dented some of the hard-won gains of previous decades, and exposed the flaws of past approaches. But the achievements of the past are nevertheless heartening evidence of what the South can accomplish.

These achievements are many, varied and substantial. The South has shown that, given a less unpropitious international environment, it can substantially increase savings and investment, accelerate growth and improve social conditions. The high rates of growth the South recorded in the 1950s, 1960s and 1970s helped to lay valuable economic foundations – roads, communications, energy supplies, irrigation systems – which are substantial assets for the future. National economies were diversified to varying degrees. Advances were made in modernizing agriculture and expanding food production. There were some notable successes in industrial transformation, in mastering technology and in competing in world markets.

The investment in human capital was also remarkable in its impact, as evidenced in longer life expectancy, lower infant mortality, improved literacy and higher levels of education and skills. Its people, now healthier and better educated, are the South's greatest resource.

These successes were not evenly spread on the map of the South. In most countries they did not create enough resilience to prevent a slide backwards when external conditions suddenly worsened. Nevertheless, the total picture must give the South confidence in its capabilities – and inspire hope for the future.

There are also other factors to buttress confidence. New sources of economic vigour have appeared within the South – in the form of financial resources, technological capacity, management skills and entrepreneurial strength. There is now a wider range of relevant development experience to draw on. The progress made by the South's two most populous countries – China and India – pursuing distinctive development paths, is instructive. So too is the success achieved by some countries in East and South-East Asia, following a different strategy and giving more emphasis to science and technology. They were all better equipped to face up to the global economic downturn of the 1980s. There are also achievements – economic and social – in other countries of the South. All these experiences offer important lessons to the rest of the South. Equally, there are lessons to be learned from the failures – mistakes that others need not repeat. There is a new flexibility in the South, a more mature, pragmatic approach to planning and policy which is the result of learning from these experiences.

Global trends

Globally too, there are some encouraging trends. The tensions between East and West have eased. The more co-operative relationship between the superpowers could help to secure a higher place for development in world concerns. A part of the resources released by disarmament – finance, technological know-how and research skills – may be made available for global purposes. The reforms in the USSR and Eastern Europe, in so far as they lead to a rise in these countries' living standards, cannot but benefit the global economy. However, there is a danger that, in their preoccupation with Eastern Europe, Western developed countries may further downgrade the priority they attach to international action to promote development in the South.

In recent years, concern about the global environment has significantly increased. Simultaneously, there has been a widening recognition that poverty is a primary cause of environmental damage in the South and that efforts to overcome poverty are vital to world environmental security. Other issues that have recently become prominent – particularly the threat posed by the international illicit traffic in drugs – also call for global action across the North-South divide.

Another trend may also point to the wisdom of greater global co-operation to combat underdevelopment. In the past few years there has been growing turmoil in the South. This, clearly, has had various causes, but an important factor is the frustration of expectations, particularly among the young, where economic stagnation or retrenchment have severely narrowed opportunities. Turbulence in the South has so far been a domestic phenomenon, but there is no guarantee that it will be permanently quarantined within national boundaries. There is a growing realization that turbulence in developing countries, caused or aggravated by poverty, unemployment, and frustration among the youth, might be fraught with dangers to international stability.

The world has become increasingly interdependent and, in a sense, integrated. But it has not evolved a system for dealing equitably with this increasing integration. The South is still in a position of subordination and dependence, and this prevents the effective management of the new global challenges. A reform of the international system – particularly of international arrangements governing the flows of trade, money, finance and technology – is therefore an essential need of the world as we approach the 21st century. A world in which one fourth of the people are affluent and three fourths are deprived hardly offers an enduring basis for peace and security. This is all the more true when the disparities between rich and poor are becoming wider. The imperatives for moving towards a less unequal world are steadily becoming stronger.

The Vision: People-centred and Self-reliant Development in an Interdependent World

The South is part of a world whose interdependence is constantly widening and deepening, and our vision is of a co-operative world made more secure for all its people.

We would like to see a truly interdependent world organized on the basis of human equality and human variety in pursuit of jointly defined common purposes; where there is peace, security and dignity for all persons and all peoples; where all can take advantage of scientific and technological advances; and where the world's resources are used in a sustainable manner to meet the needs of all rather than to satisfy the narrow interests of a few, so that poverty can be abolished without damage to the environment.

Our vision is for the South to achieve a people-centred development: a form of development that is self-reliant, equitable, participatory and sustainable. We envisage a process of development achieved through the active participation of the people, in their own interests as they see them, relying primarily on their own resources, and carried out under their own control.

The objective should be not only to secure economic growth but also to ensure that it benefits the mass of the people. Development must be conceived of as a process which enables human beings to realize their potential, build self-confidence and lead lives of dignity and fulfilment. Development does, of course, require sustained economic growth, for only in an expanding economy can poverty be eradicated. But development cannot be measured solely by the growth of the gross national product. What is produced, how and at what social and environmental cost, by whom and for whom – all this is just as important as a higher GNP. Hence, in conditions of mass poverty, priority must be given to policies aimed at ending poverty, increasing productive employment, and ensuring that the basic needs of all the people are met, with any surplus being fairly shared. Such goods and services as food, shelter, basic education and health facilities, and clean water should be accessible to all and without discrimination on grounds of gender, race, colour or religion. In addition, our vision includes a democratic form of government, together with its supporting individual freedoms of speech, organization and information, as well as an effective system of justice which protects all the people from actions in breach of just laws which are known and publicly accepted.

We have necessarily approached the problems of the South from the point of view of the South. But we do not see its interests as being in permanent conflict with those of the North. Nor does the self-reliance we counsel for the South imply a turning away from the rest of the world. We do not believe autarky is a viable course for any or all of its countries. Our call for self-reliance is a call to make more effective use of the South's own resources – human, physical, financial and organizational – as the basis of its development.

Our vision goes beyond the South to embrace the whole world. We look to a world in which there is no "South" and no "North"; in which there is not one part rich, developed and dominating while the other is poor, underdeveloped and dominated.

The Setting: The Development Crisis and the Retreat from Multilateralism

How insecure the world is for most of its people was amply demonstrated by the acute crisis which engulfed large parts of the South in the 1980s. The impact on the South of policies followed by the major industrial countries has been magnified by the skewed orientation of the international economic system. And the economic plight of the countries of the South puts them in a subservient position in the world system. They are denied any significant say in decisions about the operation of the world economy, which are more and more concentrated in a few powerful countries of the

North. In addition, the revolutionary advances in science and technology are being monopolized by the transnationals of the North.

The drain of resources from the South on debt transactions began in 1984 and still continues. It accounted for the loss of $163 billion in the five years 1984-1988. Equally damaging – and even more widespread in its impact – is the drain of capital attributable to the worsening of the terms of trade.

These trends have combined to produce a virtual breakdown of the economic order in many countries of the South. There has been nothing to halt their slide into deeper debility and instability. A number of them have shown alarming signs of social stress. In many countries poverty has been a factor in the rise in violence.

The early post-war decades had witnessed a tentative recognition of shared responsibility for action to reduce world poverty. There was some evolution towards a global development consensus and a framework of multilateral support for the efforts of developing countries to lift themselves out of poverty. The creation of IDA at the World Bank, the establishment of UNCTAD, IFAD and the regional development banks, and the provision of new facilities at the IMF were among the developments that signalled this movement.

The increasing deprivation and disarray in a large part of the world in the 1980s should have moved the world community to add to these defences. Instead there has been a retreat from global co-operation towards greater dominance in the world economic system by those with economic power. Multilateral institutions have been weakened by being denied the resources they need; they have also been made instruments for advancing in the South the ideological objectives of dominant countries in the North.

The UN General Assembly held a special session on Development Co-operation in April 1990 while we were finalizing our Report. Its results represent a limited response to the call of developing countries for a revitalization of international co-operation for development. We welcome the recognition given in the declaration adopted at the session to many of the urgent problems facing developing countries. We regret, however, that such agreement as there was, was more on what to say than on what to do. It did not translate itself into concrete commitments to action, and no follow-up mechanism was agreed.

Debt and adjustment

The North's response to the debt crisis shows how far the world has moved away from a co-operative approach to the problems of the South. Overborrowing by countries of the South was matched by overlending by banks and financial institutions in the North in creating the debt crisis. This called for a solution jointly worked out between the indebted countries and their creditors. But the North has refused to consider a solution that would be fair to both parties. It has forced debtor countries through the international financial institutions to give primacy to the payment of debt service over every other economic or social objective, including the protection of the living standards of their poorest people.

The South was compelled to adjust not merely to sharply reduced capital flows, with banks refusing new loans, but also to much higher debt service payments. These were the direct product of policies – notably monetarist policies – which were adopted by industrial countries to curb inflation and which led to a dramatic increase in interest rates. The resulting recession squeezed demand for the South's products and depressed commodity prices. The combined effect was to push up debt service ratios in debtor countries, which had to set aside a much larger proportion of their export earnings to pay their creditors.

Closely linked to the debt issue is that of structural adjustment and the tighter conditionality imposed on countries driven by balance-of-payments difficulties caused by external factors to seek IMF support. The need for economic reforms to bring their payments into greater balance and help them recover their growth momentum is not in dispute, nor that such changes must involve a measure of belt-tightening and discomfort. But the policy package the IMF has made its standard recipe has been based on a doctrinaire belief in the efficacy of market forces. Financial liberalization in conditions of inflation has aggravated inflation. Import liberalization when foreign exchange was extremely scarce has enlarged payments deficits, leading to steeper devaluations than would otherwise have been necessary. Pressure to expand exports – exerted simultaneously on a number of developing countries exporting the same commodity – has led to oversupply, causing prices and earnings to sag for all of them. While lip service has been paid to the need for adjustment to lead to growth, adjustment has invariably stifled growth and, by causing investment to contract, jeopardized future growth. The drive to secure financial balance in the short run has been at the cost of output and employment as well as of consumption. The poorest people have borne the greatest hardship.

What is abundantly clear is that the North has used the plight of developing countries to strengthen its dominance and its influence over the development paths of the South. Developing countries have been forced to reshape their economic policies to make them compatible with the North's design. While adjustment is pressed on them, countries in the North with massive payments imbalances are immune from any pressure to adjust, and free to follow policies that deepen the South's difficulties. The most powerful countries in the North have become a *de facto* board of management for the world economy, protecting their interests and imposing their will on the South. The governments of the South are then left to face the wrath, even the violence, of their own people, whose standards of living are being depressed for the sake of preserving the present patterns of operation of the world economy.

The science and technology challenge

Science and technology have been a key determinant of economic progress throughout history, and the speed of scientific and technological progress in recent decades has further enhanced their role as agents of change. But the South can take advantage of advances in this field – and avoid becoming further marginalized within the world economy – only to the extent that it has the capacity to absorb them and adapt them to the needs of its people. The development of scientific and technological institutions and manpower must be an important objective in national and collective planning for the future.

The South's progress in this sphere is also critically dependent on international arrangements. Developing countries are almost entirely buyers of technology in the international market, in which the sellers enjoy unchallenged dominance. Moreover, the present world intellectual property system – of patents, trademarks and copyrights – gives the North's sellers of technology monopolistic rights in the markets of the South. If the South is to benefit from the advances of world science and technology, this state of affairs needs to be changed to its advantage.

The South Commission Report

The South Commission's Report, compiled after three years of study and discussion, outlines the directions in which we believe the South should move to make its future more secure.

We address our recommendations primarily to the nations of the South. The responsibility for securing its development rests with the South, and it is its own efforts that will primarily determine its success or failure.

The South is not, however, a separate entity; it is a part of an interconnected world, with a multitude of links to the North, and it is constantly influenced by what happens in the North. Northern markets, technology and finance will continue to be important to the South's progress. And policies followed in the North will continue to have an impact on the South's performance. Some of our recommendations are therefore addressed to the North.

A three-part agenda

We have divided the agenda of action we propose for the South into three parts. The first concerns domestic policy within the national setting. The diversity of economies within the South precludes a uniform strategy, yet certain principles and objectives need to guide the development courses of all countries. We address the imperatives of collective self-reliance in the second part. A much more vigorous drive to strengthen co-operation among the countries of the South is of supreme importance in the present circumstances to reinforce their capacities for growth. The South's solidarity is equally essential for improving its position within the world system of economic relationships – the third part of the South's agenda. Our recommendations are designed as a comprehensive approach to the problems which the South – its countries and its people – have to overcome.

2. THE NATIONAL DIMENSION: SELF-RELIANT AND PEOPLE-CENTRED DEVELOPMENT

The South cannot count on a significant improvement in the international economic environment in the 1990s. With growth impulses in the North having only a weak resonance in the South, growth must be generated from within the economies of the South. Maximum self-reliance must therefore be the keynote of its renewed development effort. If only for this reason, the new development strategies cannot be a replica of those of the past. Pursuing a self-reliant and people-centred development strategy will require the South to draw lessons from the limitations and failures of past efforts. Their weaknesses need to be remedied by fundamental changes in approach and priorities.

An important lesson from experience is that satisfying basic needs should have priority, both on grounds of equity and to sustain economic growth at a rapid pace. Development patterns that by-pass large segments of the population, and development strategies which assume that increases in the gross national product will automatically benefit the poor, have revealed inherent limitations and contradictions; these have eventually distorted or arrested growth. Meeting basic needs is the cornerstone of a sustainable strategy of development. Where these needs are unsatisfied, governments should, as a minimum, undertake realistic programmes to make food security, primary health services and literacy all universal, and to provide basic education to all.

People-centred development also requires democratic structures and institutions, appropriate to the culture and history of each country. These are necessary if a consensus among citizens on the goals of development is to be reached, and a just and stable social system created in which both the costs and benefits of development are equitably shared. Without a democratic framework, social tensions and conflicts cannot be resolved peaceably, and could negate even those gains that may have been achieved.

The objective of people-centred development can be achieved only within a rapidly expanding economy. High rates of growth are indispensable to generate the resources to satisfy basic needs and support a progressive increase in living standards. Achieving universal food security will, for example, involve considerable investments by both governments and the private sector. Similarly, providing universal primary health care and sufficient educational facilities of a high standard require large investments.

A dynamic economy is critically dependent on a high level of investment. Given the generally hostile international environment that most developing nations face, the bulk of such investment will need to be mobilized internally. Countries will need to establish institutions and inculcate values that encourage savings – and efficiency in their use – in both the public and private sectors.

Creating an environment in which high rates of savings and investment can be realized calls for a style of development that is indigenous and in harmony with the people's cultural heritage. The South can ill afford to copy the consumption patterns and lifestyles of affluent societies. In a developing country, such patterns not only divert resources from the satisfaction of broad public needs but also, by fostering the conspicuous consumption of a few while neglecting the needs of the many, encourage social tensions and strife.

Another key determinant of a country's rate of growth is its ability to master and use modern science and technology, including the increasingly complex and rapidly developing knowledge-based technologies. Clear policies and guidelines for science and technology will therefore need to be a part of development plans in the South.

In the last two decades the "hidden" environmental costs of past development efforts have become increasingly apparent. In some countries the degradation of natural resources has gone so far as to result in the abandonment of large areas of formerly productive land. Development efforts must protect and, to the extent possible, improve the environment. It would indeed be short-sighted to put future growth – and future generations – at risk.

It is also necessary to determine the appropriate balance between the state and market forces in the development process. An important lesson from experience is that sustained development is unlikely in most circumstances to be achieved solely by the state or solely by the private sector, but requires strong public and private institutions working co-operatively for democratically agreed objectives. Finding the right balance is therefore a key task for policy-makers.

The goals of development and democracy alike call for action to reverse the tide of militarization. In some countries, governments have had to incur heavy military expenditure in order to counter insurgent or secessionist movements. External factors have played a part in some regions. Direct military threats have left no option for some countries but to step up expenditure for self-defence. But only a few countries can rightly claim that their military budgets are proportionate either to any external threats or to their resources. The countries of the South need to be more vigorous in working out ways of settling disputes peacefully. Military expenditure diverts resources from development and from actions to satisfy the people's needs. The growth of a military culture, moreover, tends to breed contempt for democracy and the rights of the people.

Another evil the South must tackle is corruption. Excessive centralization of economic decision-making and inadequate systems of public accountability are apt to create fertile conditions for corruption. The illicit traffic in drugs and the arms trade have also been factors in the rise of corruption in some countries. Governments should give greater priority to rooting out corruption and insist on higher standards of probity in public life. In the last resort, the effective functioning of democratic systems is the best safeguard against corruption.

Each country's development strategy must necessarily be specific to its stage of development, size, resource base, cultural heritage, and other national characteristics. But a strategy for self-reliant and people-centred development will need to be guided by certain common principles and objectives. In the light of the lessons learned from the development experience of the South, the South Commission has recommended a set of broad economic policy measures designed to achieve the fundamental objective of meeting the people's needs through a development process that combines high rates of growth with equity while being, at the same time, environmentally sound.

Food Security

In many developing countries, meeting basic needs will in the first instance require the eradication of chronic food insecurity. Their strategies should encompass the following:

- Land reforms which – taking account of local characteristics – lead to equitable patterns of ownership and more efficient land use and give farmers an incentive to improve productivity.

- The reorientation of investment and promotional policies in favour of small peasants and co-operatives, along with increased expenditure on infrastructure. Agricultural research and extension services should be expanded and focused on technologies that suit small farmers and protect the environment. Smallholders' access to credit has to be greatly enlarged. Special attention should be given to women as major food producers in terms of training, extension and access to inputs and credit.

- Increasing off-farm employment, both in productive rural works and in rural industries, especially in countries with limited scope for redistributing land.

• The reform of tariff, exchange rate and domestic price policies so as to offer incentives for expanding food output.

• Measures to broaden the access to food among the rural and urban poor, such as the generation of opportunities for employment and a better targeting of food subsides, and action to raise the income and productivity of the urban poor, including support for the informal sector and well-targeted basic social services.

Human Resources

Investments in human resources, by improving people's capabilities, simultaneously foster equity and efficiency; they thus have a strategic role in people-centred development. The countries of the South should undertake to achieve by the year 2000 universal primary health care, universal literacy, and education for all children of primary school age. They should also aim at a substantial increase in enrolments in secondary and higher education and in vocational and technical training. Special efforts are needed to improve education, health services, water supplies and sanitation in the rural areas.

Priority needs to be given to the creation of more extensive and more effective delivery systems in order that the services may reach the poorest people. On account of the resource constraints in many countries the expansion of education and health services will call for reforms in social policies, including a more equitable distribution of social expenditure. In providing health care, greater use should be made of traditional systems of medicine, especially those based on medicinal plants. Tighter priorities, a better distribution of expenditure and greater attention to cost-effective delivery can help to overcome resource constraints.

Rapid population growth rates present a formidable problem for most developing countries. Action to reduce them through integrated population and human resource planning can ease the pressures on the economy to provide jobs and lead to more benefits from investments in human resources. Developing countries should devise effective population policies, giving priority to improving child survival rates, expanding female education, and raising the social and economic status of women along with a rapid extension of family planning services. While the impact of measures to moderate population growth will be felt only in the long run, they must be taken now to ensure the well-being of future generations.

A commitment to improving human resources requires that the South's policies should be designed, and their implementation assessed, in terms of broader social goals than an increase in per capita gross domestic product. Such assessment involves the use of a range of social and economic indicators which adequately encompass social welfare and human development in their widest senses. The compiling of such indicators should be high on the agenda of development planners.

Industrial and Trade Policies

A rapid pace of industrialization is essential to achieve high rates of economic growth and to generate employment and raise incomes. But the past patterns of industrialization leading to small areas of affluence surrounded by much larger areas of poverty and backwardness need to be avoided. Future strategies must improve on those of the past:

- The emphasis should be on the development of a mass market for basic goods, the strengthening of industry's links within the national economy, increased and more efficient use of local resources, economy in the use of energy and imported inputs, and enhanced international competitiveness designed to increase exports, particularly of manufactured goods.

- Even though capital-intensive techniques will be required in many industries, incentives, as well as publicly-supported research and development, should favour small-scale, labour-intensive industries and rural enterprises processing local materials. These increase the employment-generating effects of industrialization, lead to beneficial links with agriculture, and help to narrow rural-urban disparities.

- Indiscriminate and excessive protection and subsidies must be avoided in order to promote efficiency and technological dynamism.

- Measures should be taken to avoid the concentration of economic activities in large urban centres and to promote their dispersal.

- Full advantage should be taken of the substantial opportunities, including export opportunities, open to the services sector. Efficient service industries can help a great deal to enhance the competitiveness of agriculture and industry.

The reform of industrial, trade and exchange rate policies should aim at building up a dynamic manufacturing export sector and efficient import substitution industries. Expanding the production of goods for export to provide the finance for imports of essential capital and consumer goods needs to be an important component of a high-growth strategy. Despite barriers in developed countries, there is still considerable scope for stepping up exports of manufactured goods from the South.

Success in exporting manufactures depends on a range of internally consistent policies:

- A stable and predictable macro-economic framework and in particular a realistic exchange rate are vital conditions.

- A flexible system of protection can play a useful role, with protection rationalized in line with long-term comparative advantage. Tariff and exchange rate policies should not discriminate against exports, and industrial policy and public investment should support export efforts.

- The public sector should establish or encourage export promotion institutions and endeavour to open up marketing channels.

Appropriate specialization in production and trade is particularly important for small countries; because of their limited internal markets, they must rely on exports to achieve industrial development. Integration with other countries in their region can help them to exploit economies of scale and to negotiate stable joint export arrangements with major trading partners.

Closing the Knowledge Gap

The scientific and technological revolution of the last two decades has created a new setting in which success in development will depend even more than formerly on the ability to benefit from science and technology. A widening knowledge gap threatens the economic prospects of the South. Closing this gap will be essential to strengthen the South's ability to make science and technology choices and use scientific and technological advances for development.

To face this challenge, developing countries need rapidly to build their own human skills and institutional capabilities so that the pace of absorption and diffusion of science and technology can be substantially accelerated:

- Science and technology need to be integrated into national development plans – with sectoral priorities carefully selected – and backed by adequate resources.

- Most countries need to spend more on research and development. For the South as a whole, spending on R&D should be doubled, so as to bring it close to the 1 per cent of GNP recommended by UNESCO.

- An effective transfer of technology cannot take place in the absence of capabilities in basic sciences. Adequate stress has therefore to be laid on education in basic sciences and an effective system of research.

- Both in secondary schools and at university level the proportion of students following courses in science and technology should be raised. The goal should be at least to triple the number of scientists and engineers.

- A science and technology culture should be actively fostered, and on-the-job technical training in public and private enterprises encouraged.

- Links between production units and research and development centres should be strengthened.

- Financial institutions should provide special facilities for entrepreneurs harnessing new technologies for productive use. In some countries, venture capital funds could provide such facilities.

National priorities should reflect the level of development, resource endowment, and the thrust of future growth. There can be no single model for all countries. None the less, the first area to be developed will usually be classical low technology, followed by applied sciences provided that some expertise in basic sciences is already available. The last area to be developed will generally be science-based high technology. Large and medium sized developing countries seeking to compete in the world market will generally have no option but to make simultaneous advances in all four areas of science and technology.

The Roles of the State and the Market

Governments need to review carefully the respective roles of the state and of market forces in development. In this context, it is necessary to distinguish between three economic roles of the state.

In all countries, the state has to be responsible for the orderly and stable management of the economy as a whole. It must apply consistent fiscal, monetary, trade, and exchange rate policies so as to create a favourable environment for investment and growth, avoiding inflation and unsustainable external deficits. While the specific policies will vary from country to country, all countries must recognize that sacrificing fiscal and monetary discipline and permitting inflation to get out of hand will harm both growth and equity. A tax system which is broad-based, elastic and progressive and does not dampen the incentive to save and to bear risks can enhance the state's development effectiveness. Tax reforms should receive high priority in a large number of developing countries.

The state's second role is in planning and in regulating economic activities. A situation in which market forces create a pattern of resource allocation or income distribution inconsistent with national objectives can justify state intervention. But how effective its intervention is depends on the state's administrative efficiency and its ability to act with speed and accuracy as conditions change. An overextended and overcentralized administrative system can be counterproductive. Decentralization and reform of the price systems can both make decision-making quicker and help to enlist popular participation in development. Most countries need to review their regulatory policies so as to ensure that they do not hamper entrepreneurship, technical advances or competition.

The state's third role – as an entrepreneur – will be influenced by the social philosophy of the government, the capacity of the private sector, and the state's management capabilities. However, we believe that for most developing countries, the state should now be more selective and discriminating – as well as more efficient – in this role. It is also important that countries assigning a large role to the public sector should pursue policies which enable it to perform its allotted tasks with efficiency. Many countries need urgently to improve performance as well as resource generation in public enterprises. These can succeed only if they have a high degree of financial and operational autonomy, a manageable number of clear commercial and social objectives, and transparent accountability. Government control should be exercised only in strategic areas such as the setting of broad economic and financial targets.

Democratic institutions can considerably enhance the state's effectiveness by fostering national consensus on the goals of development. Accountability to the public, transparency of government activities, an independent judiciary, and the freedom of the media are essential to a democratic system. They can equally help to curb corruption, which saps development efforts and harms society.

Critical to the success of the state will be institutional reforms to improve its organizational and financial capabilities:

- Administrative processes should be modernized to enable the state to perform its functions effectively. In many countries, moreover, the administrative skills of public servants need to be improved.

- The mechanisms of the state for generating and allocating resources should be improved. This involves enhancing the equity and efficiency of tax systems and strengthening the performance and resource-generating capacity of public enterprises.

- Far-reaching reforms in development planning are required to ensure a stable, balanced and development-oriented macro-economic framework, and to promote economic decentralization and the people's participation in the planning process.

Supporting the Business Sector

As important as the reform of state institutions and the improved management of the public sector is the creation of an environment conducive to entrepreneurship, both private and public. Sustained growth and development require the full and efficient participation of the business sector, including public enterprises, private firms, co-operatives, other socially owned enterprises, and microbusiness. The relative importance of these elements will vary from country to country. However, the successful examples of development in the South clearly show that economic growth is vigorous only in a climate in which the business sector – as defined above – can thrive.

The thrust of government policy should be to promote entrepreneur-ship, competition, innovation and technical progress, and to strengthen the ability of the business sector to seize opportunities in both domestic and international markets.

The success of the business sector is tied to stability and predictability in the environment in which it has to operate; governments must create a macro-economic setting which is conducive to enterprise and remove bureaucratic impediments that discourage investment and innovation.

The Gender Dimension

A development strategy committed to equity and participation must also give priority to the raising of the social and economic status of women. Throughout the South, women play a vital role as producers and agents of social progress. Yet they carry the double burden of discrimination and greater than average poverty. No nation can truly develop so long as half its population suffers discrimination. It is, therefore, essential that development programmes should purposefully seek to advance women's status in society, ensuring that women's concerns are treated in a comprehensive manner, adequate resources are made available to meet their needs, and the obstacles they face in important economic areas are eliminated.

Macro-economic policies, especially those bearing on the allocation of resources and technological choices, need to take account of their likely impact on women's productive activities. Policies ought to be pursued that enhance women's income-earning capacity and give them a fair share of social services. Women's right to social justice and equity should be legally protected. Deliberate endeavours to foster a gender-sensitive culture should support these reforms.

The Cultural Dimension

Development strategies must also be sensitive to the cultural roots of the society and promote culture -- the creative expansion, deepening, and renewal of society's cultural stock. Governments should consider the adoption of Cultural Development Charters setting out the basic rights of the people in the field of culture, the principal policies for translating these rights into reality and the role of the state in the process.

The Environment

Whilst the custody of the environment calls for a global approach, the South must itself do all it can to counteract environmental degradation. It has no alternative but to pursue rapid economic growth, and hence industrialization; it must therefore control the environmental hazards that go with growth and, through urban planning, reduce the environmental pressure in its large cities.

The countries of the South should adopt an integrated, environment-sensitive approach to their development. While in the long run what will be crucial are policies to slow down population growth, there are several directions in which governments could act to limit damage to the environment:

- The pressure on natural resources should be relieved by: improving the productivity of smallholder agriculture; the rational management of rangelands, water resources and forests; encouraging rural industry to expand off-farm employment; and a better regional balance in the allocation of resources to avoid high population concentrations in a few centres.

- There should be strict controls on air and water pollution by industries.

- The use of energy-efficient and environmentally safe technologies should be encouraged, and the North should be pressed to transfer them at a cost the South can afford. Measures to protect the environment need to be supported by campaigns to make the people aware of environmental concerns and mobilize their interest in environmental protection.

3. THE STRATEGIC ROLE OF SOUTH–SOUTH CO-OPERATION

The need for developing countries to rely on their own resources and efforts to revitalize development in the 1990s applies not only at the national but also at the South-South level. Increased reliance on the collective resources of the South, through diversified and reinforced processes of political, economic and social co-operation, will be of vital importance in the response of developing countries to the many challenges they face. By expanding the flows of finance, trade, technology and skills within the South, through stronger links which take advantage of complementary assets, South-South co-operation can fortify the development of all countries of the South.

The strength the South can gain by making more use of its collective energies will give it greater importance in the world economy and a more favourable position to exert influence on global economic management. Pursued with determination, South-South co-operation can in the long run change the world economic map; criss-crossing links within the South can mitigate the dependency that imperial rule built into North-South links.

The search for a more rational and equitable world order, which the South has pursued for so long, requires a more effectively organized South to present its case and negotiate its demands in world forums. On the issues that concern humanity in common no less than on those of special relevance to the South, it is necessary that the South should speak with one voice. It is equally necessary that its voice should not go unheard – or unheeded – because of its organizational failings.

To look for strength in solidarity has throughout been an instinct of the South. It found expression not only in the Non-Aligned Movement and the Group of 77 but also in a wide range of mainly regional and subregional arrangements for trade and, in some cases, wider economic co-operation. The 1970s were a dynamic period for co-operation among developing countries; in that period South-South trade nearly doubled as a share of world trade. OPEC's initial success demonstrated what collective action could achieve; in addition, the financial surpluses of its member countries were a significant source of development aid and investment funds for the South. In the 1980s, however, the prolonged development crisis imposed strains on the South's arrangements for collaboration.

The setbacks of the past decade do not diminish the rationale for South-South co-operation. On the contrary, the downturn in the global climate for development – and the prospect that Northern growth will provide less traction for the South – makes collective efforts even more vital. Indeed, the diversification that has taken place within the South provides more scope for co-operation. New areas of economic vitality, as in East and South-East Asia, have created opportunities for exploiting complementary resources and enlarging South-South co-operation.

The South Commission was greatly heartened by the decision by a group of developing countries in Belgrade in 1989 to set up a Summit-Level Group for South-South Consultation and Co-operation. This is an important step towards giving organizational strength to the South.

As a contribution to the formulation of a comprehensive approach to South-South co-operation, we have selected several priority areas; action in these areas should provide renewed dynamism to South-South co-operation.

The Foundations and Priority Areas for Co-operation

Increased co-operation must be built on an ethos of pride and confidence in the South and commitment to South solidarity among all sections of society. Only with such foundations can there be durable bonds of partnership between the nations and peoples of the South. The level of South consciousness must be raised, and public sentiment must be generated in favour of links within the South, by an active process involving both the educational system and the media. There need to be efforts to create a wide constituency for South-South co-operation embracing the business community, the professions, women's organiz-ations, trade unions, and other social groups. People's contacts should be fostered through professional and other non-governmental organizations, cultural and sporting exchanges and through tourism. Information flows should similarly be expanded.

The success of these efforts – and of South-South co-operation as a whole – will be determined by the vision and performance of national leaders. Professions of commitment to solidarity and collective action must be backed by wholehearted support for practical co-operation; leaders should find the political will to turn rhetoric into reality.

Greater priority must therefore be given to South-South co-operation within the machinery of government. The implementation of decisions taken by collective organs of the South, including regional agencies, rests crucially on supportive policies and institutional arrangements within each country. These could be best assured by designating a cabinet-rank minister responsible for fostering South-South co-operation, with the authority to ensure that national planning takes explicit account of the commitment to co-operation, to pursue the strengthening of South-South links and to see that national obligations flowing from collective decisions are fulfilled. This should be complemented by the creation of a national committee, of prominent personalities from different walks of life, to reinforce the national drive to enlarge South consciousness and to mobilize public opinion in support of South- South co-operation.

Educational links within the South should be expanded, with the accent on scientific, technical and vocational courses and the development of managerial and entrepreneurial skills. Selected institutions should be supported as Centres of Educational Excellence to provide training for students from the South. A foundation should be set up to offer at least 10,000 South Fellowships a year for study within the South; a proportion of these should be set apart for students from least developed countries. Exchanges of staff and teaching materials among universities, particularly in the newer scientific fields like molecular biology and genetic engineering, should be part of the programme of South-South co-operation. These should be complemented by a programme of collaborative research pooling scientific capacities within the South.

Finance and Debt

South-South co-operation, especially in trade, requires substantial finance. Increasing the resources available for this purpose is therefore an urgent task.

- Additional resources should be provided to clearing and payments schemes so that their effectiveness is improved by the ability to extend credit.
- Existing export credit facilities should be enlarged, and new facilities should be created to serve regions that now lack them.
- The regional development banks should give more support to schemes of subregional and regional co-operation; support should include the refinancing of export credits, and finance for subregional and regional projects and programmes.
- The World Bank should set up a facility to refinance export credits given by developing countries, and should fund an increasing number of projects involving two or more developing countries.
- The IMF should establish a facility to support schemes for trade liberalization and expansion among developing countries.
- The UNDP should use a significant proportion of its funds to support

South-South co-operation, including the Global System of Trade Preferences (GSTP) and associations of commodity producers.

- Developing countries in a strong economic position should extend development assistance of varying degrees of concessionality to poorer countries.

Determined efforts should be made to establish a South Bank. Such a bank, under discussion and study for many years, could help to fill critical gaps in financing needs. OPEC surpluses have dwindled, but there are sources of capital within the South that could be mobilized through appropriate arrangements. A bank of the size and scope first envisaged may not, however, be feasible; the South should lower its sights and set up a bank initially to provide finance for exports and for clearing and payments arrangements. In due course it could widen its operations. Pending participation by all developing countries, the bank should be set up by a broad group of countries.

The wide-ranging support for co-operation within its region offered by the Arab Fund for Economic and Social Development illustrates how useful a multilateral bank of the South could be.

An equitable solution to the debt problem, with debt servicing reduced to levels that allow economic recovery to take place, is crucial to development and, in many countries, to social and political stability itself. A solution is more likely if the debtor nations stand together in defence of their interests. Such action, consonant with the collective self-reliance we commend to the South, is necessary to change the present situation in which individual debtor countries stand alone in facing a phalanx of banks, countries and international financial institutions. Recent developments give added relevance to the South Commission's call for a debtors'forum, made in its Statement on External Debt in February 1988. Through such a debtors' forum countries could consult each other, co-ordinate their debt management policies, and consider the possibilities of concerted action. It would also help them to make a common stand at the international conference on debt which we propose. Co-operative action involving both creditors and debtors is undoubtedly the preferred course. In the absence of a jointly agreed solution, however, such a forum would help debtor countries to undertake the defensive unilateral action as the sole option left to the South.

Developing countries are being forced to rely increasingly on the IMF and the World Bank, and to accept conditionality and performance norms of a far-reaching nature. Not all countries are well equipped technically to negotiate with these institutions and secure the best possible arrangements. In view of this, the Group of 24 should set up a group of experts to assist developing countries which require advice in such negotiations.

Trade and Commodities

The Global System of Trade Preferences (GSTP), which became operational in 1989, is based on the advantages to be gained from promoting trade within the South as a whole. Its establishment is an important achievement. It offers a framework for expanding trade by lowering tariff and non-tariff barriers, and for reducing the heavy dependence on markets and suppliers in the North. A framework is, however, only a start; the South must now give it substance, and aim to have a significant proportion of South-South trade liberalized under the GSTP by the year 2000. A technical service should be set up to assist the scheme's implementation; it should draw up a timetable for enlarging GSTP activities in the 1990s.

State trading agencies should be used more actively to step up South-South trade. They should work jointly in import purchases, export promotion and marketing, warehousing, freight and training. The Association of State Trading Organizations should prepare a programme for extending such co-operation in the 1990s.

Developing countries should study the scope for making more use of counter trade, including buy-back arrangements; they should also consider forming an organization to act as a broker for counter trade transactions, eliminating the use of intermediaries in the North.

Primary commodities are still the mainstay of many economies in the South. Their extreme vulnerability was further confirmed by the sharp fall in commodity prices in the 1980s, and technological advances in the North will continue to pose threats to the competitiveness of export commodities. Many attempts to achieve producer/consumer co-operation in securing stable markets for commodities have failed, while competition among producers has pushed prices further down. Developing countries producing commodities for world markets in which the South accounts for a predominant share should form associations with a view to obtaining remunerative and stable prices through supply management or market intervention. In due course, these associations could set up a joint body to co-ordinate action for a range of commodities.

Tropical beverages are produced wholly in the South. Countries producing tea, coffee and cocoa should take the lead in introducing rational and fair systems for their international marketing

Co-operation among commodity-producing developing countries should also extend to consultations among themselves with a view to establishing common positions in negotiating international commodity agreements and in dealing with consumer countries.

Business and Industry

While trade liberalization and expansion are important, joint action to promote investments and stimulate agricultural and industrial production is also necessary to unlock the full potential of South-South collaboration. It must serve to exploit the South's complementary resources in finance, natural resources, technology, markets and managerial talent. With the advances made by many countries in the South, there is now more scope for involving the business sector, both public and private, in joint undertakings. This is a vital direction for future co-operation.

There are now many multinational companies in the South, with impressive financial, technological and managerial capabilities. They are an important asset, opening the way for joint production arrangements in many areas. There is scope for joint ventures in, for example, the fertilizer, petrochemical, energy and capital goods industries, as well as in the manufacture of basic consumption goods. The joint production of generic drugs in common use could, for instance, lower health service costs in countries that now depend on Northern suppliers. Programmes of industrial co-operation should lay emphasis on the need to assist the least developed countries to expand and diversify their exports.

Developing countries should give investors from the South more favourable treatment than they give to foreign investors generally. In return, the investing companies should agree to observe the norms advocated by the South for transnational companies from the North.

Consortia of consultancy and design firms and of industrial research institutes should be set up, and a network of consultants able to undertake feasibility studies in other developing countries should be established.

United Nations agencies should maintain rosters of experts and consultancy firms in the South and make the information available to governments. Measures should be taken to increase the use of experts and firms from the South and there should be annual reports on the number of such experts and firms employed and their proportion in the total.

The efforts to establish an Association of Third World Chambers of Commerce and Industry should be intensified. The association should be given sufficient resources and institutional support to be an effect- ive instrument in business co-operation. The flow of information on investment laws and practices, manufactures, markets, technology, and services in the South should be improved.

The Group of 77 and the Non-Aligned Movement should set up a standing committee to review co-operation in business and industry and suggest measures for its enlargement.

Services

Many developing countries are unlikely to be able to make significant headway in the services sector on their own. The development of this sector should therefore be pursued through the South's economic co-operation arrangements. Important objectives should be the creation of an adequate infrastructure, particularly in telecommunications and informatics; the development of producer services with close links with the productive sectors; and the improvement of the trade balance in services. The expansion of such services as banking, insurance, telecommunications and transport can be vital to efficiency in the industrial sector as a whole.

Food Security

Action to improve food output and security should have an important place in co-operative efforts. Agricultural and agro-industrial projects should be among the joint enterprises promoted by the South. Joint ventures in farming, particularly between food surplus and food deficit countries, should be encouraged. Similarly, co-operation in research, taking advantage of the advances made by some countries in agricultural technology, particularly for arid zones, should be strengthened and extended to the field of biotechnology. Full use should be made of the network of institutions under the Consultative Group for International Agricultural Research (CGIAR).

Long-term supply arrangements between food surplus and deficit countries are desirable; so is a commitment by food exporting countries to give priority to supplies for countries facing critical shortages. The practice of holding regional food stocks for use in emergencies – as already happens in a few regions – should be extended to other regions.

The South should initiate a long-term co-ordinated programme to help Africa modernize its agriculture and become self-sufficient in food.

Science and Technology

Co-operation within the South can substantially assist national efforts to narrow the knowledge gap in science and technology with the North and build up capabilities in applying the advances of science to its development needs. A priority task should be to prepare a strategy for scientific co-operation.

The Centre for Science and Technology of the Non-Aligned and Other Developing Countries should, in co-operation with other institutions in the South, draw up a programme for co-ordination and co-operation in scientific and technological research, identifying areas for joint activity.

Core activities should be selected for collaborative research at regional and inter-regional levels in conventional areas like agriculture and energy as well as in such new areas as biotechnology and micro-electronics. Partnerships between scientific institutions should be complemented by links with productive enterprises that could lead to the commercial use of research results.

Higher education, particularly in the scientific, technical and professional fields, calls for the extension of collective self-reliance. Many countries cannot hope to be self-sufficient in educational facilities at this level. There is also a clear need to reduce the costly dependence on institutions in the North. This could be achieved by making wider use of the many universities and technical colleges of high standing already established in the South. Our proposals for a network of Centres of Educational Excellence and a foundation to offer scholarships are designed to lead to a significant expansion in South-South flows of students. Technical and vocational training could be improved by technical assistance schemes under which newly industrializing economies are able to offer teachers and apprenticeships to other developing countries. Over time exchanges of students and trainees will also prove valuable in raising the level of South consciousness.

Attention should also be given to setting up jointly funded, specialized, research-cum-training institutions in different parts of the South to offer able scientists from developing countries the opportunity to work in the South and for the South. Developing countries should support the efforts to create a South network of 20 centres of advanced research specializing in high technology and environmental sciences. The work of the Third World Academy of Sciences and the Third World Network of Scientific Organizations in promoting South-South co-operation should also have the support of the South.

Developing countries should undertake joint studies of the implications for them of advances in such new technologies as micro-electronics and biotechnology and in the use of new materials, robotics and fibre optics.

The Environment

In their efforts to protect the environment, developing countriescould co-operate with each other in several directions: in managing shared natural resources, especially river basins, coastal areas, forests and wildlife; in such activities as offshore oil exploration, the management of exclusive economic zones and the prevention of desertification; and in such areas of research as renewable energy, especially biomass and solar power, and the efficient use of energy in industry, agriculture, transport and homes.

The South should adopt a common approach in negotiating with the North to ensure an equitable management of the global environment and should sponsor arrangements for sharing technologies that help to conserve energy and reduce environmental pollution

Information and Communications

Efforts to build up South consciousness and solidarity as well as to strengthen economic co-operation will benefit from improved flows of information within the South.

Links between the media in the South and South-South flows of information through the media should be intensified. Advances made by individual countries as well as in collaboration between countries should be widely publicized. Links should also be strengthened between national data banks in the South, reducing dependence on Northern sources for data in important areas. The South should use the opportunities provided by South-owned satellites to improve communications and information links within the South.

People-to-people Contacts

People-to-people contacts should be strengthened through cultural and sporting exchanges and other activities, as well as through links between voluntary organizations in a wide variety of fields.

Restrictions on tourist and business travel need to be greatly eased. Visa requirements should be eliminated on a reciprocal basis. Where foreign exchange is a severe constraint, special clearing accounts should be set up to facilitate tourist travel.

Regional Co-operation

The subregional and regional organizations of the South set up in the past few decades are a vital set of building blocks for collective self-reliance. Paradoxically, while the North has been seeking new advantages through regional groupings, a number of the South's initiatives have been allowed to weaken. The pressure of domestic crisis management during the past decade was the main factor accounting for this decline. The adverse global environment, however, makes it incumbent on the South to revitalize these instruments of co-operation. Each of them should work out well-defined action plans up to the year 2000, with clear priorities and goals.

Governments should increase their support for regional and subregional trade expansion schemes by reducing exchange controls and trade restrictions, widening the range of products covered by preferences and deepening preferences.

Trade expansion should be supported by the regional co-ordination of investments in selected fields, and the regional organizations should identify opportunities for efficient import substitution. Each grouping should move towards harmonization of development plans and policies within its region.

The larger and more advanced countries within each grouping should pay particular attention to the needs of the least developed members, and assume a degree of responsibility for their progress.

The countries of the South should make more vigorous efforts to resolve conflicts and preserve peace in their regions. The organizations established to promote economic co-operation could provide a setting for consultations to ease tensions or act as channels through which countries not party to a dispute can offer their good offices.

A Secretariat for the South

The South's collective endeavours have been seriously hampered by the lack of any permanent mechanism to provide intellectual, technical and organizational support in negotiations with the North and in promoting South-South co-operation. Neither the Non-Aligned Movement nor the Group of 77 has anything more than rudimentary arrangements for support. Hence, the South is at a great disadvantage, particularly in dealing with the North, which has, besides strong national resources, the backing of the well-staffed OECD secretariat, with its extensive facilities for research and consultations. The increasing range and complexity of issues on which the South must safeguard its interests, formulate common positions and engage the North make it essential that the South should have a secretariat at its collective service. There is an equal need for institutional backing for the South's efforts to enlarge South-South co-operation, particularly at the inter-regional level.

We are convinced that a facility of this nature is vital for the success of the South's collective efforts and that the South should address this matter with a high sense of urgency. The formation by 15 developing countries of the Summit-Level Group for South-South Consultation and Co-operation, whose leaders will meet regularly, makes the case for a secretariat even more pressing. We envisage a secretariat being at the service of this group as well as of the Group of 77 and the Non-Aligned Movement – as a secretariat of the South.

Our Report outlines the main functions this secretariat should carry out in supporting the South's efforts to realize its collective objectives. While we very much hope that the proposal for a secretariat will receive widespread support, we do not believe that its establishment should depend on unanimity among the countries of the South. So long as there is substantial enough support to make its setting-up feasible, a start should be made.

4. NORTH-SOUTH RELATIONS AND THE INTERNATIONAL SYSTEM

The debt crisis, the collapse of commodity prices and growing protectionism in the North have amply confirmed that the present relationships between South and North are inimical to the progress of the South. The enormous and increasing difference in economic power between North and South is a reflection of the international division of labour, which has condemned the South to specialize in low value-added, low technology production and exports.

We believe that sustained development in the South necessitates a fundamental restructuring of the international economic system. We also believe that, in the process, a fairer, more rational and more lasting world economic system can be built. Just as the South cannot develop without a more favourable international environment, lasting stability in global relations calls for progress in the South and greater global equity. International economic reform, while being a demand of the South, is equally a need of the international system. The reform must cover the international financial, monetary and trading systems. A central need is to set up arrangements to provide for the transfer of adequate resources from developed to developing countries to accelerate development in the South. These should include contingency mechanisms to ensure the orderly continuation of development efforts in the face of unexpected shocks. The reform of the international trading system should give priority to improving the access of developing countries to the markets of developed countries. The new global system also requires fair international régimes for science and technology and for the management of the environment and the global commons. International institutions should be made more democratic, more effective and more supportive of development.

Debt

The revival of development in a large number of developing countries requires international action to reverse the present trend in resource transfers which has prematurely made these countries net exporters of capital. It is a long-accepted principle of international economic policy that developing countries should be able to expect a positive net flow of resources to supplement their domestic savings. The present situation is the reverse: an absurd and intolerable transfer of resources to the North.

This state of affairs must be changed as an urgent priority through an equitable solution to the debt problem. The point must be accepted by the international community that, for reasons beyond the control of developing countries, their external debt is not repayable in full, and its nominal value will not be paid.

The Brady initiative is only a cautious first recognition of the force of this argument. Its limitations have been revealed in its implementation so far, and it is clearly inadequate. What is needed instead is a concerted approach to achieve debt reduction and debt service reduction simultaneously. Negative resource transfers should be ended and debt service related to the ability of the economy to pay and to grow. The amount of debt service should be determined by the level of resources a country needs to revive growth and sustain it at a rate that allows per capita income to rise by at least 2-3 per cent a year. The issue should be the subject of intergovernmental negotiation. We reaffirm the need for an International Debt Conference with the participation of the debtor governments, the governments of the creditors, and the international financial institutions. Its mandate would be to arrive at a binding international agreement on a framework solution.

A global solution to the debt problem must include relief for the least developed countries. Their total debt is not large in absolute terms. However, in relation to the size of their economies and their exports, their debt is a heavy burden in most cases. A solution to the debt issue should lead to a reasonably quick resumption of growth in those economies. It should involve the full write-off of their bilateral official debt - already done partially by a number of donor countries - the extension of debt cancellation to other low-income countries that may be less poor but are still heavily indebted, and the refinancing on concessional terms of the non-concessional bilateral official debt, as well as the multilateral debt, of all countries concerned. The establishment by the World Bank of a debt reduction facility for low-income countries that have access to its resources only through its soft-loan affiliate, IDA, is welcome, but the sum of $100 million being made available to the facility is insufficient. A substantial increase is needed.

Financial Flows

In the long run, the countries of the South should be able to generate enough savings for investment from their own resources. However, in the initial stages of the resumption of growth, long-term external finance will be needed, particularly for the poorest and least developed countries. Experience shows that the private sector by itself cannot fill this need adequately. The international system should therefore provide for the transfer of the needed external capital to the developing countries.

This requires several decisive steps. Developed countries should fulfil the target commitment of 0.7 per cent of GNP for official development assistance adopted by the United Nations in 1968, and of 0.15 per cent of GNP in aid to the least developed countries accepted by most donors in 1981. Efforts should be made to double official development assistance to LDCs by 1995 and to increase it to 0.20 per cent of GNP by the end of the 1990s.

A higher proportion of financial flows should be channelled through multilateral agencies; financial institutions, notably the World Bank and the regional development banks, should have a larger role in meeting the requirements for development finance.

For many developing countries, multilateral concessional assistance will continue to be of critical importance. Concessional assistance should be doubled by 1995, and a larger share provided through multilateral institutions (IDA and the "soft windows" of regional development banks). The additional resources should be devoted to food production, the satisfaction of other basic needs, population control, energy security, and other environmentally sensitive sectors.

Difficulties are invariably encountered in negotiating replenishments of IDA's capital; the replenishment cycle should therefore be extended to five years from the present three.

In view of the limited funds available to IDA – the ninth replenishment is no higher than the eighth – and the pressing claims of sub-Saharan Africa on these funds, the World Bank should revive the Third Window it opened temporarily in the 1970s to offer loans on terms halfway between those applying to its regular loans and IDA loans.

A comprehensive rgime for direct foreign investment should be introduced. International action is needed to adopt the Code of Conduct for Transnational Corporations, under negotiation since 1976, as well as a set of rules to control restrictive business practices. Joint ventures and other forms of association between small and medium-sized firms in industrial countries and the business sector in the South should be encouraged.

The governments of developed countries should co-operate with the governments of developing countries in identifying and instituting judicial proceedings against those responsible for illegal flows of capital from the South.

International Monetary Issues

The lack of a mechanism for creating international liquidity in an orderly way has become a major problem for the world economy as a whole. Meanwhile, there is a growing privatization of international liquidity, and this particularly hurts countries with low credit ratings. Thus, while there is ample liquidity, the developing countries have very limited access to it. This calls for a greater use of SDRs – the reserve currency created by the IMF. There is immediate need for agreement to allocate a reasonable amount of SDRs on a regular basis exclusively to developing countries over and above their small IMF quotas. In the long run, SDRs should become the main reserve asset for the international monetary system.

International arrangements should be adopted to reduce misalignment and volatility in the exchange rates of the principal world currencies. A target zone system for these currencies is one possible arrangement. There should be effective multilateral surveillance of the exchange rate arrangements, and the macro-economic policies, of major developed countries.

Interest rates should be brought down to historical levels through international action. Pending a decline in interest rates, developing countries should be insulated from the effects of excessively high levels.

Uncertainty and instability have greatly increased in the world economy. It is therefore essential to have international arrangements to cushion developing countries against unexpected shortfalls in foreign exchange earnings or sharp increases in payments as a result of changes in interest rates or exchange rates. Agreement on the need for such arrangements has existed since the early 1960s, when the IMF established a Compensatory Financing Facility. The conditionality attached to assistance under the facility was considerably tightened and access was reduced in the 1980s, making it much less useful. It should be a priority of reform of the international financial system to reduce this conditionality, and to return the scheme to its original quasi-automaticity, at least in offsetting foreign receipt losses beyond the control of developing countries.

The 1980s witnessed a sharp increase in the conditionality associated with the provision of external finance to developing countries. While this trend is now a universal fact of life, unlikely to be reversed, the content and mechanisms of conditionality call out for major reform. If the set of policies a country is obliged to follow is to be viable, it needs to be country-specific and free of ideological bias. Devising and carrying out structural reforms are complex operations as differences can and do arise in drawing up an optimum mix of policies. It is therefore necessary to ensure that the performance norms stipulated for developing countries by the international financial institutions are based on objective analysis and not influenced by the ideological prejudices of the donors. Only a depoliticization of the process through the introduction of independent international evaluation of development performance can inspire the respect and confidence of both donors and recipients.

A panel of experts, independent of the IMF and the World Bank but operating as an advisory committee to them, should be formed to assess the needs of developing countries and the conditions appropriate to each of them. These two institutions should also set up regional councils to advise them on the broad framework of their policies and programmes.

Trade and Development

The prevailing approaches, rules and disciplines of the world trading system, as embodied in the General Agreement on Tariffs and Trade (GATT), are based on the principles of open, multilateral, transparent and non-discriminatory trading. However, developing countries face an entirely different reality when trading with the North. Protectionism in the industrialized countries now affects a very large proportion of the South's exports of processed products and manufactures.

Sustained growth in the South will need a substantial expansion of exports to the North. As world trade is unlikely to grow as fast as it did during the 1945-79 period, this will require deliberate action by developed countries to keep their markets open. A reformed international trading system must enable developing countries to step up their share of world trade in products in which they have a distinct comparative advantage; it must as well support the growth of trade among developing countries themselves. It should treat sustained development in the South as a central objective, reiterating the notion of preferential and more favourable treatment and limited reciprocity.

We believe the time has come for the world community to take up again the idea of an International Trade Organization. It should be equipped to deal with the new needs of the world trading system in a comprehensive and integrated fashion. Its mandate should include both a regulatory role in the world trading system and the promotion of development.

The trade in textiles and clothing must be returned to GATT rules and disciplines as a matter of urgency. Equally, sector-specific quantitative restrictions affecting, for instance, steel, leather goods, footwear and consumer electronics, which discriminate against manufactured exports from many developing countries, must be eliminated.

A satisfactory outcome of negotiations on some of these matters is linked to the reaching of a comprehensive agreement on safeguards,that is, on temporary import barriers imposed by individual states in order to protect industries at risk. Non-discrimination in applying safeguards should be a sine qua non of such an agreement. Over the last few years, there has been a convergence of views on several aspects of safeguards; agreement on these aspects should be pursued vigorously. Any attempt to introduce selectivity in applying safeguards should be resisted, as selectivity would allow them to be used essentially against imports from the South.

The application of traditional norms governing the trade in goods to the trade in services could seriously undermine the ability of developing countries to promote and regulate their service industries. Services such as transport, communications, banking, insurance, health and education have always been regarded as critical for sustained development. The new "producer" or "business" services – a by-product of advances in information and communications technologies – also have a profound impact on competitiveness in many economic processes and products, for instance by improving inventory management and quality control. To be consistent with the objective of promoting development, any new multilateral framework for the trade in services must provide opportunities for the creation of a strong producer services sector in developing countries. It must also facilitate the growing participation of developing countries in the world trade in services.

The inclusion of "trade-related investment measures" (TRIMs) on the agenda of international trade negotiations involves serious threats to the developing countries. Seeking to restrict the freedom of developing countries to regulate foreign investment, the proposal for TRIMs is essentially an attempt to introduce a multilateral regulatory system that would further strengthen the North's transnational corporations.

Clearly, all countries need screening procedures to block unacceptable and counterproductive activities or projects and to modify the terms of their operations to make them consistent with national development objectives.

The Commission attaches special importance to the need to reform international commodity trading. The crisis in commodities is as dramatic as that in the international financial system. Efforts are urgently needed to overcome the crisis in commodity markets in ways that will prevent its recurrence. The setting-up of mechanisms to regulate the international commodity economy should be high on the agenda of the world community. The essential goals of UNCTAD's Integrated Programme for Commodities remain valid, namely, improvement of the terms of trade for commodity-exporting countries, stabilization of prices, compensation for shortfalls in commodity earnings, as well as commodity development through increased productivity, domestic processing and participation in marketing and distribution.

There is a distinct trend towards the formation of large trading groups among developed countries, as evidenced by the Canada-United States Free Trade Agreement and the moves by the European Community to create a unified market by the end of 1992. It would be wholly objectionable if these groupings were to result in reduced access for the South's exports. Reasonable measures should be introduced to preserve, and indeed expand, the preferential access of the developing countries to these extended regional markets of the North and to avoid the potential marginalization of many countries of the South.

The prospective integration of the USSR and the countries of Eastern Europe in the world economy could offer significant opportunities for building a better world for all. In the shorter run, however, the prospects are more uncertain. With their greater freedom, Soviet enterprises are likely to seek more competitive sources for their imports. This could place some developing countries at a disadvantage. Conversely, in the short run, the USSR's stated objective of significantly increasing its imports of consumer goods could benefit those countries of the South that are able to export consumer durables and light manufactures at competitive prices. Should the Eastern European countries progressively multilateralize their trade and payments arrangements, the scope for trade could expand, even though some transitional problems may arise for developing countries heavily dependent on markets in the USSR and Eastern Europe. In the short term also, more competition from Eastern Europe in world markets and for the world's surplus savings could create problems for the developing countries. We remain deeply concerned that both attention and resources could be diverted from development. However, in the longer run, the entry of these countries into the international financial institutions might contribute to greater balance and objectivity in the functioning of these bodies.

Science and Technology

Measures to make it easier for developing countries to develop their domestic capabilities in science and technology and to acquire new technology from abroad should be a prominent part of new international arrangements to be negotiated between North and South. They should provide for the control of restrictive practices of transnational companies and include the following features:

- United Nations agencies, in particular UNIDO, UNESCO, the International Atomic Energy Agency (IAEA) and the UN University, should play a more prominent part in building up a scientific infrastructure in their areas of competence with a view to contributing to scientific and technological progress in the South.

The UN Commission on Science and Technology should identify the priorities for international policy in this area. Scientific centres for agriculture, such as the International Centre for the Improvement of Corn and Wheat in Mexico, the International Centre for Insect Physiology and Ecology in Kenya, and the International Centre for Biotechnology and Genetic Engineering in Trieste and Delhi sponsored by UNIDO, provide models of institutions engaged in applied research. In basic research, the experience of UNESCO and the IAEA in relation to the International Centre for Theoretical Physics (ICTP) in Trieste should be explored with a view to setting up other centres of advanced research and training, sponsored by United Nations bodies in disciplines relevant to their activities. The decision to set up, with the Italian Government's support through UNIDO, three new research centres in Trieste – one for high technology and new materials, one for pure and applied chemistry, and one for earth sciences and the environment, which together with the ICTP will constitute the International Centre for Science – is a welcome development in this direction.

- A network of research and training institutes for the development and application of high technology should be established in the developing countries, and this should be supported by the multilateral financial institutions, notably the World Bank. The proposal by the Trieste Centre for the creation of 20 new centres around the world provides a basis for developing such a network.

- Centres of technological information should be established in the countries of the South to facilitate access to scientific literature; these centres should have comprehensive collections of scientific and technological books and journals either provided by governments of the North or supported by bilateral or multilateral aid.

- There should be a link between total international aid and aid for science and technology. Donor countries should agree to provide a given percentage of their ODA as an additional sum to finance R&D activities in developing countries.

- The new arrangements should provide for the transfer of technology from the North on terms consistent with the development interests of the South. Financing should not be tied; there should be controls to check transfer pricing; the ability to export should not be restricted; and there must be freedom to diffuse the technology within the country. The negotiation of an International Code of Conduct on the Transfer of Technology to Developing Countries and revision of the Paris Convention should be completed in a spirit of accommodation between North and South. Holders of patent rights must accept corresponding obligations to facilitate the development of links for the absorption of technology by the developing countries.

● Technologies that help to preserve the environment and conserve natural resources should be treated as international public goods, and technologies with potentially dangerous social consequences should be internationally monitored and controlled.

The Environment, Oceans and Energy

Evidence of the global risks arising from damage to the environment provide another reminder that North and South are parts of one human family sharing one fragile planet. The custody of the environment calls for a co-operative approach based on global interdependence.

The damage so far done to the environment has been overwhelmingly caused by the pattern of economic development in the North. Poverty is, in contrast, at the root of environmental degradation in poor countries, where the compulsions of survival lead to improvident use of the land and other natural resources.

Multilateral arrangements for protecting the environment should therefore recognize that poverty and underdevelopment must be overcome for the environment in the South to be protected; such arrangements should have the removal of poverty in the South as a central objective. It would be wholly unacceptable if the North were to seek to force the South to choose between development and environmental protection.

The adoption of environmentally sound policies and technologies will clearly involve more costs than the South can bear unaided. The international community should share these additional costs as part of a global plan for saving our endangered Earth. The South's readiness to join in a campaign to preserve the ecological heritage is reflected in the proposal made by India at the Non-Aligned Summit in Belgrade in September 1989. This envisaged a UN-administered Planet Protection Fund to which all countries, except the least developed, would contribute 0.1 per cent of their annual GDP. The South Commission commends this proposal to the international community.

All countries that have not yet done so should ratify the Convention on the Law of the Sea in order that it may enter into force as soon as possible. A forum should be created within the United Nations system for the discussion of ocean affairs in an integrated manner, as they are closely interrelated and should be considered together. The management and possible utilization of the global commons, such as Antarctica and outer space, must be based on their acceptance as a part of the common heritage of humankind. The 1959 Antarctica Treaty expires in 1991; it should be succeeded by a treaty inspired by this spirit.

The global economy needs an internationally agreed rgime for energy that is stable, that is, without disruptive fluctuations in supply and prices, and is fair to both producers and consumers by ensuring reasonable and remunerative prices as well as access to reliable supplies. It should ensure that the development of the South is not impeded by the failure to provide for an orderly expansion and fair allocation of energy supplies.

Global Economic Management and the UN System

True peace and security in the world cannot be assured without action to make the international economic environment more equitable, predictable and supportive of development in the poorer parts of the world. Such action has to be a global responsibility. The United Nations, as the principal forum of the global community, should have a central role in guiding the world towards this objective.

Ways must therefore be found for the world community, through the United Nations and at the highest level of world leadership, to make assessments of global trends and their consequences for development as well as for the environment. We recommend that periodic summits of a representative group of nations from both North and South should be convened by the United Nations for this purpose. They should set guidelines for action by the UN and its agencies and other important components of the global system.

Action to improve global economic management and decision-making also requires a reform of the voting structures in the IMF and the World Bank. These should be changed to achieve a better balance between developed and developing countries in their policy-making bodies.

Peace and Development

To beat swords into ploughshares has been one of humankind's noblest and most enduring dreams. In recent times, the hope has been that part of the vast sums spent on preparations for war would be diverted to the war against world poverty. An opportunity for making this a reality is offered by the thaw in relations between the two superpowers and the start of a process of disarmament. The need for it is made more acute by the high cost of preserving the environment and the global habitat while at the same time allowing developing countries to achieve an adequate rate of growth.

The South Commission believes that a Peace and Development Fund should be established into which a substantial part of the resources freed by the scaling down in arms budgets should be channelled. This fund should use a significant proportion of its resources to assist developing countries to meet their technological needs, through such means as the establishment of centres and schemes of scientific and technological training, and collaboration between institutions of learning and research. A major thrust should be to improve technological capabilities in areas relevant to efforts to satisfy the basic needs of the billion poorest human beings. The possibility of combining this initiative with the proposed Planet Protection Fund mentioned above should be explored.

A Six-point Programme for Immediate Action

There is today a new combination of powerful political, economic, ecological and moral considerations which justify a Six-point Global Programme of Immediate Action to combat world poverty in the interest of sustainable development worldwide and the promotion of global peace and security. This programme needs to address some urgent issues, whose resolution will help to revive growth in the South and also be a first step towards a more basic restructuring of the international system designed to ensure a more equitable management of global interdependence, in the interest of both developed and developing countries. The programme should have the following objectives:

- Action to stop the net transfer of resources from the South to the North, to remove the overhang of the external debt of developing countries and to scale down their debt service to levels that would allow growth to be sustained at a rate that would yield annual increases in per capita income of at least 2-3 per cent.

- The establishment of multilateral arrangements for protecting the global environmental commons and ensuring sustainable development. These arrangements should recognize that poverty must be overcome in order that the environment in the South may be protected, and should respect the freedom of governments to set their own national priorities and policies.

- A doubling of the volume of concessional resource transfers to developing countries by 1995, priority being given to transfers through multilateral institutions (IDA and the "soft windows" of regional development banks); the additional resources should be devoted to food production, the provision of other basic needs, population control, energy security and other environmentally sensitive areas.

- The establishment of independent international mechanisms for evaluating the requirements of developing countries, the norms and indicators for performance, and the criteria and conditionality appropriate to each country. These mechanisms, acting in an advisory capacity, could help considerably to depoliticize the negotiations between international financial institutions and developing countries, the laying down of performance norms and the assessment of performance.

- A timetable for lifting protectionist barriers that adversely affect the growth of developing countries'exports to the developed countries, bringing the textiles trade under normal GATT disciplines, and removing various "grey area" restraints affecting developing countries' access to markets in the developed countries. Provision should be made for the stabilization and support of the international prices of primary commodities of special export interest to developing countries by a commitment to negotiate international agreements for these commodities. International assistance should be made available to developing countries in diversifying their commodity sectors.

- The incorporation of contingency provisions in international arrangements with a view to protecting developing countries against excessive fluctuations in international interest rates, exchange rates and terms of trade.

If a programme on these lines is to be realized, political initiative at the highest level will be needed, in order to impart the necessary momentum. The leaders of the South's nations should meet and agree on a programme for immediate action, and then use their influence to convene a global summit to discuss it with the leaders of the North. These North-South discussions could, at the same time, reopen the process of negotiation for a longer-term, fundamental reform of the international system.

5. TOWARDS THE 21st CENTURY

The globalization of economic, social and political processes now under way is likely to acquire further momentum in the years to come. Knowledge, and the application of science and technology in society, will become still more powerful determinants of wealth and power in the world.

The emerging world setting offers tremendous opportunities as well as risks. New knowledge harnessed properly can become a potent instrument for freeing humanity from poverty, ignorance and disease; but unequal access to knowledge can lead to the further marginalization of the South.

The South has to be effectively mobilized to face these formidable challenges. The objectives and policy recommendations we have outlined in our Report should assist the South in this gigantic task. They retain validity well beyond the 1990s. To recapitulate, the South must harness all its energies for the following tasks:

- A fundamental reshaping of its economies, polities and societies leading to institutional structures and value systems which prize creativity, innovation and a spirit of enterprise as well as a deep concern for social justice.

- The mobilization and enhancement of the potentialities of the people through the pursuit of development strategies and patterns which put the people at the centre and aim at raising the quality of life for all.

- A strong commitment to closing the knowledge gap with the North, through improvements in education and the development of capabilities to take full advantage of advances in science and technology.

- An effective population policy, based on a vigorous social development strategy.

- A long-term commitment to rational and prudent management of the environment and use of scarce natural resources, particularly land and water.

National policies are the foundations for the successful pursuit of development objectives. However, no less important is the challenge of South-South co-operation. With the increasing importance of cconomies of scale and expenditure on research and development, South-South co-operation may well become the most cost-effective means for the South to reach the new frontiers of science and technology. Its strategic role will increase just as opportunities for co-operation can also be expected to grow.

The restructuring of the global system is equally essential for an equitable management of global interdependence, for a progressive narrowing of the North-South divide, and for assuring peace, dignity and security for all. This can come about only after a prolonged struggle. But the South must consolidate its solidarity and improve its organizational capabilities to wage that struggle and to bring it to a successful conclusion. Through organization and commitment to an agenda inspired by universal human values, the South can influence the future evolution of the world system.

II. CRITICAL PERSPECTIVES

6. THE SOUTH AND THE NORTH: NEITHER DICTATORSHIPS NOR INTERFERENCE

Ahmed Ben Salah

Introduction

The Report of the South Commission offers an account of the situation in the South, presented on the basis of a deliberately sympathetic global view of that part of the world, with its setbacks and handicaps, its differences and potentials and its responsibilities and hopes. In all these descriptions, in the analyses of the facts, and throughout the study of North-South relations and the various proposals concerning the South's future and its future relations with the North, the economic factor is always predominant. The North is likewise seen as continuing to dominate and to act by virtue of its economic strength and the imprint it has managed to impose on its relations with the South and on the organization and operation of the international system and its institutions. But, despite the experience of the four decades since the Second World War, should the political reasoning behind the North's behaviour, behind its direct and violent or indirect and efficient interference in the countries of the South be concealed?

In particular, should we ignore the basic problem which arises more and more violently in most of the countries of the South concerning the nature of their political authorities, their leaders and their structures? This is, in short, the problem of political régimes whose record in essential fields is steadily becoming more negative and oppressive. They constitute explosive obstacles to the freedom and socio-economic and cultural development of peoples, and inhibit or prevent any genuine and effective association among the countries of the South and any improvement in relations between the South and the North.

In other words, the problems created by the attitude of the North, the political régimes of the South and the relations between North and South are primarily political in nature. The persistence of these problems cannot fail to block or impair any progress towards a situation more consonant with the rising consciousness, aspirations and demands of our time.

These problems can be solved, or at least dealt with, through political action which should, if possible, be carried out jointly, in an organized fashion and simultaneously in both the North and the South.

Background and Present Situation

Negative developments

During the post-war decades and particularly at the time when many countries of the South had just achieved independence, the world scene was essentially dominated by the Cold War, in which opposing arguments kindled or fed regional conflicts, wars of liberation, resistance movements and various other upheavals. In the economic field, the positive effects of various reconstruction plans, particularly in the countries of the North, were beginning to be fully felt by the 1960s, a decade of prosperity, progress and international co-operation for the world economy.

It was against this background that the process of independence got under way, opening up different paths towards decolonization and development. Certain countries chose alignment with the liberal economic policies of the countries of the North, more particularly the former colonial powers. The leaders of these countries in fact paid no attention to decolonization and allowed the economic "systems" in force before independence to continue and develop.

Other countries, instinctively or deliberately wishing to achieve independence through a complete break with the past, or because of the ideological training of their leaders, launched themselves straight into the mechanics of Eastern dogma, proclaiming adamantly that they were freeing themselves scientifically from colonial and capitalist oppression.

Yet others, though less numerous, after some cautious hesitation, opted for a policy of autonomous, nationalist and progressive non-alignment.

Overall, therefore, at the economic level, there was, on the one hand, alignment with the colonial and liberal North or with the Marxist East and, on the other, an effort to achieve authenticity and non-alignment. At the political level, all the countries concerned found themselves, in varying degrees, progressively shaped in very similar moulds: the single party, "the father of the nation", sham parliaments, strong-arm police, a subservient press and "national culture"... On the surface and sometimes to some extent in reality, there was a certain good-heartedness, an occasionally enlightened paternalism and a cult of the "father figure" at times carried to extremes. However, some of the elements in this trend became increasingly active, completely dispelling all the euphoria and revealing a situation characterized by frustration, indignation, opposition and violence.

In many countries of the South, the presidents, whether civilian or military, "legitimate" in law or otherwise, imposed a personality cult. The main effect of this kind of anachronistic mania or pathology is to diminish the values and demands for reform of society as a whole, its aspirations, cultures and freedoms. This was combined with a cult of the entity that became a state, a nation or a fatherland, whose identity was asserted, above all through rivalries. There was conflict between neighbours, brothers and other entities, often floundering in bloodshed, poverty and the divisions of the colonial era. For reliance was placed on the agents, advice and military forces of the North or the East.

At the economic level, development tended to take the form of speculative investment, rapid amassing of excessive wealth, accelerating corruption, and pomp and splendour: with arrogantly splendid palaces, mausoleums, villas and shiny limousines. At the same time, an unbearable level of underdevelopment was reflected in inadequate schools, anachronistic or borrowed and unsuitable curricula, destitute hospitals, famine, degraded, offensive and ostentatious lifestyles among the currently "favoured", together with increasingly overpopulated and impoverished shanty-towns and queues of those seeking flight or emigration, uprooted at home even before their departure for new agonies abroad.

In many countries independence closed like an ever-tightening vice manipulated by civilian or military chiefs or by *nomenklaturas*. Some of them were imbued with the conviction that they were the lite bringing civilization, modernity, efficiency, production and profitability. Others were full of faith – apparent or real, but in any case intransigent – in their mission as the bearers of Marxist or ultra-Marxist ideologies of salvation, always extremely verbal and often warlike, cynical and lucrative.

This negative and profoundly destructive trend blocked or distorted and falsified any genuine, constructive development nationally as well as in regional or international groupings striving together to give new life to peoples and restore the balance of power throughout the world and in international relations.

Improvements and action

As can already be seen in this review of the past, which is mirrored in the present situation, no country of the South was able to escape under-development and political and police obscurantism, even – and perhaps especially – when the initial choices were sound and are still in essence the most suitable ones in their fundamental approach. The two reasons for the inability of these countries to succeed are, let us repeat, first the immediately or gradually perverted character of their governments and, second, the various forms of interference in their affairs by some countries of the North.

Reference will be made here to the policies or "experiments" initiated and implemented by a few countries of the South, occasionally for several years, with acknowledged qualitative success and quantitative changes, which enable the just struggles of today to continue.

The main bases of these policies, which have become the common denominators of several countries, and of several political trends which transcend their historical and natural differences can be defined as follows:

- Decolonization, the initial process of transition towards full liberation of the country and society, which permits the regrouping needed to effect a change in the balance of power, both within the country and in international relations.

- Changes in thinking and socio-economic structures through the abolition of curbs and impediments to the liberation and advancement of all citizens without distinction. Structural reform through the introduction of various appropriate systems of education, vocational training, instruction of teachers and literacy campaigns; through the gradual introduction in all sectors, at the local, regional and national levels, of new structures to eradicate feudalism, obscurantism of all kinds, indifference and fatalism, as well as fear of responsibility, work and organization; elimination of epidemics and plagues; continuing preventive action.

- The launching and implementation of a national programme of economic, social and educational development based on decolonization and structural reform, having regard to the contribution of these factors to the real knowledge of the society concerned and to its aspirations. Recognition of decolonization and structural reform both as pre-requisites for, and as continuing measures forming part of the national development programme, based on the broadest possible consul-tations at the local, regional and national levels and adopted by a genuine, substantial and vital consensus, broader in scope than mere legal or institutional endorsement.

- On the basis of these consultations, a simultaneous development of freedoms, accompanying, supporting or correcting the measures for implementation of the programme and its specific and assessed social, economic and financial forecasts. Extension of freedoms is still the essential factor for ensuring the success of any development programme, its continuity, 'adaptation and modification. The greater freedoms that accompany development enable society as a whole to undertake the establishment of traditional or modernist bases for a social, economic and political democracy that reflects the development and maturity of citizens and society as a whole.

- Regional and international co-operation which consistently respects the options made and development programmes chosen and their adjustment to the changing world, enabling the peoples of the South to make an invigorating contribution to international life within the framework of a balance of power that is and must be constantly maintained.

The policy orientations to which such foundations give rise were frequently proclaimed in most of the countries of the South and still are. In reality, however, what has happened and is still happening in practice is the direct opposite of what is proclaimed and this is what has led to the unhealthy and explosive situation that prevails today.

There has nevertheless been a genuine improvement, rich in achieve-ments and lessons, in some countries of the South, thanks to the nature of their liberation struggle or the tenacity of their opposition to dictatorship of all kinds, and because of the awakening of their peoples, the competence of their professionals and the quality of their leaders, some of whom remained loyal to their struggle and to their promises. For many years, the policy bases described above were really the result of their efforts, the way they managed the situation and the positions they adopted at the regional and international levels.

This is true in particular of Algeria, Chile, Egypt, Tanzania and Tunisia. As a general rule throughout the 1960s and the first half of the 1970s, projects, achievements and expectations were a source of confidence, pride, enthusiasm and hope. Starting from conditions of endemic poverty or extreme weakness resulting from wars of liberation or sporadic regional conflicts, these countries, and some others as well, had to tackle virtually every kind of obstacle simultaneously. At home, there was impatience, lack of understanding and resistance to change, even though change was desired, intended or trustfully accepted. Abroad, there were the prejudgements of a few "big shots" in the North, those who claim to "know best" and always wish to "guide", while at the same time mocking in ambiguous language the people actually trying to do something positive and their still fragile achievements.

There have also been other even "bigger shots", who have never been officially received by the authorities of the countries in the South but have always worked behind the scenes, manipulating certain officials to ensure that, in practice, they are always "in favour of whatever is against and against whatever is in favour!" There have been the opinions – always expressed "from a scientific standpoint" – of phoney gurus who blithely practise their deception, working only in the background. All these wonderful people, appointed thanks to bilateral and sometimes international "co-operation", and their allies within the countries concerned, who were more readily recruited after independence and during the difficult and austere transitional periods, had ready access to the media of the countries of the North. Their views were further disseminated and "embellished" by reporters, correspondents and editorialists who vented their spleens on those bringing about real change in the countries of the South that were really engaged in genuine decolonization.

Those who really worked for co-operation, the real intellectual guides in the countries of the North, were no longer able to neutralize the frenzy of these agents of hatred, contempt and deception. Both at home and abroad, as decolonization progressed with changes being approved by large majorities, so the denigration and harassment were stepped up with a view not only to creating obstacles, doubt or distrust, but also actually overthrowing those in power, sometimes by violence.

Leaders in countries of the South were taken in hand by their "courts", which had links with the remaining feudal forces still active in the country and with various elements of the undercover services. Some of these leaders surrendered blindly. There was, for instance, the case of a head of state who publicly denounced the entire policy which had been carried out under his authority for many years. In so doing, he "laid the blame" on certain members of his staff and, without heed to the collective memory, forgot the policies he had been advocating only a few days before and his earlier praise of the quality of his staff. Furthermore, in his public denunciation of the past, no reference was made to studies carried out by national experts or to any meetings of political bodies, institutional or otherwise. The only clear and striking reference made was to a report by the ambassador of a colonial power disparaging the development policy in no uncertain terms and predicting catastrophe if that policy were pursued. Overnight, the party in power, the press and the media as a whole ceased to refer to development, to meetings and to discussion of the various issues confronting the country, and mentioned only the topic prompted by an ambassador who was thus able to take considerable revenge for the "unbearable" years of decolonization he had experienced in the country.

Things became even more grotesque and this marked the beginning of the moral and political crisis now experienced by that country, which had in fact made substantial progress along the difficult path towards development, reform and advancement of large sectors of the population. A spate of effusive messages was cabled by the chairmen of political parties in the colonial North and comments in the press contained deceitful and malicious justifications, encouraging leaders who had turned against their own country to embark upon an irreversible course of repression, the massacre of workers and a string of endless trials.

Only a few years later, on the other side of the world, another country was also to suffer the tragic assassination of its democratically elected leader. The nature and consequences of these scenarios were very similar. There and elsewhere in any case there was a return to exploitation, accompanied by the rise of régimes which did not hesitate to commit violation after violation of the rights of large sectors of their populations, particularly those of the militants and activists.

In these two cases, as in others, the reversal of genuinely national policies, that were an in-depth expression of the aspirations of the societies concerned, is still today responsible for a situation of non-development, destruction of what has been achieved in various sectors and deteriorating social relations. The reversal of these national policies has given rise to a liberalism that is uncontrolled because it gives complete freedom to the strongest to amass wealth, enjoy the "delights" of corruption and the delusions of an "entente" with the great of the world: that is, the First World. This untamed liberalism allows no freedom for others, who have made efforts and who have hoped. It precludes all progress towards a democracy that is other than spurious, repressive and fed by submission to indebtedness, waste and the satisfaction of the continuing paternalistic censors of the colonial North.

This deplorable trend continued for many years in certain countries of the South and still persists in others. This is due to several factors; first of all to feelings, attitudes of mind and cravings for power at home or abroad, factors which are not, of course, taken into account in economic calculations or in any rational assessment. Complexes of various kinds, the desire to dominate, hatred and contempt are, however, very effective and potent elements. Almost everywhere, in different societies, they conflict with the desire for freedom, dignity, justice, respect for others and self-respect. The confrontation is more intense in the countries of the South where the moderating influences found in the everyday life of most of the countries of the North have not yet had time to develop.

Second, economic and ideological justification and motivation for this negative development or messy situation are not lacking. In the context of the Cold War, the main idea was not only to ensure that acceptance of the ideologies of the East was prevented, but to obstruct any movement in the direction of economic progress and a just organization of society which might indirectly improve the standing of those ideologies. Yet in many countries of the South where the kind of reversal referred to above occurred, the leaders were and remain above suspicion in this area because of their training and the way they behaved. In some cases, moreover, the leaders of these countries were convinced that economic progress and a just organization of society were more likely to be achieved with them and their peoples who had fought long and hard for their liberation. Politically they did not have to be or seem to be "professionally" anti-communist, but they had to develop structures which did not need a communist ideology in order to be just and to meet the aspirations of their peoples. In this, some of them at least were closer to the socialists of Northern Europe than to the communists elsewhere. But the Cold War had its mechanisms and its networks, and the nationalist and progressive leaders of the South could not escape the vice-like pressures nor the justifications of that war.

Third, and in addition to these contradictory and often grotesquely false justifications, arguments were advanced to secure the support of some élites and businessmen, who were often already susceptible to such arguments as a result of their university or business training and their refusal or inability to take a straightforward non-aligned national stand.

These well-worn arguments touch upon a number of familiar subjects. The role of the state is presented as excessive statism; the nationalizations called for by decolonization are presented as communist action heralding the stifling of private enterprise and the private sector; structural reforms, even though quite successful, are presented as overly hasty and imposed from above; while profitability, productivity and efficient management are brandished as major arguments, with total disregard for the point at which the countries concerned began their development and the fact that times have changed since the developed countries, some of which achieved development several centuries ago, embarked upon that process. Nevertheless, in many countries of the South public enterprises were springing up and there were increasing numbers of professionals trained in modern management, with experience in both the public and the private sector, itself often the result of the evolution of public enterprises.

However, it was not difficult to see the structural changes taking place in society, which were reflected in particular in the progress achieved by broad strata of the population which had risen from poverty and despair. It was also possible to see considerable confidence in the future based on work and well-deserved pride in achievement and construction.

It is these achievements and the other quantifiable and recognized successes mentioned earlier, as well as the moral, social and material progress made, that have enabled peoples to develop their awareness and to combat domestic shortcomings and foreign interference. Today, despite the cynicism of some and the stubbornness of others, and despite repression and torture, the struggle for the "second liberation" is under way – a struggle for the independence of countries, for the organization of regional solidarity, for action to combat all the forms of expression used by the blind Powers and their allies, for a joint contribution to the necessary change and renewal of international relations. The fight has begun; neither the structural adjustment programmes, nor the strong-men they generate under very questionable protection can halt the peoples' developing awareness of the legitimacy of their aspirations for freedom and well-being, and of their struggle for a second liberation.

The North and Global Transformation

It seems reasonable to ask whether the overall situation in the South, very summarily described here as being either in collision or in collusion with the practices of the North, did not become an anachronism some time ago. Should it not have rapidly been superseded, or even avoided or sublimated? The answer is "yes" – through a natural and correct interpretation of the lesson to be learned from the collapse of the Nazi and fascist dictatorships and the agony of the colonial era. The North and the South contributed, separately or together, to the start of a great global transformation. Together, they had an obligation to assume the ethical and logical consequences of this development, which was essentially the birth of an era of liberation and progress. Together they could have prevented the rise of new dictatorships and helped to remedy profound imbalances. But the break, the change of course were already inherent in the victory, which has become exclusive; it was the victory of the North, or of a certain North. Reconstruction plans were being drawn up and new international institutions established just as colonial occupation was being strengthened and wars were being waged against peoples rising in strength to regain their freedom. The North, short-sighted, sectarian and triumphant, was rejecting and shattering the logic of history, of an historical era.

For two decades the North succeeded in prolonging the agony of the colonial era by again turning its military arsenals against the peoples of the South, thus aggravating the historical backwardness of a large part of the world that was in the process of liberating itself. At the same time, the North was not only unable to prevent the rise of a powerful totalitarianism, but even gave it room to grow in the South. It was this growth which finally served as the catalyst in the gradual and then accelerating change in the North's attitude towards the colonized countries struggling for independence. With the exception of India, it was at the beginning of the 1960s and throughout that decade that countries gained either formal or real independence one after the other. Peoples acceded to independence and became aware of the time they had lost, in other words of their intolerable backwardness in all areas of life.

Various forms of international and bilateral co-operation were then conceived; some were beneficial, others conditional or even detrimental. The latter, together with the action of the malevolent Powers, shaped the extensive weakness of the South. The North was incapable of overcoming its complexes and its short-term vision and of grasping and guiding this first global transformation of the century, despite the sound efforts of the forces of justice and progress in the North and despite the constant struggle of the popular majorities in the South.

Now, a fresh opportunity dawns for a second global transformation as the 20th century draws to a close. It has been a century with a heavy burden of war and failure, but full of potential for the growth of a world of spiritual and material values, real justice, closeness to nature and strong worldwide solidarity.

The revolution in the East signalled the collapse, not of a religion or an ideology, but of systems of relations and of management which people, castes and armies had tacked on to that religion or ideology, in a manner wholly and consistently out of keeping with the values inherent therein.

The revolution of the peoples of the East is a revolution of great universal values, and one hesitates somewhat to compare it with the anti-colonial revolutions so commonly snapped up, taken over and diverted by the various mechanisms and actions of both the North and the South, just as the first Soviet revolution was diverted. Regardless of the case or the time, the lesson is inflexible, ever-present, loud and clear: the few fundamental values which enable people to live together – freedom, dignity, justice and the right to continuous progress – cannot be killed.

What will the North do? What is it doing now? What will the South's attitude be? What lesson will the South learn? Will it accept the North's interpretations? Will it let slip this great opportunity and give in in an effort to adjust the machinery that constitutes the fabric of its relations with the North? Or will the South wake up, as it did when the real anti-colonial struggles took place, so that, within each country, the inflexible lesson can be relearned and applied through genuine and straightforward work for the second liberation? Such action will be of great help in ensuring the success of this second global transformation and in counterbalancing or redirecting the sometimes ravenous appetites which ultimately will totally ruin this opportunity for restoring the world to equilibrium in peace, or through conflicting ideas or competing approaches with respect to justice and solidarity.

The North does not seem to be taking this course at all. It was sickened by the existence and the growth of communism and is today even sicker because of its overwhelming desire to feel that communism is dead and, along with it, socialism, which in general has adopted an intelligent attitude towards the dictatorships set up in the name of communism.

There are many, in the North, who are already making triumphant declarations or, at a more technical level, are preparing their take-over of the countries of the East while they are still weak. They are doing this in the name of solidarity and even of fraternity, but not in the name of civilization, a term "appropriate" elsewhere, further to the South.

Here again the predominant factor is neither cultural nor political in the sense of a policy of freedom, independence or democracy, but rather economic, in other words economic liberalism. This means first and foremost a market economy for good and *right away*, so as to be sure that what is at stake is freedom and democracy, and of course strategic positions and renewed profits.

But here the North, and today Europe in particular, is revealing itself, and in a light, moreover, where memories are stronger. In the present competitive context, countries will of course emphasize that they are European and that their object is to "contain" the power of the United States, and particularly that of Japan. The internal divisions that seem likely to occur everywhere in the East will create untenable situations hardly likely to remove the threat of wars or even general warfare. In the vacuum created by the palpable absence of an international organization that is free of vetoes and committed to reform to end its lop-sided composition – in an economic situation that is almost everywhere becoming extremely critical – the worst is now possible, particularly since, as a precaution, the kind of "unfortunate mistake" to which certain election campaign practices may give rise should be anticipated.

Surely the North as a whole, together with the South, should have been able to initiate a renewal of the United Nations in order to settle or examine the dangerously overheated situations which exist today? It could then have continued to use all possible means to ensure the success of this transformation worldwide, or at least show it had the international will to protect humankind from the minor upheavals which will culminate in conflicts and war, rather than in justice, freedom and progress.

Prospects and Struggle

The whole South is sinking further into a situation of extreme weakness. In most countries of the South, the authorities in power are simply aggravating the situation and making its consequences unbearable for all their people, including their youth. They react against the people with constant repression, merciless violations of freedoms and relentless attacks against national opposition forces offering new policies. These anachronistic and incompetent authorities shelter behind the reasoning, advice, programmes and diktats of the major interests of the North and the machinery that has been established to impose them – but also to support these authorities as far as possible, by holding them hostage if necessary. The principal aim always seems to be to prevent or delay any change which the peoples concerned and their élites, with faith in their values and their dignity, will not fail ultimately to bring about. It is still recognized today that, at the global level, economic, political and military indicators continue to confirm that forces in the North remain in a constant state of confrontation vis-à-vis the South. They persist in erecting, in the South, all kinds of walls to prevent development of the peoples, cultures and economies of the South. For these forces, the fall of the Berlin Wall has no relevance to the South or the walls erected there. The conflicts, explosions and migratory movements concern them so little that the just in the North itself appear to be crying in the wilderness in their reports, analyses and appeals. In fact, these forces, with their gross appetites, their "know-how" and their fears, are looking towards the East and its vast space and vast market and no one can foretell what will become of the European edifice which has been so patiently constructed, given the haste and dogmatism of these arrogant forces.

Even if, like those of others, the foregoing arguments are presented in oversimplified North/South terms, it is obvious that the prospect of change in the relations between the two will depend on the necessary distinction between the forces in both the North and the South. It is, however, a joint struggle that must unite the forces of progress and justice in the South with those in the North, even if, from time to time, they find themselves in the minority or defeated. There are some "South" elements in the North and some "North" elements in the South. There are also opposition forces in both North and South. There are many areas for dialogue and co-operation, particularly concerning the future of the equilibrium of tomorrow's world, over and above today's anachronisms, blindness and confusion.

The struggle of the forces of liberation and progress in the South, and the supportive struggle of the forces of justice in the North, will make it possible to change present conditions and create new opportunities for a lively response to the aspirations of all peoples to peace in justice, freedom and progress.

In the struggle of the forces of freedom and progress in the South and the North, the stakes are primarily political. The basic opportunities for economic progress in the South and for renewed relations with the North will depend on whether the necessary changes in the nature of the political forces in power in the South actually take place. These forces bear the responsibility for the steady weakening of the South and for the deterioration of its relations with the generally democratic North. What would happen in the South, and also in the North, if by some misfortune the North should fall into the hands of certain forces that are increasingly visible on its political scene?

It is in this spirit and having regard to the unavoidable efforts that must be made if the challenges facing the South in particular are to be taken up, that a number of points are submitted briefly by way of conclusion:

- All the necessary measures must be taken to provide the minimum conditions for renewal of the South, which is itself capable of contributing greatly to a continuous adjustment of North-South relations.

- Efforts must be made and action taken to end the stifling of freedoms in the countries of the South and to ensure, under international supervision if necessary, that lawfully elected governments finally gain control in those countries.

- Once these new governments are in place, thanks to their legitimacy and self-confidence, a process of subregional and regional association must be initiated so as to create viable spaces for economic and cultural projects that will respect the individuality, values and traditions of each member of such groupings.

- Such subregional or regional groupings established in freedom and independence, in addition to developing their internal relations and exchanges, might then be in a better position to call on subregional or regional groupings in the North to join them in a partnership for economic and cultural development.

- It will also be vital for the South and for a healthy development of relations with the North and the achievement of a just balance of power, to work and strive for in-depth adaptation of all the United Nations institutions to the present-day world and the world of tomorrow. A United Nations truly representative of authorities that are themselves representative could become an essential guarantee of progress for each individual country and for humankind as a whole. It could also be a noble instrument for correcting political errors committed within states or in their relations with other states. The United Nations would also be better placed than the IMF is at present to put forward programmes for political change that would ensure that appropriate decisions were taken in the economic and monetary fields.

- There might perhaps be a general call for the South Commission or such institution into which it might develop in independent circumstances and with appropriate resources, to serve as a focal point for initiating and co-ordinating action and policies designed to aid and support the struggle of the peoples of the South, together with their trustworthy and upright officials, to enable the South to set an example with its own cultures, traditions, ambitions and renewal.

7. THE SOUTH: GLOBAL CHALLENGES[1]

Christian Comeliau

After the Gulf War, North-South relations will never again be what they were, or what they were believed to be, before that war. Opinions may differ on the causes and consequences of and responsibilities for the war (depending on whether the focus is on surprise or, on the contrary, "I told you so"). Analyses and proposals for development and co-operation strategies may continue or, on the contrary, come to a halt. Professional experts may manage to preserve development as an area of expertise and as a livelihood; or they might revert to less ambitious and more lucrative subjects. The fact remains that a deep, unavoidable and irreversible fissure has opened up; it will swallow the blind, and could stop all the others. But the divorce between the reality of development and the debate to which it gives rise can no longer be ignored.

Though it predates the Gulf crisis, it is in this context that the South Commission Report should be considered.

The Report may be considered exceptional testimony, as it should make it possible to answer a central question: on the eve of the outbreak of the crisis and of the Gulf War, how did the South itself analyse the past and envisage the future? If it can be argued that the official attitude of the North at this critical moment was, and still is, unbelievably narrow, blind and timid, how does one judge the South's attitude as reflected in the position taken by distinguished political and intellectual personalities from the Third World who, though no longer in power, still have considerable influence and who shared their thoughts during the three years before the crisis? What image, what "vision" of the South does the Report convey that could explain the break and, above all, enlighten the reader about prospects and options for the future?

The following analysis is meant to be constructive, it seeks nothing more than to start a dialogue. My central theme is that the Report of the South Commission is deeply disappointing, not because of any inept or unwarranted observations, but because it falls far short of the demands (extraordinarily heavy, true) of the present situation, and because it adds no new bases and no fresh practical proposals to the analysis of this situation and to the political options that this requires. It offers no vision peculiar to the nations of the South as to the nature of the development of

North-South relations. On the contrary, it would seem as though the development of the South implied its integration – almost copycat integration – into the North-dominated system.

The Report of the South Commission is not the first of its kind. Even though their membership was explicitly North-South, Jan Tinbergen's RIO Group in 1976[2], and the Brandt Commission, which produced two reports in 1980 and 1983,[3] represent comparable ventures, particularly as their approach links them to what might be called an "enlightened social-democratic" trend, and because they are at the borderline of intellectual reflection and political responsibility. Dudley Seers, writing about the Brandt Commission's first report, sharply criticized the ambiguity of such studies in which, because of the initial community of ideas, it is possible to avoid all clashes and, hence, all the quarrels which those in power actually have to face.[4] Perhaps the ambiguity might be lessened if these works were conceived of as a sort of ongoing reflection rather than oriented towards turning out a single report.

It is not the personality of the members of such groups, or their technical competence, let alone their intellectual integrity which is at issue. Yet the fact is that most of them have acquired their experience in the state apparatus; their training and experience in multilateral organizations have forged in many of them an approach to development and international relations that is Westernized, economicist, and marked by the intellectual and diplomatic modes of this very special milieu;[5] and thus the catalogue of questions dealt with strangely resembles, in short, the table of contents of all the reports that preceded this one.

This last point is largely unavoidable, and is probably, after all, of only minor importance. If the Report really fails to convince, it is not because it resembles its predecessors in vocabulary and table of contents. Nor is it because it contains a good number of commonplaces: it is sure to be reproached for this, but one must be wary of such charges in such a field, since such commonplaces must be repeated today to counter the omni-present "prevailing wisdom" of the World Bank and comparable institutions. For the South to repeat its attachment to the principle of people-centred development, for example, or its right to a certain protectionism may be a commonplace, but it is a necessary commonplace. For it to proclaim that the purpose of development is the promotion of the well-being of the people is perhaps an obvious point, but one that needs to be repeated at a time when the term "development" also serves to justify mixing business with politics, or military power. The reaffirmation of general principles, even the least unexpected, does not necessarily lead to platitudes. Why, then, does the Report make such boring reading? And why does it fail to present truly convincing theses?

The reasons are threefold. The first is more one of form than of substance. In its concern to be taken seriously, the Commission consulted numerous experts, and one can find echoes of their texts in the final Report. But what the Report gains in expertise, it loses in political impact, and above all in concentration around some key ideas that would have better summed up the positions of the South and hence its ideology (in the strongest sense of the word) in the present international context.[6] These ideas are not totally absent, but they are given insufficient weight.

The second reason, seen too often – alas – in this kind of publication, lies in its "economism", in the undue weight it attaches to the strictly economic – and even macro-economic – dimensions of the issues raised, although the Report does mention some concerns such as the cultural dimension or people-to-people relations, but fails to give them any specific weight. Even what is said about the informal sector and about enterprises barely differs from what has been written a thousand times elsewhere. At the same time, the macro-economic approach strikingly resembles that which is to be found in any outdated textbook, without even underscoring the exceptionally timely questions, such as structural adjustment. To be more specific: too macro-economic, too state-oriented, the Report fails above all to situate the political with respect to the economic, and to use the economy to clarify alternatives open to political leaders. The clarification of these relations between the political and the economic remains an essential condition for removing some of the ambiguities of international relations.

But the third reason why the Report is not convincing is the most serious, especially because of the contrast with the initial aims: quite simply, with respect to positions currently adopted in international debates, it fails to offer an alternative philosophy as an approach to the general problems raised – development, identity and cohesion of the South, the future of North-South relations. True, many ideas are put forward in these different areas, but they smack too much of a mere updating of the claims of the 1970s. What is lacking is the general link and above all the scent of novelty that would give the reader the impression of finally escaping from the wilderness of theory and from the repetitions of the prevailing doctrine that have been blocking international debate at least since the early 1980s, that is, since the beginning of what may be called the "financial decade".[7] It has been said that the future has begun to look so bleak over the last few months of 1991 that this fresh start is more necessary than ever.

This lack of alternative philosophy will become clearer through two examples, which also constitute two themes of central importance in the body of the Report: "common interests", and relations with the world system.

The affirmation of a community of interests between the parties that are to be brought together through greater solidarity is a recurring theme in this kind of report. For example, much the same argument was made in the Brandt report on the subject of North-South relations and on the common interests which "ought to" bind them. In the present case, the argument is first applied, as was to be expected, to the cohesion of the South itself, but it falls very short of the scale of the problem raised. It is a commonplace to speak of the growing differentiation of the Third World. But have the consequences of this differentiation on the internal cohesion of this Third World been sufficiently analysed? The Report of the South Commission makes a lengthy analysis in economic terms of this problem and of the related problems of South-South co-operation – and this was necessary. Still, the question arises how these economic interrelations – known to be weak, compared to the links of dependence with the North – can lead to political solidarity sufficient to mobilize the forces of very diverse countries in the "service" of a general interest of the South ("to serve the South"). What would be the substance of this general interest? How could it be mobilized since there is practically no common policy decision-making centre, not even a secretariat for the elaboration of economic policies (as is the OECD for the countries of the North)? If the South Commission wanted to create – or contribute to creating – South-South solidarity, surely it ought to have supplied more material for building this solidarity. To be more specific: are these economic interests sufficient to create a political interest capable of mobilizing the diverse forces, or must there first be an enhanced political awareness – in an international crisis, for example, like that of the Gulf – for these economic interests to be taken into consideration?

These questions concerning the South's strategy and tactics are not touched upon in the Report, and the treatment of the basic problems of these common interests is probably too superficial, especially in political terms. But if this is so, can the Report be expected to lead to great progress? Is it enough to keep on harping on the theme of the common interest of the South, if serious thought is not given to the new problems of exclusion and rivalry that may crop up within the South as regional powers come into being? There is no shortage of disturbing examples on this theme, and it is not the proliferation of institutions and bureaucracies that will settle such questions. The South Commission could have proposed some lines of thought on the positive part that these regional powers could play with respect to their neighbours, but there is scarcely a hint of this.

Is the ambition of solidarity any better defended with regard to North-South relations? The stated principle is that the South must first of all be self-reliant, but that does not preclude the search for collaboration with the North, in order to "change from exploitation to shared benefit, from subordination to partnership", stressing that the South needs the North but also that the North needs the South. Hence the proposal for a "pact of solidarity". These are obviously desirable perspectives, but the Report does not make clear on what tangible bases they could be built. And the facts offer even less evidence of a change in the North's attitudes with regard to such perspectives; the international situation today shows that these are as remote as they possibly could be from its major concerns.

Besides, it may not be very realistic to speak of North-South relations without specific reference to the nature of the world economic system, whose decision-making centres are essentially in the North but which is spreading a model of development designed to dominate the entire planet. A presentation in these terms may appear to be excessively theoretical and general in an analysis meant above all to be pragmatic. On the contrary, I do believe that without a constant awareness of the nature of the system it is impossible to achieve realistic policies.

The persistence in such a report of the idea of "catching up" – the gap to be filled progressively between the South and the North – is somewhat surprising. Admittedly, this reasoning is warranted on many specific points, for example, in the case of demographic and social indicators. However – to generalize – it means but one thing: that the world system is accepted as it is, with its underlying values and guiding rationale, and therefore with the inequalities and exclusions for which the South reproaches it today. This implies a readiness to repeat the basic error of the 1970s: the call for a "new international economic order" exactly similar to the old order, except in the sharing of power. It was not a matter of reducing injustice, inequality or exclusion, but merely of shifting the impact. Today, it is rather regrettable that with its exceptional intellectual "strike force" the South Commission was not able to come up with a more critical view of the nature of this system, its advantages and costs, the potential scope for adapting or even transforming it, with a view, for example, to promoting a more equitable world or more sustainable development. Nowhere does such analysis feature in the Report.

The consequences with regard to many special problems are evident; a few examples selected from the most important ones will suffice. For example, no critical thought was given to the price of modernization or to the extremely serious situations – already well-known – caused by the expansion of consumption-dominated growth in the large cities of the most advanced countries of the South, or to the harm caused in their ecosystems through ignorance of the energy costs. Nor was any critical thought given to the requirements of maximal integration in world trade, requirements referred to in all the recommendations of the multi- lateral organizations, and, more generally, what are known as "international strategies of development". Liberalization of trade is brought up, and its drawbacks in services are analysed, but the main attack is aimed at the protectionism of the North; nowhere is a solid case made for development-oriented, selective and sound protectionism. Why does the South so thoroughly interiorize the dominant conventional wisdom?

Nor is there any criticism of the consequences of the capitalist relations of this world system, of its logic based exclusively on profit-making. There is the usual bundle of charges against the malpractices of multinational firms, but also arguments favouring these very same companies when they are based in the South. Is it likely that their capitalist mentality will be fundamentally transformed just by virtue of their geographical origin? Likewise, there is no new practical proposal in such vital and necessary areas as the role of the state, the role of planning, the relative roles of public and private enterprises. On this point, here again, and regrettably, the report does not go any further than the World Bank.[8]

Overall, the attitude to the world system is extremely ambiguous. There are the familiar criticisms whenever there is talk of the costs borne by the South; but the essential point is overlooked, namely that it is very likely that the mechanisms of exclusion will recur as this system extends to the South and favours certain countries, certain sectors or certain groups of activity to the detriment of all the others. In other words, according to this attitude, the world system is wrong not because it foments exclusion, but wrong just so long as it generates exclusion to the sole benefit of the countries of the North. What then are the chances for the emergence of this "rational and development-oriented international system" which the Report calls for? Now that the hopes of "real socialism" have vanished in the East, are there no other solutions left than a blind acceptance of dominant neo-liberalism? Surely, further thought should have been given to the opportunities of pluralism opened up by certain *selective* uses of the world system. This approach might have made it possible to present a truly political critique of the world system, without at the same time conducting an academic analysis which would of course be out of place in this context. The critique could have taken the form of multiple positive proposals on GATT and protectionism, IMF and debt, the World Bank and structural adjustment, or the role of the United Nations and its specialized agencies.

The main criticisms of the Report of the South Commission concern the "missing alternative",[9] the lack of a new philosophy of development and international relations. The term "missing alternative" was coined in connection with structural adjustment. In view of the practical importance of this adjustment, one could hardly fail to have strong views on the subject. Yet the Report devotes only a few (far from original) pages on the consequences of adjustment, but none at all to its design. Has the South no alternative proposal on this matter? What is to become, then, of the brave efforts and critical thinking of the Economic Commission for Africa on the subject?[10] Why, on such a vital issue, strengthen further this impression of intellectual paralysis affecting the thinking centres of the South with regard to the crisis of the world economic system?

I shall mention one last – and not the least surprising – example to illustrate this absence of an alternative philosophy: the attitude concerning transfers of financial resources from the North to the South for development. It is quite normal, of course, to stress with indignation the paradox of a reverse transfer from South to North. But after two oil crises, three decades of ineffective aid, and on the eve of a war officially estimated to have cost 500 million US dollars a day, for the South to reassert its claims on development finance, by recalling the all-too-familiar target of 0.7 per cent of GNP which the countries of the North ought to be transferring to the South in the form of official development assistance,[11] speaks volumes on the general disarray regarding this matter and on the lack of imagination of the South's leaders. As to debt – and it is certainly right not to link it to the problems of development – here again there is no fresh proposal, not even an appeal for greater solidarity among the debtors of the South.

This critique may seem to go too far in that it calls for what no one is yet able to propose, namely an alternative philosophy of development and international relations. But if there is one need which is highlighted by the recent worsening of the international situation and the darkening of the long-term prospects of North-South relations, it is surely the need for such a fresh philosophy. There is no other way out of this dead end. We must think quickly, and in depth. If each of the individuals and groups concerned feels unable on its own to make progress in this field, perhaps once again co-operation between these individuals and between these groups should be increased and they should – modestly – get back to work.

The South Commission has submitted its Report on the challenge to the South. But times change quickly – North and South are already confronted with a much more profound challenge.

Notes

1. This text was prepared for the Delphi Forum in Poros, Greece (1-9 June 1991), and included in the published proceedings of the meeting: Sophia Mappa (ed.), 1992.
2. RIO, 1976.
3. Brandt Commission, 1980 and 1983.
4. Dudley Seers, 1980, pp. 681-693.
5. Is it possible to imagine for a moment, for example, that the South Commission failed to speak of "sustainable" development, the "cultural" dimension of development, and all the other buzzwords in recent international conferences?
6. If A.O. Hirschman has made such a great mark on development economics, it is not due to his technical analyses but because each of his articles brings a striking idea, disputable perhaps, but which cannot be brushed away. Perhaps there were some new Hirschmans in the South Commission, but the Report did not give them much space.
7. I develop this idea further in Comeliau, 1991.
8. Even less, judging by UNDP, 1991, which at least has the merit of nuancing and presenting its case in this field.
9. The phrase was proposed by Tony Killick with regard to structural adjustment. It is used here in a broader sense. See Tony Killick and M. Sutton, 1982.
10. ECA, 1989.
11. Announced and repeated regularly since the 1970s, this goal was reached only by a few small countries. The average amount of official assistance from the OECD today is hardly one half of this percentage. But this goal may be criticized from different angles: technically, because it is a rate and because this rate says nothing about the effectiveness of the transfer in the beneficiary country; economically and politically, for today it is clear that international conditions of development go far beyond the question of "aid" which does more harm than good.

Bibliography

Brandt Commission (Independent Commission on International Development Issues)
    North-South: A Programme for Survival, Pan Books, London, 1980.
Brandt Commission (Independent Commission on International Development Issues)
    Common Crisis. North-South: Co-operation for World Recovery, Pan Books, London, 1983.
Comeliau, Christian
    Les relations Nord-Sud, collection Repres, Dcouverte, Paris, 1991.
ECA (United Nations Economic Commission for Africa)
    African Alternative Framework to Structural Adjustment Programmes with a View to Recovery and Socio-economic Change, Addis Ababa, 1989.
Killick, Tony and M. Sutton
    "An overview", in Tony Killick (ed.), *Adjustment and Financing in the Developing World: The Role of the IMF,* Washington, published by the IMF in association with the ODI, London, 1982.
Mappa, Sophia (ed.)
    L'Europe des Douze et les autres: Intgration ou auto-exclusion?, Forum de Delphes, Karthala, Paris, 1992.
RIO
    Reshaping the International Order: A Report to the Club of Rome, Dutton, New York, 1976.
Seers, Dudley
    "North-South: muddling morality and mutuality", *Third World Quarterly,* Vol. II, No. 4, October 1980.
World Bank
    World Development Report 1991, Oxford University Press, New York, 1991.

8. PEOPLE-CENTRED DEVELOPMENT THROUGH COLLECTIVE SELF-RELIANCE

Johan Galtung

For someone who for decades has argued that development has as its real goal the development of human beings, starting with the basic human needs of those most in need, and basically through collective, solidary action of those hit by maldevelopment, it is hard to restrain enthusiasm for the Report of the South Commission. Here people-centred development, eradication of misery, collective self-reliance come out on top. Included are so many of those factors missed by the economism that has marred the field since the 1950s: people, human beings with their very basic needs, living in a civil society that is neither state nor capital, neither plan nor market but simply people in all their varieties, with all their networks and organizations; and here are women and the gender factor in general; here we find culture; environment.

It is all here. In other words, this Report is so much more realistic than the single-minded efforts to reduce development to economic growth, with saving ratios, investment, productivity, capital formation and GNP. They are also here, but never alone.

So, kudos for the South Commission. But how could it be otherwise, given its composition? Among the 29 members we find six of the most dedicated development politicians in the South; and two of the most celebrated women specialists (there could have been more). True, there are 16 economists. However, they are not single-minded neo-classicists but very broad-minded humans defying any classification. We had reasons to expect the best.

Another very positive point: the Report is not identified with the name of any one person, politician, economist, whatever, as are so many reports from the North. How does this cult of personality in the North square with its self-proclaimed democracy, and how does the collective and egalitarian nature of the South Commission's work square with the alleged authoritarianism of the South? Good, eloquent symbolism. Leave it that way.

The Commission should also be praised for burying the "Third World", an expression used in their Report only in references to some of the older institutions. South is "in" – geographic, it is true, with the usual problems of placing Australia, New Zealand and some others, but so much better than the numerology of the "Third" world, which so obviously alludes to third-class, third-rate, and which is only marginally acceptable in the biblical sense of the last becoming the first. Actually, if what this Report recommends is translated into practice that may eventually be the outcome.

However, anyone working in this field has comments, some of them critical, but mainly complementary to the complimentary. My comments are grouped under four headings: *South, People-centred, South-South* and *South-North.*

South

To start right there: the underlying geopolitics of the division of the world into North and South. No objection to two catchy compass terms. But where does the South Commission place the former socialist countries, in the former Soviet Union and Eastern Europe? Today they are more South than North, rapid "thirdworldization" of the former "Second World" soon being an accomplished fact, with élites negotiating on cosy terms with the "First World", with a vertical division of labour and capital and R&D on terms dictated by them, with an increasing gap in material living standards between high and low, and endemic unemployment and imminent misery at the bottom.

Not long ago the world had two career patterns for countries to choose from, or to be pushed into: the market road and the central planning road. The second career ladder has now been removed. Of course, we would then expect more pressure to enter the higher echelons on the single available ladder. This is the strategy so far chosen by Eastern European countries trying to join the European Community at least in associate status, and by Mexico in joining the North American Free Trade Area. But the West has admitted one and only one obviously non-Western country so far, the first country in the South/ "Third World" to have made it: Japan, even to the point that people forget not only race and culture but even geography, referring to Japan as "Western". And look at what happens: accusations, calumnies, Japan-bashing.

I do not think the Club wants to admit more countries like the highly successful mini-Japans, precisely because they are successful. Rather, there will be a stampede, like on the roof of the American Embassy in Saigon that day in April 1975, till the ladder is pulled up. The rest will know their place. Individuals will try to arrive by plane or boat or other means; countries will not.

This is also the South, also non-members of the Club. And the correct name for the Club is not "North". It is, has always been and will for a long time remain the West (or, more correctly, the North-West). In the whole Report the countless "North-South" problems are in reality West-South relations, and the former socialist countries are heading for the same problems. Only racial and cultural arrogance, and geography, will prevent them from seeing that staik reality still for some time to come and joining "periphery" countries in the South.

Potentially this makes the South even stronger than the Report indicates. The West, meaning the OECD countries, the trilateral of North America-Western Europe-Japan, with 2+4+1=7 constituting the self-appointed Group of Seven, acting as executive committee not only for the West but for the world economy (imitating the United Nations Security Council), is strong economically. But demographically these countries constitute only 15 per cent, and are declining. From this, three conclusions can be drawn: the West might be well advised to be less arrogant and domineering; the South will prevail in the longer run, and it is to be hoped that it will not treat the West so badly as the West did the South. Japan might also do well joining the South, meaning most of the human race. There is enormous dynamic potential there.

People-centred

The development models we have had so far usually derive from national economics, not from nature, human or world economics; and not from non-economics. To give top priority to such basic needs as food, clothing and shelter, health and education, "los bienes fundamentales", is people-centred; to give top priority to GNP is country-centred. From there the step to lite-centred is usually a very short one, given the importance for GNP growth of processing and marketing, and hence of industry and trade, and also of industrialists and traders. We have been labouring under GNP growth for far too long.

But then there is another dimension, people-generated versus lite-generated, which is barely touched by the Commission. In general, people will secure their livelihood in the way open to them, meaning with intensive labour and traditional technology, and élites will do it with capital intensity and modern technology. The two do not exclude each other, as the Commission points out. But the concrete proposals favour the latter, and the evidence from the technological shift in agriculture, fisheries and silviculture is far from reassuring. In the North these technologies came slowly and their application was the work of many people; in the South they come from above, through investment and assistance, depriving the traditional sector of well-to-do markets and thus making them even less able to afford the new products. Inevitably, the result is the impoverishment so well documented in the Report, and an increasing distance between high and low (no data about this in the Report).

Of course, the South should go ahead and use modern technologies and develop centres of excellence. But at the same time, realistic development today should probably promote three sectors at the same time: modern, traditional and intermediate, protecting the traditional resource base while at the same time introducing new technologies. Such themes are left unexplored in the Report.

Since the strategy will probably be lite-generated and as a consequence only rhetorically people-centred, the only known way of squaring that circle is to make products available outside the market, for example, free of charge or heavily subsidized. This may be incompatible with the conditionalities to which many countries in the South are subject. The alternative is structural fascism.

South-South

Clearly the South is competitive in the South in so far as factor prices (nature, labour) are low and transportation distances short. But there are some basic hurdles to be overcome before trade and other types of exchange can flourish, and one of them is the self-defeating colonial notion that only products from the West (and Japan) are worth having. South consciousness and solidarity, so well argued by the Report, are all indispensable in this respect.

The Report also attacks head-on the hurdle of hard currency, one of the major tools whereby the countries of the West protect the status quo: they define their own currencies as convertible, and those of most others as inconvertible, thus forcing the South to export to the West on their terms. There are many alternatives: barter, bilateral ad hoc exchange rates, multilateral clearing. The basic point is that the South must not be prisoner of the idea of "badly needed hard currency", for the sake not only of increasing direct South-South exchanges, but also of decreasing dependency on wildly fluctuating dollar rates. The Report is imaginative, but also cautious in its optimism, given the record of some of the clearing schemes in the past.

Another vital factor is transportation. Countries in the South are connected to the rest of the world through very good air links for travel by and products for the lite; surface transport for travel by, and products for, ordinary people is very deficient (except for the haj pilgrims: they must be the true experts in the field). The Asian and Pan-American highways, when completed, will or should have good multiplier effects; so should two or three good African North-West and East-West highways. What a fine task their construction would be for development agencies with much conscience money to spend, and few projects not doomed in advance. It should not be a cause of concern that the means of transportation using those new roads may be primitive; so they were in the West to start with. Much worse is no travel at all.

On the other hand, if problems of transportation can be solved, the questions of currency convertibility and trade with the West lose some of their importance. The requirement of rapid communication is more easily satisfied, being a necessity for the élite.

North-South

As optimistic as I would be for South-South relations, as pessimistic am I for North-South relations, precisely for the many reasons cited from recent history in the Report. The track record of the countries of the West is mostly negative, for they have a tendency to manipulate all schemes in such a way that they somehow end up working in their favour. What reason is there to believe that this tendency would suddenly change?

Let us take a sober look at what makes for development, defining that tortured concept simply as growth plus distribution, both of them sustainable. There has to be growth, and there has to be distribution; both of them have to be considerate so as not to generate counterforces that will destroy the whole exercise. This means showing sensitivity not only to nature, but also to humans, to the social structure and to the world structure. The socialism in Eastern Europe and the Soviet Union that was very insensitive to nature, humans and the social structure has now collapsed; the capitalism of Western Europe and the United States is similarly insensitive to the world structure and also to nature, humans and the social structure, but manages to place most of the pressure on the South. Socialism exploited itself and collapsed as a result of inner revolts; capitalism exploits somebody else and is able to contain outer revolts. In other words, capitalist countries are smarter, though this does not mean in any way that capitalism is development, being neither distributive, nor sustainable. Both capitalism and socialism have failed; the detrimental effects being experienced throughout the former socialist world and in the vast periphery of capitalism.

But there has to be growth; societies have to become richer in order to have something to distribute. There are three basic rules:

(1) High C/N, culture over nature; high degree of processing.

(2) High Q/P, quality over price; good quality for the price.

(3) Balanced R/F; synchrony between the real and the finance economy. How does the West react to strategies of development on that basis?

A Strategy of Development = Sustainable Growth + Distribution

(1) There has to be a start, a new beginning, brought about by war, natural catastrophe, revolution, elections or any general social change leading to some redistribution of domestic power.

(2) There has to be a reshaping of some part of the international system, leading to some redistribution of international power.

(3) A major objective is redistribution of production factors to all, domestically and internationally, to produce many producers:

Nature: land reform, access to communal waters, fields, forests. Labour: improving human quality through health and education.

Capital: access to credit on affordable terms.

Technology: appropriate for the people using it.

Management: appropriate for the existing social structure.

(4) First production priority: the satisfaction of the basic needs of those most in need. In practice this means the provision of food, clothes and housing, if possible produced locally to avoid dependency. This is crucial: if human beings are not provided for, what is the purpose of development and, by implication, of growth?

(5) Second production priority: production and consumption tools:

for food: walking tractors, biogas converters, pots and pans;

for clothes: spinning, weaving tools;

for housing: manufacture of bricks and other building materials.

And similarly provision must be made for health, education, transport and communication.

(6) Third production priority: production of goods for inner/outer trade. The basic rule would be not to export unprocessed natural goods but to take up the challenge of processing, locally and nationally, aiming to introduce certain products into a prestigious market niche, high on C/N and Q/P; the former creating challenge-response sequences, the latter leading to higher market shares. The top product is non-material, pure culture (art, science), distributed through teaching/learning.

(7) Keep control over distribution, not only over production. The challenges deriving from distribution are equally important, for what is the purpose of products if they do not reach the consumers?

(8) Always improve production factors, which in practice means:

for nature: improve, enhance nature's eco-balance (like forestry);

for labour: ever higher levels of health and education (for Q/P);

for capital: check real economy/finance economy synchrony (R/F);

for technology: invest in the creativity of everybody (for C/N);
for management: the participation of everybody.
(9) Always check that development does not slip into mere growth:
for nature: by internalizing eco-cycles, linking cause and effect;
for humans: by internalizing challenges, taking on the difficult tasks;
for societies: by retaining the eradication of misery as first priority;
for world society: by sharing negative and positive externalities;
for the future: by not discounting the future, diachronic solidarity;
for culture: by high priority to cultural production and distribution.
(10) And if it fails: start again, possibly from the beginning!

Many comments, or a whole book[1] can be devoted to these points. But
the reader will understand the general gist of this commentary: eclecticism,
combining capitalism, socialism, social democracy, "Japanism" and "green"
strategies, in a certain sequence. Many of these objectives can best be
achieved through the market, provided that the market is ethically
sufficiently enlightened. But much has to be done by other agents, like the
state or local government. This method should not be confused with the
characteristics of Stalinist economics,[2] which are: (a) centralized planning
of consumption as well as production; (b) domestic priority to large-scale
projects and the production of capital goods; (c) foreign trade giving
priority to large-scale projects and the buying of capital goods; (d) little
or no opportunity for public discussion and influence.

But the basic point here is not the countless comments but the question
stated at the outset: how will the West react, particularly in its present super
market-mood, one might almost say supermarket mood? Will the reactions
be friendly, helpful or hostile, trying to stop the South from doing what the
West has always done, but prefers to do without competition, as witnessed
by the reaction to a competitor from the South, Japan?

What the West wants is rather constant: access to raw materials and cheap
production factors for processing under its control (not necessarily in the West)
and marketing, also in the South. The countries of the West call this "free
trade", and have an ideology called "economics", and a strategy called
"development assistance" to achieve their purpose. All three are highly
attractive to élites in the South who engage in trade, learn economics and
benefit from development aid.

Consequently, the countries of the West would be opposed to most of the
ten-point plan above, so much so that they might be looking for pretexts for
violent intervention, if past experience is a guide. A new beginning is not for
the South to decide; the start was made when the West awakened it. No
redistribution of domestic and international power is necessary, only freely
operating markets, that is, power to those with economic assets and the

political and military power to back them. A free market does not distribute production factors; they are bought by those who can afford to buy for the purpose, among others, of ousting local competitors. A market is not concerned with basic needs and not-so-basic wants, but with demand, backed by cash. Even if goods can be produced more cheaply locally, the situation can be changed so profoundly by controlling nature, capital and management that this production ceases to be cheap. And when it comes to production for export with high C/N and Q/P, this is for the West to undertake according to the ideology of comparative advantage, the South being condemned to engage in nature- and labour-intensive production. Again, by controlling technology the West can outcompete the South in a "free" market. An additional objective is to retain the control of distribution that dates from colonial times. Under these circumstances efforts to "improve production factors" essentially controlled by a West mainly interested in classical division-of-labour policies are beset by great difficulties, except in the niches producing for the West.

Then there is the crucial point (9): the vulnerability of the South, the enormous population pressure etcetera, all conflict with "economics", so blind on negative and even on positive externalities, leave alone on equal sharing, particularly of challenging tasks and pollution/depletion.

Is all this "old hat" critique of the West, even with a touch of Marxism? Certainly, and as valid as ever and very well proven by the case of the country said to have more economic freedom than all the others, the United States (possibly recently joined by the United Kingdom), which is even unable to eradicate the appalling misery within its own borders. But tempered by experiences, many of them very positive, from social-democratic, "Japanist" and "green" economics, a truly free and ethically conscious market could come into being. The South can ill afford not to use the whole spectrum of human experience of economic activity. And here it is worth noting that, whereas command capitalism operates through the market and command socialism through the plan, the other three systems use both, and hence are less vulnerable. The traditional economy (of which green economics is an updated version) uses both, but at the local level; the social-democratic economy uses both by restraining both, and the Japanese economy uses both by developing both further in dialogue.

The best system is probably a combination of these three; using the local economy for basic needs (point (4) above), the social-democratic for softly directing national priorities (point (5)), and the Japanese-style economy for international markets (point (6)).

The West will not take anything like this lightly. All North-South conferences, inside or outside UNCTAD, have added up to very little, partly because of Western procrastination, partly because certain countries in the South have played up to the West by accepting more stable (and if possible higher) prices for raw materials/commodities instead of trying to change the division of labour, which is what the West is most afraid of. Taken in this narrow sense the Prebisch thesis has had a negative impact.

The Report of the South Commission has strong and wise words about the catastrophic decade of the 1980s. But the Report has failed to note how catastrophic were the 1980s also for the carriers of the ethos of the 1980s, the United States and the United Kingdom, with their trade deficits and foreign debts, and stable misery and unemployment inside their own borders. Neither country is doing well on C/N, exporting less and less processed products; not too well on Q/P either, as is shown by the way they are outcompeted by East Asia (and not only by Japan); and the R/F situation is awful, reflecting transitions from a production to a speculation economy (also in Japan, but its C/N and Q/P are robust enough to compensate).

In short, the South cannot expect or learn a great deal from the West. The South may also consider phasing out ODA, but keeping people-to-people co-operation, and particularly in cases where the South also can do something for the West in return. An example would be missions to analyse the predicament of the West together with Western experts and to make constructive proposals, something the West loves to do for the South, but usually to the South rather than *with it*. Here the South has a comparative advantage: being bicultural it often understands the West better than the West understands the South.

There is so much that can be done. But the road forward for the South does not pass through the West. Hence, South, go ahead! Nobody else is going to help you develop, you do it better yourself. And the Report of the South Commission is a fine step in the right direction.

Notes

1. Johan Galtung, forthcoming.
2. See George Mathew, 1991, pp. 9–15.

Bibliography

Galtung, Johan
   Development Theory: Goals, Processes and Indicators, forthcoming.
Mathew, George
   "Socialism is dead, long live socialism", in George Mathew (ed.), *Dignity for All,* Ajanta, Delhi, 1991.

9. TOWARDS A POLITICS OF THE SOUTH

Rajni Kothari

In this paper I take up the theme of the challenge to the South as portrayed in the Report of the South Commission and build further on it by taking up aspects of this "challenge" which are implicit in the Report but which need further and candid elaboration. I do this partly because of the way I perceive the problematique of the South, partly because of the dramatically changed situation globally, and partly because the very idea of thinking of the world in North-South terms is in jeopardy after so many countries of the South have knuckled under due to global pressures. I shall attempt to do this on the basis of my view of world history and its current unfolding.

As I see it, the human condition in the modern age exhibits a curious paradox. Both the science and the philosophy of "modernity" had announced perpetual progress and happiness born of access to a growing quantum of resources, both material and moral. It was also predicted that, as material well-being expanded and enveloped all human beings and all societies, a larger sense of unity would appear based on prosperity shared by all and on confidence in the future of the planet as a whole. Instead, there is growing conflict between classes of human beings and between societies in diverse geographical settings. Economically, and in other material senses too, modern man has produced a deeply divided world which is marked, in addition, by growing exploitation and worsening inequities as more and more people and some entire societies are excluded from the development process. In turn, this state of affairs has produced severe social tensions and confrontations between classes, regions and ethnic identities, giving rise in several countries to fundamentalist appeals based on a total rejection of the modern secular worldview.

In the countries of the South it was hoped that the anti-colonial struggles and the achievement of independence by a large number of former colonies, which had in several cases also been accompanied by nationalist uprisings and cultural renaissance with the object of making their entry into the modern world authentic and creative, would make them capable of charting new paths towards "progress". This hope too has been belied, and instead these countries' condition is one of growing dependence on the dominant centres of the world. This condition of dependence has in many respects been far worse than that of colonial subjugation. Moreover, paradoxical as it may sound, it is a dependence that has become more real with growing aid, transfers of technology and assistance for furthering economic development of the so-called developing countries. And today (that is, for the last several years), these countries are being advised to become integrated into the world economy, to become competitive internationally and, for this purpose, to draw upon the bounties which transnational corporations have to offer.

It is a cruel joke being perpetrated on countries and cultures which were not so long ago engaged in the task of translating political freedom into economic self-reliance and cultural autonomy and, with this in view, sought to "delink" themselves from global structures of corporate capitalism. Increasingly the very élites and governments of these countries that were engaged in such a task are beginning to accept defeat and to join this chorus of economic integration and political interdependence. In consequence of the collapse of the Soviet Union and the opening up of the whole of Eastern Europe to the transnationals, and as a result of the way the United Nations was used by the United States during the Gulf War, the capacity of these governments to participate meaningfully in the global arena, individually and collectively, has been eroded. So has the power and influence of collective institutional structures meant to promote the interests of the South, like the Group of 77, the Non-Aligned Movement, OPEC and several regional formations inspired by the ideas of the New International Economic Order (NIEO).

The challenge that the South faces, then, is altogether different in kind from that considered, for instance, by the Brandt Commission when it addressed the North-South issue or from that meant to be dealt with by the strategies for the series of United Nations Development Decades, worked out with the assistance of the secretariats of UNCTAD, the ILO, UNICEF and UNESCO. The challenge that the South faces today will have to be met in an institutional and political framework altogether different from that which existed in the 1960s and 1970s and which came crashing down during the 1980s. Any attempt to face the "challenge" during the 1990s on the basis of the earlier strategies and assumptions will be unrealistic. Instead there is a need to consider frankly why both the dominant model paradigm of development and the resulting approach to issues of poverty and injustice proved to be misplaced.

The basic flaw in the last 30 or more years of development has been a complete failure on the part of the countries of the South to address the fundamental political issue that they, as peoples and states, faced when they became independent and still continue to face. It has been a mistake to think of the achievement of independence or liberation from colonial powers as the dawn of freedom for these lands and peoples. Independence entailed no more than a transfer of power from one régime to another, mostly a transfer of administrative power including, of course, control over police and army operations. In some cases, no doubt, the movements for national independence generated a great deal of struggle which involved the participation of large numbers of people and long- drawn-out and pitched battles against the imperial régimes and their agents and armies. This often led to a fair amount of mobilization and the growth of a deep sense of identity between the leaders of the movements and the people at large. But even where this happened the "transfer of power" was essentially a transfer from one régime to another, usually at the apex of the administrative structure. Almost everywhere it meant the end of the movement and the beginning of the exercise of state power by small élites.

The political task that faced these élites consisted of providing democratic content and socio-cultural roots to the state. This meant both that the power that was transferred to the élites was to be shared with the people at large and that new structures and institutions had to be created and organized so that freedom and "self-rule" (what the leaders of the Indian movement called *Swaraj*) became real for the people. It was on the basis of such realization of freedom from the grassroots to the apex of the system and the development of institutions for this purpose that participation in regional and global structures was to be pursued. International expertise and know-how were indeed relevant but only in so far as they could be used by the people through the institutions of self-governance that would have come into being if the political task of translating independence of states into freedom of peoples had been achieved.

"Development" would then have meant fulfilment of both the needs and the aspirations of the people, to be realized at levels and in locations where the people lived, not something handed down by some superstructure. This would also have enabled these countries to draw upon time-tested traditions and knowledge systems (including sciences and technologies) that were already there and, taking these into account, to examine imported ideas and techniques for what they were worth. Similarly, community lifestyles and ecologies that had survived for centuries could have been made part of the new design for development. There was no need to think of traditional societies being antithetical to the new enterprise called development. Nor would they have been so conceived if the basic political tasks of ensuring freedom and self-determination to peoples and to diverse communities had been undertaken, which also would have entailed removal of inequities forming part of the traditional order. Nor would there have been much scope for the new inequities that the modern concept of development brought into being. (Today, what exists is one set of inequities reinforcing the other.)

Since there has been a failure to establish a democratic and truly federal political system in which peoples, communities and regions might have taken an active part, development has become both a centralized activity and one that, because it has served mainly the élite's needs and fostered alien lifestyles, produced deeply divided and tension-ridden societies. The current preoccupation with disparities between the rich and the poor countries has taken attention away from the even more glaring disparities within Third World societies. Many of these are, of course, a product of dependency relations between rich and poor countries, but even these have in large part been promoted by the élites of the poorer countries. Deep schisms producing increasing turmoil and violence are overtaking these countries, while their élites go round the capitals of the affluent world and global financial institutions asking them to help bail them out of such a scenario. It follows that the cure for the phenomenon of growing poverty and inequality in the world cannot come from talk about narrowing international divisions; what is needed first is action to deal with structures of inequality and destitution that obtain within societies and, on the basis of greater equality and justice in those societies, to endeavour to reduce inequalities internationally. The excessive focus on North-South relations has provided an escape route for the élites of the Third World who may wax eloquent in international fora but whose record at home is one of exploitation and repression.

The other major flaw in the thinking on challenges facing the South has been an almost exclusive preoccupation with Third World régimes rather than with the people and the civil societies – or communities – of which they are an integral part. Much of the discussion on development and other issues like the environment, peace and human rights has remained apolitical, largely because of this over-emphasis on governments as supposedly the main actors in the international arena. This has even been the line of thought of intellectuals and statespersons convinced of the need for charting alternative strategies of development for creating a more just and equitable world. This is particularly true of Western thinkers who are committed to the cause of the South in its confrontation with the North. Willy-nilly, their efforts in international fora tend to support Third World s in their overall desire to promote the cause of the Third World, including quite often the interests of s that are highly élitist and oppressive at home, so much so that raising real issues of democracy and human rights is found embarrassing. This, incidentally, is one of the main reasons why dissenting groups in the South find the global movement for alternative development at once too abstract and too élitist.

One further consequence of the preoccupation with Third World governments has been that very little attention has been given to the link between global corporate capitalism and national chauvinist and fascist tendencies that are drawing upon both global structures and conditionalities and endogenous influences. The simultaneous attack against working- class and other social movements of the dispossessed and against the secular nature of the state has not been sufficiently gauged. Correspondingly, little attention has been given to the restructuring of civil society without which no major transformation of either individual states or the state system can make much headway. Each of these societies faces contrary pulls of globalism and local chauvinism, of modernity and ethnicity, of technocracy and ecology. The challenge facing the South involves both these dimensions.

Today, at the beginning of the 1990s, the scenario is grim. In the West itself there has been an almost complete marginalization of dissent, for the market has fashioned not only preferences but also opinions; consumerism has been the bane of Western society far more than of the Third World, except of course for its outward-looking élites. In the Third World these élites, psychologically overpowered by the demonstration effect of Western lifestyles and conspicuous consumption, have become alienated from their societies and have become part of the global middle class; this is what "globalization" in effect means. In the socialist world, the long shadow of the market and Western lifestyles as well as the possibility of large doses of capital investment by the multinationals have all meant that the torch-bearers of *glasnost* and *perestroika* have been reduced to begging to be bailed out of their economic crisis by the West, in the process also giving up the global diplomatic and strategic role that history had carved out for them. At the other end of the erstwhile power spectrum, the one and only superpower that is left has managed to gloss over its serious economic crisis by flaunting its military and technological might, paradoxically rendering, in an era of demilitarization for which it claims credit, its own military strength the arbiter of world politics. The Gulf War established this position beyond any doubt. It sent out a clear signal to the rest of the world: let no one dare challenge the supremacy of the United States in the management of world affairs.

When the OPEC powers made their dramatic dbut on the world scene in 1973 and after, sending shivers around Western capitals, many analysts advanced the theory that economic and financial power was far more important than the military and strategic power of the Western alliance. Today the opposite seems to have been proved, in that the No. 1 power of the world continues to be No. 1 despite massive diffusion of economic power – Western Europe, Japan, the new industrializing countries of Asia

– largely on account of its continued superiority of military might, now unchallenged even by the Soviet Union.

All this is relevant in considering the challenges facing the South, for beyond simple appeals for reducing North-South disparities one must get to the root of the crisis facing humanity in consequence of the growing homogenization of the world from the top downwards, thanks to the road-rolling of the market and the powerful ideological package of globalization through privatization and privatization through globaliz-ation ("integration into the world market"). In this, the role of the state in intervening in order to reverse the trends towards growing poverty and unemployment will be neutralized by the very élites that control these states.

I have argued in this paper that the basic challenges facing the countries of the South are internal and that it is a mistake to lay the blame for the crises in the South on external factors. But there is one aspect in which the global impact must be fully assessed and faced. This is the growing permeation of the countries of the South – as well as of the socialist world – by ideological fixations and, consequently, technological fixations, both together undermining the political process which alone could respond to the democratic upsurge round the world. In large parts of the South the urge to "catch up" technologically has been gaining ground, quite often as a substitute for engaging in social and political transformation. To this has now been added the ideological package of privatization and globalization. The result will be the gradual erosion of the autonomy and sovereignty of independent nations. Such a philosophy of integration in a global economy will also necessarily centralize power, both economic and political, within societies, while the centres themselves will become vulnerable to global influences. But as the élites that control these centres will be the net beneficiaries of this entire process, they are not likely to resist encroachments on the sovereignty of their states. The main cost will be paid by those who are excluded from the market and indeed from the development process as a whole and, where fundamentalist elements have gained ground, by those excluded from civil society as well.

In all the discussions on the condition of people in the South and on the role of the North in contributing to it, very little attention has been paid to the true import of the model of technological modernization that had been advanced quite a while ago, the fixation on technology that followed it during the 1980s, and the fixation on the ideology of privatization that was built upon it. All this while Gandhi had been completely forgotten, and it is only now that his warnings against the technological fixation of the modern mind are being heeded when perhaps it may be too late. Most of the critiques of development strategies that have been advanced until recently, whether of the Marxist variety or arising from the environmental critique, have been rooted in the mind-set of modernity and the development paradigm conforming to the worldview of modernity. None of them has been able to grasp the phenomenon of systematic exclusions of millions of people round the world, largely because they thought of development as something to be acieved by the élites for the people rather than by the people themselves. If they had made the latter the focal point of their efforts, they would have given primacy not to technology but to politics and to social transformation to be brought about through the political process.

The challenge that faces the South, therefore, is fundamentally political, primarily within each of the societies composing the South and only secondarily a challenge for the South as a whole. But there is no doubt that thinking collectively for the South as a whole will also have to be in political terms. This means that the countries of the South, in various regions and across these regions, will have to overcome their differences without undermining their rich diversities and plural identities, and refuse to be individually co-opted by the North or by corporate capitalism.

This cannot be done without resisting the temptations that the ideology of privatization and globalization has been holding out and the various "compacts" for transferring capital and technology that are being offered. The latter will only accentuate divisions within the South, creating a "North" within the South. The issue is not how to make the North more understanding and compassionate. The task is, rather, once again to chart a path different from that followed so far, once again to reaffirm the need to delink from the global market-place. It is only by adopting a more autonomous and democratic path in which the enormous power of the peoples of the Third World is harnessed that these countries will be able to act collectively and, on that basis, to be in a position to resume the "North-South dialogue". The dialogue that has not yet even begun and has long been overdue is the dialogue with the people: and then, the dialogue *between* the diverse peoples, first in the South, then across the South and the North.

What I have presented in this paper is a predominantly political analysis with very little attention to the technical details that one usually finds in development analysis. This has been done deliberately. For I am convinced that, without political will and without a mobilization of people's energies, the crisis of development that the governments of these countries face cannot be dealt with. Such mobilization will involve alignments across the whole of the South, but these will not materialize if the only basis of acting together is resistance to the power and stratagems of the North. Today the only thing that holds the nations of the South together is the common debt trap in which they are all engulfed – hardly a condition for collective action. The "South" is fast becoming more a myth than reality.

I shall end on a rhetorical note: let those engaged in the struggle for survival and sustenance of the South make up their minds. Are they going to permit their diverse populations to work for the basic social and political transformation of their societies – and of the world at large – or are they going to remain content with joining lite dialogues within already established frameworks of discourse?

10. WOMEN: THE MISSING ELEMENT

Hilkka Pietilä

In the South Commission there were three outstanding woman members, and one would have expected to see much more influence of women's thinking in the Report. Yet the Report manages to assess the whole development record, its flaws and achievements, without paying any attention to the fact that all along so-called development seems to disadvantage women or benefit men and women very differently – in the so-called developed countries as well as in Southern countries. There is plenty of information on this.

Maybe the most pertinent assessment is that made by Southern women themselves in the famous DAWN Report produced by DAWN (Development Alternatives with Women for a New Era), an international network of primarily Southern women researchers, which has developed to incorporate a few thousand women worldwide. Entitled *Development, Crises, and Alternative Visions: Third World Women's Perspectives*, this pioneering critical report on development was received with great enthusiasm at Forum '85, the parallel NGO conference in Nairobi in 1985 in connection with the United Nations World Conference to Review and Appraise the Achievements of the UN Decade for Women. It has since been one of the basic documents on development. The DAWN women's network evaluated the development process, both in theory and in practice, and came to question the whole underlying process of development as it has been understood. It has been implicit in that understanding

> that women's main problem ... has been insufficient participation in an otherwise benevolent process of growth and development. Increasing women's participation and improving their shares in resources, land, employment and income relative to men were seen as both necessary and sufficient to effect dramatic changes in their economic and social position. *Our experience now leads us to challenge this belief.*[1] [emphasis added]

In DAWN's opinion, this challenge is equally relevant to the more industrialized countries. It coincides with the distinction between two divergent approaches in the international women's movement. The perception of development as described above has been and still is prevailing in the so-called "equality movement", which aims only at equality of women and men on existing, that is, male terms.

This approach, however, has been found very detrimental both to women themselves and to society. And it thwarts the whole potential of women to be agents of positive change in their societies. The challenge proposed by DAWN is now shared by the most advanced part of the women's movement.

The malignancy of the prevailing type of development for women as well as for nature – for that matter, women and nature share the same destiny – is confirmed also by another extraordinary source of information, the *World Survey on the Role of Women in Development* produced in 1984 by the United Nations system, for the Nairobi Conference in 1985.[2] (This was subsequently updated in 1989.[3]) These reports are not as analytical as the DAWN Report but their findings support each other.

The United Nations 1989 survey points out that the issue is no longer to look only the situation of women in such areas as education, employment and health; instead one "should analyse the role of women in relation to the key developmental issues as envisaged in the International Development Strategy for the Third UN Development Decade, focusing in particular on trade, agriculture, industry, energy, money and finance, and science and technology".[4]

The impact of improvements in the role of women upon the achievement of overall development goals is explicitly addressed in the survey:

> Improving women's role in development has the immediate effect of *increasing equality between sexes*. It has also the effect of accelerating the process of *agricultural development*, increasing the level of *national production* and the supply of food at the national and local levels. Simultaneously, it has the effect of *making development more responsive to human needs*.[5] [emphasis added]

Still the tone – traceable even in this quotation and emphasizing how useful, productive and materially beneficial it is to improve the status of women – is degrading to women as such. Equal dignity and rights for women, as for every person, are causes in their own right and need not be justified by productivity and efficiency!

DAWN defines feminism as a political movement that is "geared to human needs through wider access to economic and political power. Equality, peace and development by and for the poor and oppressed are inextricably interlinked with equality, peace and development by and for women." As a matter of fact, the majority of women in the world are poor, and the majority of the poor in the world are women!

DAWN concludes: "... we cannot propose a social/political economic programme for women alone, but we need to develop one for society, from women's perspective."[6]

This is what the South Commission failed to realize.

Doves and Hawks

Women in the South Commission attempted to introduce alternative development ideas which were more sustainable, humane, democratic and feasible. "There are 'hawks' and 'doves' in development as well as in disarmament talks and continuous battle between them," one of the women members of the Commission has commented. The "doves" are those

> who propose a more dispersed form of growth, a growth which may not show itself in the trade statistics ..., but goes on in the large traditional zones of the poor countries. The doves would emphasize the production of health and food, and provision of basic education as necessary preconditions of economic growth and the growth of human capability... [The "hawks" are those] who would push and pull the economies and societies of the poor countries towards high rates of growth accompanied by the manufacture of industrial products and their exports.

They would see "progress" and "modernization" in terms of presence in the world market.[7]

The little attention devoted to women in the whole South Commission Report – three pages out of almost 300 – addresses women as objects, not subjects in their own right. The Report speaks about women, for women and to women, but not with them, nor does it let them speak on their own behalf.

However, women's equitable participation in all walks of life, nationally and internationally, is no longer only their legitimate right but a social and political necessity in the process towards a more balanced, humane and sustainable future.

One of the basic conditions for the realization of a self-reliant approach is "the self-identification of the developmental role of women... The desired role of women in development should be defined largely in the first place by women themselves, both through their more intensive general social and political involvement and through their proper organization." Taken from the *United Nations World Survey on the Role of Women in Development* (1986), this passage is bold enough to add that "it is only by changing the role of women in society that society itself can be changed".[8]

Women, with their "dovish" approach to development thinking, have had very little say in development planning and policies in the past, both in the North and in the South. Therefore they could now provide an untapped and fresh source of ideas and priorities, which:

- could help the industrialized countries to rectify and humanize the lifestyle and development in these countries,

- would help the developing countries to find better alternatives for their development path instead of repeating the trials and errors of the North, which so far have created enormous damage and suffering the world over.[9] [10]

For us women in the South and North, the challenge is whether we go along with the prevailing line of order and development or listen to our own institutions, experiences and values. Are we ready to face this responsibility, have we done our homework?

My recent experiences in Finland – in connection with talks with women concerning the prospects of European integration – is that they care seriously about the foreseeable consequences also for the countries and peoples outside Europe. I take this as one more indication of the values of women. Consciously or intuitively, they have as the point of departure for their judgements:

- justice and solidarity towards the poor and disadvantaged in general as part of their concept of *equality*,

- reverence for life in all forms – particularly children – as part of their concept of environment and *ecology*,

- *peace* understood as the elimination of violence in all its forms, from direct violence (and violence against women and children) to all forms of structural violence.

I assume these values are shared by women the world over, which gives grounds for hope. This is the ground from which I work for solidarity and justice and the preservation of life on this planet. This is my contribution to solidarity towards the South.

Notes

1. Gita Sen and Caren Grown, 1987. Since this publication comprises the DAWN Report referred to earlier in the text, subsequent references to DAWN and the DAWN Report are in fact references to Sen and Grown, 1987.
2. United Nations, 1986.
3. United Nations, 1989.
4. Ibid.
5. Ibid.
6. Sen and Grown, 1987.
7. Devaki Jain, 1991.

8. United Nations, 1986.
9. Hilkka Pietil, 1984.
10. Hilkka Pietil, 1987.

Bibliography

Jain, Devaki
"Can we have a women's agenda for global development?", *Development*, Journal of the Society for International Development, 1991:1.

Pietil, Hilkka
"Women as an alternative culture here and now", *Development*, Journal of the Society for International Development, 1984:4.

Pietil, Hilkka
Tomorrow Begins Today: Elements for a Feminine Alternative in the North, IFDA Dossier 57/58, 1987.

Sen, Gita and Caren Grown
Development, Crises, and Alternative Visions: Third World Women's Perspectives, Monthly Review Press, New York, 1987.

United Nations
World Survey on the Role of Women in Development, New York, 1986 (Sales No. E.86.IV.3).

United Nations
1989 *World Survey on the Role of Women in Development*, New York, 1989 (Sales No. E.89.IV.2).

11. INVENTING THE FUTURE

Edgar Pisani

The Report of the South Commission provides a good deal of information and useful insights. It is not the "revelation" that was hoped for. We must try to understand why, before considering some particularly important problems to which the Report does not provide a conclusive answer.

The very idea of forming and convening a commission made up of women and men of the South to discuss the identity of the South and the difficulties it has in developing an awareness of itself vis-à-vis the North was very appealing. The idea answered a clear need, because when the South Commission was established the concepts of development and of an international economic order seemed to be taking on – and were actually taking on – a new meaning and tenor.

It was interesting to make a new Bandung: not at all in the enthusiasm of newly won independence, but in the bitterness of the financial, economic, social and cultural marginalization of the Third World after 30 years of effort. It could be useful to take up the work of the Brandt Commission on the New International Economic Order in a new climate and with a conflictual and not unanimous approach.

But the very composition of the South Commission, the long and arduous negotiations leading to its formation, prevented it from providing the dazzling visions and the unbearable scream without which no new world could be born. This was because – and this must be understood – the holders of power, knowledge and wealth do not want to change the world. They are living very well, and with the East changing its language and behaviour, they today cherish the dream of an integral North, unified ideologically and organized to survive and flourish without any true relation with the South.

Vis-à-vis this North, it is not the men and women educated in universities of the North, living like people of the North and working in the international institutions dominated by the North – it is not these men and women who could draw up a report shaking the eternal order of the world, which is the order of the powerful. There is no reason to be surprised that the style of the Report resembles too much the style of the innumerable documents drawn up by the international institutions, for the chances of success of the political event which the world none the less needs to come about.

Once again, on the international scene the South is speaking through the voice of women and men who no longer resemble it: their concern is to be heard by the North, and in order to do so they must speak like the North, with a success that is, alas, easy to assess.

The South Commission, which stressed the necessary democratization of the countries for which it aspired to speak, really felt this. But, here again, it could not find the routes of authentic renewal. In reading the text, somewhat quickly no doubt, as a citizen of the world and not as a researcher, one gets the feeling that, in order to democratize, the South must do ... like the North! This is not appropriate for two reasons at least: the North itself, which is none the less proud of its democratic systems, is now starting to question its ageing, the indifference it now inspires in citizens, the ways and means of a new pact between the civic society and the institutions that govern it. The concept of the nation state is reeling under the combined attacks of an economy that is becoming globalized, imposing its criteria, and the emergence of nationalities aspiring to a cultural expression of their own.

But the real reason for the criticism of an imitative democratization process, copied from that in the North, is different: political texts are not the result of a revelation, but of a conquest. It is not by translating into Pachto, Kiswahili or Arabic the Declaration of the Rights of Man and the Citizen, it is not by translating into the same languages or others the constitution of the United States, of Federal Germany or of Japan that a democratic adapted to the needs of the South will be created: it is by inventing the means of finding in each culture the elements of its legitimacy and the application of some simple, universal values. The Declaration of 1789 is a document that goes to the very heart of things but which also owes much to the historical and cultural conditions in which it was written. There are in the Arab *majlis*, or in the council of elders found in so many continents, the bases for a reinvented democratic practice at the time it is won. And here is the most important point: democracy is not imported; it is won and invented at the same time.

Invent, win – these are undoubtedly the key words which the South Commission Report does not use enough. It is as though the members were dreaming of copying or receiving. What is true in politics is also true in education, science and technology. Transfers have been referred to as though the sale of computers would absolve the multitudes of the South from taking the long road travelled by the North until the invention of these diabolical and wonderful machines. It is to mock the concept of culture to believe in the mechanical transferability of knowledge and its tools. Here, too, one must be wary of revelation and favour the conquest of oneself. As is well known, a large number of teachers, researchers and scientistsfrom the South fill and enrich the universities and laboratories of the North. Very few return home, because they do not find there the conditions for intellectual growth and for a life in keeping with the requirements of their work. The phenomenon favours the North: it is in the North's interest to train people from the South, to pass its knowledge on to them, to let them participate in its intellectual growth to the extent that, once having brought them into line, the North is sure of holding on to them. And the North does not hold on to them so that they can contribute through their work to the solution of the many problems of the South, but, on the contrary, so that they can contribute – often to the detriment of the South – to the advancement of the scientific mastery of the North, at a time when knowledge and power go hand in hand.

The South must choose to be more self-reliant and self-defined than it appears to be in the Report published in May 1990. It must know that it has the choice between two paths: imitation, which means deculturation and submission, and invention, which is control of oneself and a bridled revolt against the troubles of the world. It must know that acquiring a patent is useful for an enterprise only when the enterprise is about to deposit it itself: a patent allows it to gain time and money, not knowledge. The same is true for the South: the recipes of the North will be profitable to it only if they enable it to move more quickly on the long road of development and democracy. The South must know that development and democracy – but this the South Commission says quite clearly – are linked processes: linked because the one cannot go on without the other; processes, because neither development nor democracy are stable equilibria, but moving disequilibria, constant evolution and conquest.

One final point: there is no reasonable hypothesis for the future of an uneasy, demographically expanding world if the North does not recognize that its tendency to waste must be reduced. But there will be neither a decrease in inequalities nor the safeguarding of the global environment if the South does not recognize that its ambition must be not to copy the consumption pattern of the North but to wrench the multitudes from misery to assure them security by sobriety and solidarity.

There is no future without political invention.

12. "THE CHALLENGE TO THE SOUTH"?A CHALLENGE TO HUMANKIND AS A WHOLE!

Tamas Szentes

I set out below first my views on the nature, timeliness and importance of the Report of the South Commission; second, my opinion on its main theses, general philosophy and approach; and third, my opinion on some points where minor inconsistencies, slightly biased or relatively weak argumentation or certain old illusions seem to appear in the text.

The Report was published at a time when we witnessed not only complete disillusionment concerning earlier hopes (so fashionable in the 1970s) for a "New International Economic Order" and for the so-called "Development Decades" (often coupled with concern over the very notion of "development"), but also the final collapse and transformation of the "Second World" (a total failure of the "state-socialist", Stalinist systems both as "socialist" and as modernization projects, advertised as alternatives to "Western capitalism" and "Southern underdevelopment"). The concomitant radical changes in the international political and economic situation may temporarily divert attention away from the North-South gap, and weaken the voice of the critique of the prevailing international economic order even more than in the 1980s. The return, by means of privatization and deregulation, of those economies previously called "planned" or "socialist" to the single path of capitalist market economies marks not only the defeat of Stalinism (a deformed, dehumanized and substantially militarized order of society).[1] It seems also to mark the triumph of the philosophy of the spontaneous market over the idea of social control, regulation and planning, which for the weaker, less developed economies may appear to foreclose all options, except those of remaining at the mercy of the world market and its oligopolistic forces and servile adjustment to the dominant economic powers.

At such a time and in such a climate, under such conditions, a report like that of the South Commission, if it presented merely the earlier and often repeated argument in favour of using reforms to make the international economic order more equitable, in favour of the demands of the countries of the "South", would hardly be able (however just the argument and however populous the South) to attract the attention it actually deserves.

The Report of the South Commission, however, goes far beyond the repetition of old demands and complaints. It does not simply accuse the North of being responsible for the widening of the development gap. It stresses the responsibility also of the South, while refering to common threats and interests.

Contrary to its modest title, it is really about the challenge to humanity as a whole!

In the name of the South (a still somewhat idealized entity) it speaks about the indivisible commons and the South's commitment to a global approach,[2] about the vision of an undivided world and the need for joint North-South efforts[3] to save the common heritage. It calls for a new global dialogue to solve global problems and appeals to the common interest in and shared responsibility for a really sustainable development of world society and all nations, which would cover all human beings and would, in addition, save nature for future generations.

Never has an appeal been more timely, and never have we had such an opportunity for a new global dialogue as we may have today. With the fading away of the East-West dichotomy, ideological hostility and military confrontation which until recently camouflaged or overshadowed the fundamental problems and real condition of humanity, now the world situation appears with its true face, in all dimensions and full depth. It becomes obvious that this reality is not only "morally unacceptable"[4] but also dangerous for humanity's future, even if an arms race and armed conflicts could be avoided.

Whatever our philosophy, ideology or religion, when reading this Report we cannot escape the question: can we and our children live safely in a world "in which a large proportion of the people is without enough food while a small proportion indulges in superfluous consumption; in which massive waste coexists with pervasive deprivation; in which the majority of the people have little control over their fates and futures, but are essentially at the mercy of trends, processes, and decisions in the centres of power of the industrialized world"?[5] And do we have the right to benefit from a world order which excludes millions of humans from any benefits?

If there was a "world educational centre", a "transnational world university" with the primary task of shaping an identity for the whole of the human race and promoting such a "planetary consciousness" (as national universities normally shape national identity and consciousness), or if there were at least some "common courses" on the global problems of world society at the universities or schools of the member states of the United Nations,[6] the Report would be – in my opinion – one of the most appropriate readings. (As a matter of fact, students in the North would need it even more than those in the South.)

It follows from what I have said above that I fully share the global approach of the Report. Not only because of growing interdependence, increasing transnationalization, and the spread across frontiers of mutual effects, interlinkages of cultures, lifestyles, environment pollution, human and social diseases, violence, terrorism, etcetera, that is, those trends to which the Report correctly points,[7] but also because and as a consequence the scope of national policies has considerably narrowed. In the words of the Report, "the ability of governments to control events within national borders is drastically constrained by the external environment".[8] We are indeed facing problems that require global solutions.

All the facts and figures, statistical data and quantitative illustrations that the Report presents about the state of the South[9] and North-South relations,[10] about the development crisis, increasing poverty and marginalization, growing indebtedness, mass unemployment and food insecurity, market instabilities, ecological dangers, resource wastages, income and educational gaps, the brain drain and "perverse" resource flows, etcetera clearly show that these are symptoms of a "disease" which, though mostly afflicting the South, is rooted in the global system as a whole and can hardly leave intact, safe and secure any other part of the single organism of our world society.

In the most developed countries it was recognized long ago, particularly after the rise of fascism, that unless some benefits of economic growth are also shared by the poor and unprivileged strata of society, unless effective welfare and redistributive measures reduce poverty, unemployment and social inequities, it is hardly possible to avoid the threat of violence, ultra-radicalism, social unrest and revolts. What is needed is that the family of nations should recognize fully that the same is true also on the world level and to act accordingly.

Though declaring substantially different ideologies and political aims and being supported by opposite social forces, both fascism and Stalinism originated from the problems of internal and international conflicts, from the public awareness of sharp social inequalities and of the need to catch up with the more advanced nations, that is, from the urgent need to find a solution simultaneously, and at the expense of one or the other, to the double historical problem of social and national emancipation.

While Nazi-fascism appealed to militant nationalism and to the myth of national superiority, Stalinism appealed to class consciousness, to proletarian messianism and the dogma of an inevitably sharpening class struggle. Despite obvious differences, however, both used similar methods of violence, oppression and terror, both militarized the entire social order, all spheres of social life, including the outside world. Nazi-fascism caused the Second World War and the tragic Holocaust. Stalinism victimized millions and subordinated the peace of the world to its ideological aims and interests. One may meditate on where Stalinism could have led if its disintegration had not been brought on by internal resistance, revolts and reforms after Stalin's death and by external counterforces. The human, social and international costs of both have been enormous.

Though both failed to solve the above-mentioned double problem, and were defeated, it would be most foolish to conclude from their failure that they were mere "historical incidents" which cannot recur, since world society happily returned to its "normal conditions" after their demise. As long as the basic problems which were responsible for the rise of those régimes remain unsolved, similar régimes, though probably with different ideologies and in different parts of the world, may once again come into existence and threaten peace, security and human dignity.

Besides such threats, the growing dangers for the global indivisible natural environment that are due to the greenhouse effect, nuclear radiation, deforestation, desertification, soil and water degradation, air and marine pollution, urban squalor, etcetera and the hazards threatening the similarly indivisible world health that are caused by the spread of AIDS and the illicit traffic in narcotic drugs, etcetera[11] likewise point to the imperative need for global solutions.

Thus the Report correctly refers to common North-South interests and to the need for joint efforts, though it seems to be (quite understandably in the light of past experiences) rather pessimistic about the willingness of the North to act accordingly.

Most of the propositions presented by the Report in its three core chapters seem to reflect the lessons of past experiences fairly well and thus go far beyond not only the conventional paradigms of the past but also any kind of biased, one-sided doctrinarianism.

Though the Report pays primary attention to economic problems, fully recognizing the need for "fast and sustained economic growth",[12] it is free of an economistic approach and any disciplinary bias. Instead of relying on one of the available economic theories and (mis-)using it as a quasi-religious ideology to support its argument and proposals, the Report makes implicit use of the relevant accumulated knowledge of all scientific thoughts, that is, of different schools of economic theory, as far as they reflect or help to shed light on the objective reality.

It is indeed high time to recognize what the Report seems to recognize: that none of the theories should be used as an ideological weapon or apologetic instrument, and that all of them have some real value as well as limitations. As a matter of fact, the different theories of economics, the various "schools" in social sciences not only contradict but also complement each other. Since they approach reality from different angles, from different viewpoints, any one of them is valid only under certain conditions and at a certain time and in a certain place, and each sheds light on certain parts of reality only, for being based upon abstraction it necessarily neglects some other parts. Hence none of them reveals the whole, none of them is totally right and none possesses the full truth as such. It is only the fanatic doctrinarians and some ideological servants of the prevailing political or economic power, paying cynical lip service, who believe or want us to believe that one particular theory alone, advocated by them, is the exclusive vehicle of truth.

Once a social science theory is claimed to monopolize truth, once it is considered capable alone, without and in contrast to other theories, of encompassing the entire social reality, and once it is used to legitimate the prevailing order (of any kind), it necessarily loses its scientific character, and becomes no more than an apologetic ideology. If, however, applied correctly, that is, within the limits of the basic assumptions and of the conditions of time and space, and consistently, namely without making concessions according to political or economic interests, each theory may serve better to understand and also to improve reality by a critical analysis of reality or by the concepts and methods it provides for such an analysis. This applies to the classical and neo-classical theories of economics just as well as to Marxism and Keynesianism, or their revised versions.

Actually, a critical or uncritical approach to the prevailing contemporary world economic order follows from a sincere and humanistic or from a hypocritical and selfish viewpoint, respectively, rather than from the difference between liberals, Marxists, Keynesians or others.

Classical economics advocated international free trade with its consequent mutual advantages, and assumed sovereign national decisions on export specialization and also perfect competitive markets.

Neo-classical economics also assumed free competition, free of monopolies and artificial barriers, and international equalization and equilibrium resulting from the free mobility of both capital and labour, in other words a fully integrated world market for these factors of production based on perfect mobility of labour and capital, or, as a perfect substitute, an international market in products.

The Marxist theory advocated the elimination of exploitation both within and among nations, "full" remuneration for their value-creating labour to all workers and nations, and the subordination of production to the needs of consumers rather than to profit interests.

The Keynesian theory recommended indirect regulation of the market by the state, income redistribution in favour of the poorer strata with a lower savings propensity, and welfare measures to reduce unemployment and improve social conditions, etcetera.

It hardly needs to be shown that in the modern world economy:

- trade is severely hindered by protectionism; the Ricardian comparative advantages cannot always be realized mutually; markets are not perfect and competitive but oligopolistic;

- unlike capital, labour is not mobile enough internationally, its flow is hindered by a great many obstacles and discriminatory practices; there is no integrated labour market on the world level; international trade cannot perfectly substitute for factor mobilities; moreover "paradoxical" trade structures[13] appear contrary to the Hecksher-Ohlin theory, and the "perverse" flow of capital[14] also contradicts the assumed equalization;

- neither the unorganized workers, nor the weaker, economically less developed nations can enjoy a "full" or even a "just" remuneration for their work; world production, while causing over-supply and wastages, is still failing to satisfy basic human needs;

- on the world level there is no state-like institution regulating the market indirectly; income redistribution (if any, and if at all in the required direction) is not institutionally organized, and no "safety net", no systematic welfare measures are applied.

The Report illustrates all these facts, fully in accordance with the theories, without however being swayed by any of them. There is no sign in the Report of a quasi-religious belief in the spontaneous market mechanism with its "invisible hand", nor of a belief in a state- commanded, centrally planned economy eliminating or restricting the operation of the market.

It correctly points out that "by their very nature unregulated market systems pay little or no heed to such strategic areas as basic industries, health and education services, scientific and technological research, and the preservation of the environment and natural resources"[15] and also refers to the poor "record of direct state management of enterprises in the productive sector",[16] to their inefficiency resulting from "the lack of operational independence" and from their monopolistic status, and to the high social costs, in general, of the state subsidies provided to uneconomic industrial activities.[17]

The Report recognizes both the need for a vigorous private business sector with entrepreneurship, creativity and competition-driven technological innovations, and the need for the economic roles of the state under social control. Without any ideological bias it agrees that privatization in the economy may lead to greater efficiency, but adds that it may be "impractical or undesirable in some sectors".[18]

While stressing the responsibility of the state for macro-economic management and its planning and regulatory role,[19] the Report criticizes the overcentralized and bureaucratic planning mechanisms, the neglect by state authorities of "recognized economic principles" which result in the misallocation and inefficient use of scarce resources.[20]

Drawing conclusions from the negative experiences of the former "socialist" countries, the Report warns that overcentralization which is often rooted in economic circumstances, and characterized by an excessive role of the state and its top-down approach, leads to "widespread apathy within the society", to alienation and, in the absence of an effective system of public accountability, to corrupt practices and authoritarian tendencies.[21]

The Report suggests that countries will have *mixed economies* in which the state and the market mechanisms will have to complement each other.[22] It says that the role of the state in the management of development will remain essential even if the market is chosen as the primary instrument for resource allocation.[23]

This stand taken by the Report on the role of the market and the state is not, however, merely a realistic compromise, since it is complemented by a call for "innovative approaches – extending *beyond* the domain of *both* the market and the traditional welfare state".[24] Thus the Report seems also to visualize a "third system" in which neither the market nor the state can dominate the civil society,[25] and society, by making use of both as instruments to control and countervail each other, is able not only to protect itself against the alienating effects of both but also to humanize them and make their operation socially transparent.

Seeking new innovative approaches while accepting the world of plurality, that is, the fact of diverging views, interests and conceptions, and pointing to the limited validity of each theory as well as all theoretical and empirical models, the Report seems to reflect non-alignment also in an ideological sense, refusing doctrinarianism and the copying of models. In that way it avoids one-sidedness in other fields as well and, in addition, points to some of the shortcomings of the available theories or their methodology, to what they failed to recognize or to apply consistently.

For example, it correctly criticizes the methodology of national accounts, whether it originates in the neo-classical or in the Marxian theory, for not reflecting environmental costs. It also refuses "the persistent misconception" about the value of women's contribution to the economy and to society, which is particularly strange to find in such theories as, as for example, Marxism, which considers human labour the only value-creating factor of production, but fails to apply this principle to the very production of human labour itself, to child care, family education and to household activities.

The Report does not accept the biased overemphasis on capital as a productive factor either, but when stressing the role of the human factor in general it does not forget the importance of the natural environment, and perceives humans as parts, not "masters", of nature.

It seeks, in general, a new balance, a progressive compromise between contradictory or temporarily conflicting options, between seemingly mutually exclusive alternatives. It suggests combinative, integrative solutions where earlier the conventional wisdom had seen only "either-or" alternatives, such as choices between economic growth and social justice, between efficiency and equity,[26] between planning and market,[27] between industrialization and agricultural development,[28] between the application, in some key sectors, of capital-intensive and knowledge-intensive technologies and the use of labour-intensive methods of production,[29] between export-orientation and import-substitution,[30] between an open-door policy and the protection of national sovereignty, between self-reliance and international co-operation,[31] etcetera.

The Report, it is true, does not offer a recipe for reconciling such contradictory principles or methods and one may consider this a weakness. But is it possible at all to prescribe a universal recipe for so many countries living under different conditions? It is the art of politics and the responsibility of decision-makers to find the most appropriate compromises and ways of reconciling conflicting aims or interests.

Most (if not all) of those principles, aims and criteria of development recommended by the Report for national policies in the South may apply also to the North. It is probably due to the modesty of its authors that recommendations are addressed only to the governments of the South. As a result, however, a certain conceptual inconsistency may follow from the Commission's decision to draw a dividing line in respect of development criteria.

Development can nowhere be identified merely with economic growth, it must everywhere meet the criteria of sustainability, serve the satisfaction of basic human needs,[32] and the improvement of the social and economic well-being of people,[33] enabling "human beings to realize their potential, build self-confidence, and lead lives of dignity and fulfilment", freeing "people from the fear of want and exploitation",[34] ensuring the realization of all human rights and the protection of nature.

People (as well as nations), however, cannot realize their potential and cannot be free of exploitation unless they all have relatively equal opportunities to develop and relatively (according to their talent and diligence) equal access to economic or "physical" as well as to "political" and "intellectual" capital (that is, access to means of production as well as to political participation and to education, skill and information). For this purpose it is necessary everywhere to eliminate all those monopolies which act as a barrier to exclude certain social strata (and nations) from such access to that "capital", and to ensure that everybody enjoys economic, political and cultural rights on equal terms.[35]

Development everywhere has to be people-centred and participatory, that is, "an effort of, by, and for the people".[36] The humanist as well as the "gender" and cultural dimensions of development[37] must receive universal priority. The transparency of government activities[38] and social control over both the state and the market are not less important criteria in the North than in the South.

Even if for historical reasons several countries in the North are, no doubt, far ahead in meeting such normative principles and criteria of development, it is only ideological apologetics that would deny their relevance also in the case of the North in general. It is in the North that business-motivated wasteful, environment-polluting conspicuous consumerism,[39] selfish individualism, "a media culture manipulated for the purposes of money-making, the abuse of drugs",[40] etcetera originate and that unemployment and poverty (though to an incomparably smaller extent than in the South, as only "pockets of persistent poverty"),[41] and other social ills also exist or reappear.

Without adequate changes and structural and behavioural "adjustment" also in the North, many of the normative principles of national policy recommended by the Report to the South may remain naive illusions. Surely, it is hardly possible to avoid the "uncritical imitation of Western models"[42] and to shape economic development according to "what the people themselves perceive to be their social and economic interests,[43] or "to reduce and perhaps even reverse the brain drain",[44] to save the real values of people's own traditional cultures, to eliminate corruption, etcetera in an increasingly interdependent world where demonstration effects from the North influence people's perceptions of their needs, demands and aspirations, and where business interests and material values predominate over the cultural and spiritual ones.

A really global approach to global problems, such as the North-South gap, requires a completely new way of thinking We can hardly go beyond the conventional recipes concerning economic growth and adjustment coupled with international aid which have failed for decades, unless the required correlate changes, extending also to the North, are taken into full account.

This raises two fundamental questions: (a) Who can be the agents, actors and motive forces for such changes? (b) What is the primary level of the required changes and actions today, to meet the challenge faced by humankind to achieve an undivided and peaceful world? Unfortunately the Report is too modest to give a definite and consistent answer.

If objectively, that is, in the light of empirical reality and of the common wisdom of social sciences, freed from the influence of partial interests and ideological biases, the Report can be criticized at all, then – in my opinion – criticism can be directed at a few slight logical or methodological inconsistencies which may give rise to some illusions or weaken its argument.

The Report, on the one hand, notes the "increasing diversity within the South",[45] the widening social inequalities, the growing gap in income, knowledge and power,[46] the existence of "islands of affluence",[47] and a stratum of the rich and powerful enjoying the lifestyle and consumption patterns of the North,[48] and refers also to the "temptation separately to seek remedies for pressing national situations" which counteract solidarity.[49] On the other hand, the Report still presents the South as "a basic unity"[50] which is to take "a common stand vis-à-vis the North".[51] It believes in a common ethos and "mutual trust" not only among the peoples of the South but also among governments, the various régimes (whether they are democratic or dictatorial, military or civilian), without pointing to the misrepresentation by many governments of the real interests of the people, to the tragic hostility and ethnic, religious and other conflicts among the misled masses, and to the ties and alliances between some of those having political or economic power in the South and those having such power in the North.

In a similar way, and contrary to the correct statement that "the North too is not homogeneous",[52] that is, there are "divergent interests and views"[53] in the North and also "countries and groups ... that are sympathetic to the South",[54] the Report often treats the North as "a well-organized and united" group of countries with "a common front" vis-à-vis the South.[55]

The oversimplified identification of the real dichotomy of the world economy, that is, its unequal structure, asymmetrical interdependence and tendencies towards increasing inequalities, with the confrontation of two geographical entities, leads to some other inconsistencies, too.

This identification may explain why the Report pays little attention to the prospects for and practical means of achieving "people-to-people contacts" and the co-operation of NGOs in North-South relations (while correctly stressing their importance in South-South relations), even though many of the obstacles set by governments against free access to markets, technologies, know-how and information, to the flows of technological innovation and new research results could be more easily overcome if direct North-South contacts were established among chambers of commerce, research and information centres, professional organizations, groups of scientists, teachers, technicians as well as individuals. Governments, because of their very nature and their responsibility for defending the supposed "national interest", or rather for "*raisons d'état*", are less co-operative and generous vis-à-vis their partners.

The Report seems to display a certain inclination to idealize South-South relations and to contrast their nature with that of North-South relations. Without spelling out what "exploitation" means in concrete terms and forms[56] and how it can be avoided, it simply declares that "South-South links must avoid reproducing within the South the exploitative patterns which have characterized North-South relationships".[57]

The deeper roots of the unequal North-South relations and the structural problems of the international division of labour are likewise discussed in a slightly inconsistent way by the Report.

The inherited global division of labour and the "heavy reliance of the developing countries on the export of primary products" are merely attributed to a deliberate colonial policy,[58] even though colonialism was only one of the causes (no doubt, the major one) of the distorted, one-sided specialization in primary products. In several non-colonialized countries as in some decolonized areas under post-colonial régimes it was the selfish policy of the local ruling stratum which chose or continued to promote such a specialization, benefiting from the export earnings of the primary commodity producing enclaves operated with cheap unskilled labour. For the primary commodity exporting countries, local labour represented part of the costs only, but not of effective demand: the export earnings were mostly spent on imports rather than on industrialization or other productive investment oriented towards the domestic market.

In many cases the choice of a one-sided specialization in primary production was not only made – quite contrary to the assumptions of classical economics – by entities other than sovereign nations, it also did not correspond to real comparative advantages, if comparative costs are calculated at the macro level for the national economies concerned. Both economic history and progressive economic theory[59] have proven that such a specialization has a disintegrative effect on the economy of the countries in question, and dooms them to lose, instead of realizing, comparative advantages in international trade, and to lag behind the industrialized countries. By its very nature export-oriented primary production fails to provide similar opportunities for the economy to develop its productive forces, to expand the domestic market, to promote technological progress, to realize internal and external economies, and particularly to improve the quality of labour.[60]

The Report points to the vulnerability of the many developing countries which gradually became net importers of food [61] concurrently with their agrarian export orientation, and stresses correctly the need for "a shift in the pattern of production and exports from raw materials to manufactures and, within the latter, to products with high and medium R & D intensity",[62] that is, "the creation of dynamic comparative advantages based on the transformation of economic structures".[63] Nevertheless, some paragraphs may create the impression that "traditional comparative advantages" had really been enjoyed by the primary exporting developing countries in the past and have suffered erosion only recently, due to the new advances in science and technology,[64] and that only since the late 1970s "the North is no longer a reliable or sufficient motor for generating sustained growth in the South".[65] In my opinion (as explained elsewhere[66]) the theory of comparative advantage has never justified the continuing one-sided specialization of the South in primary production, and the North has always been both an engine for and a brake on the development of the South. What matters is the unequal nature of the division of labour between industrial and primary producing countries, the consequent increase in inequality, as also its irrationality from a global point of view.

Unfortunately, the Report also fails to extend some of those correct normative principles and aspects recommended for national policies, such as the cultural dimension, to the criteria for the prospective restructuring of the global division of labour. Though it refers for example to the cultural values and heritage of the South,[67] while realistically adding that "some traditional cultural traits are inimical to development",[68] it tacitly accepts the false conventional concept which restricts the division of labour among countries to material products only or at best to services related to material production.

In a single world society undivided by frontiers, the concept of the division of labour would obviously extend to all social activities including cultural ones, and it would be completely foolish to force or advise all people to do the same industrial or agricultural work. (Not less foolish than a proposal to force all artists, scientists, musicians, teachers, priests and physicians to become industrial workers or farmers within a nation.) This is by no means an argument against industrialization even in the least developed countries or against the importance of domestic food production, but a timely call for a really global and rational approach to the problem and future pattern of the world division of labour. (Timely indeed not only in the light of accelerating transnationalization but also of the growing recognition of many neglected values of traditional cultures, arts and skills, for example, natural medicine.)

Certain inconsistencies in applying a global approach appear also in some other respects. On the one hand, the Report fully acknowledges the empirical fact of global interdependence and the limits of national policies and sovereignty. It also stresses the mutual need for co-operation of both the South and the North,[69] and correctly states that "the issue for the South is not whether to cut its links with the North, but how to transform them".[70] Thus it seems to be free of the ambiguous concept of "delinking" (which in practice has proved not only counterproductive, harmful and risky, as the example of the East has shown, but also increasingly unrealizable in modern times). On the other hand, however, in some places the Report still speaks about how the nations of the South might become "really independent",[71] and seems to accept the conventional priority of a national approach to development, and heavy reliance, accordingly, on the activities of the state as the primary actor. It places both responsibility and trust in the governments of the South, that is, in the states acting within the national frontiers and – it is hoped – co-operating with each other.

Admittedly, no one can question the reality of the division of world society, the "single human family", by frontiers (often artificial ones) and consequently the major responsibility of governments acting within these frontiers or the importance of inter-state co-operation. However (and even apart from the illusions shared earlier by many of us[72] about successful alternatives, merely within national borders, versus the dominant rules of the game), if the challenge outlined so well by the Report is taken seriously, and if it is the security and future destiny of humankind which are at stake now, then it is high time to transcend the conventional beliefs in "national states", in their capability and willingness as well as their democratic nature in general. If "the world community as a whole should transform radically the institutions and arrangements",[73] then other scenarios and actors (other than those tied to national frontiers and state structures) have also to be taken into account and mobilized.

The Report suggests "a reconsideration of the role of the United Nations"[74] and a reform of institutional arrangements, including the multilateral financial institutions. Unfortunately, however, it takes a narrow view of such a reform by limiting it to "the reform of the voting structure" in order to give "increased weight to the South".[75] However justified this demand may be, the Report apparently fails to touch on the crucial problem of the system of representation in general of the world community, which is still based exclusively or primarily on the representation of states only.

Though the Report refers to "a vast field of relations between the South and the North that do not necessarily involve governments" and to "links and contacts among groups and individuals" as well as "grass-roots organizations",[76] it hardly draws conclusions as to how to transform the international institutional system.

If within national societies a mixed economy coupled with a social welfare state and a pluralistic democracy seems to be the best among the realistically available alternatives for the time being, or even in the long run, then internationally, too, that is, for world society as a whole, a similar pattern is to be approached and the possible ways how to reach it have to be explored.[77]

A mixed economy involves both a private and a public sector. On the world level, however, there is no real public sector, despite an ever-growing transnational sector of the private economy.[78] A social welfare state possesses a social safety net and takes regular measures to reallocate resources and redistribute, through taxation, income in favour of the poor, unprivileged and unemployed. Such a safety net and institutionalized reallocation and redistribution hardly exist as yet internationally. A pluralistic democracy presupposes the articulation, representation and reconciliation of the diverging interests of all the different segments, strata or classes of the civil society and their proportionate participation in the process of decision-making and control over public issues. But the world's civil society does not have such opportunities and rights. Consequently, the countervailing forces, which are so important if a brake is to be put on the concentration and centralization of power in the hands of a few, are either lacking or organized in dubious ways as alliances of some states versus others, with the risk of inter-state military conflicts.

Human rights, which it is fashionable to mention nowadays, appear also in a false context, as the rights of citizens within their own country, to be respected and protected by their own state only. Thus they are totally confused with citizens' rights. While the latter are tied to citizenship, human rights in a real sense must belong to *all* members of humankind, of the world's human society, independently of citizenship, national, ethnic, caste and family origin, gender, social status, class, or religious, cultural or other differences.

Human rights in such a real sense are not yet respected even by the most democratic states. While they may fully guarantee citizens' rights to all their own citizens, they enforce severe regulations to prevent the citizens of other states from exercising human rights in the territory under their sovereignty and control. Human rights include not only the right of emigration but also the right to immigrate, to choose freely one's place for living and working.[79]

Human rights, which also include the right to security and development, to a peaceful and decent life, to a clean environment, to remunerative employment and to satisfy basic needs, to develop one's potential, to access to education and information, and to participate in a democratic way in public affairs, to representation and to take part in decision-making, etcetera, can be realized only if they are guaranteed on the world scene, too, and respected all over the world. This is the only way to eliminate completely discrimination and exploitation, to make the world market really competitive and integrated also in respect of labour, to liberalize the flows of and access to all factors of production, to all products and services, including cultural ones, internationally too, and to democratize the governance of global interdependence.

To reach such an aim before it is too late is indeed a great challenge, not only to the South, but to humanity as a whole.

Notes

1. For a detailed critical analysis of the nature, roots and characteristics of Stalinist systems, see T. Szentes, 1990, p.151; or T. Szentes, 1989, p.16.
2. South Commission, 1990, p.260.
3. Ibid., p.213.
4. Ibid.
5. Ibid.
6. Several years ago at the Task Force meeting of the United Nations University some of us recommended that the Rector should initiate such courses and organize an international network for them, involving all national universities that co-operate with UNU.
7. South Commission, 1990, pp.4-7.
8. Ibid., p.283.
9. Ibid., chapter 2.
10. Ibid., chapter 5.
11. Ibid., pp.6-7.
12. Ibid., p.82.
13. See, for example, the famous Leontieff paradox in the case of the US economy in W.W. Leontieff, 1956.
14. See, among others, Thomas Balogh, 1963.
15. South Commission, 1990, p.114.
16. Ibid., p.115.
17. Ibid., pp.125-126.
18. Ibid., p.127.
19. Ibid., p.114.
20. Ibid., pp.93-94.
21. Ibid., pp.48-51.
22. Ibid., p.81.
23. Ibid., p.276.
24. Ibid.
25. The ideal civil society, freed from domination both by the state and by the market but making use of them for human development, has been eloquently described in Marc Nerfin, 1987, pp.170-195.
26. South Commission, 1990, pp.275-276.
27. Ibid., p.15.
28. Ibid., pp.83 and 138.
29. Ibid., pp.92 and 94.
30. Ibid., pp.96-99.

31. Ibid., p.221.
32. Ibid., p.279.
33. Ibid., p.11.
34. Ibid., p.10.
35. One of the lessons to be learnt from the failure of communist régimes is that economic rights cannot be fully realized without political rights, and that socially free access to "physical capital", to the main means of production, cannot be achieved via the ownership of the latter by a state that is not socially controlled and democratically operated.
36. South Commission, 1990, p.11.
37. Ibid., pp.128 133.
38. Ibid., p.117.
39. Ibid., p.272.
40. Ibid., p.46.
41. Jan Pronk, 1991, p.31.
42. South Commission, 1990, p.46.
43. Ibid., p.11.
44. Ibid., p.110.
45. Ibid., p.201.
46. Ibid., p.38.
47. Ibid., p.282.
48. Ibid., p.38.
49. Ibid., p.21.
50. Ibid., p.1.
51. Ibid., p.21.
52. Ibid., p.3.
53. Ibid., p.20.
54. Ibid., p 204.
55. Ibid., pp.20 and 202.
56. For an investigation of the forms and mechanism of the regular income and resource losses suffered by countries in the international economy, see T. Szentes, 1971.
57. South Commission, 1990, p.18.
58. Ibid., pp.26 and 143.
59. See, for example, the works of Ral Prebisch, Gunnar Myrdal, Hans Singer, Celso Furtado.
60. See H.W. Singer, 1960, and T. Szentes, 1985.
61. South Commission, 1990, p.38.
62. Ibid., p.109.
63. Ibid., p.247.
64. Ibid., p.41.
65. Ibid., p.153.
66. See T. Szentes, 1971.
67. South Commission, 1990, p.133.
68. Ibid., p.132.
69. Ibid., chapter 5.
70. Ibid., p.211.
71. Ibid., p.12.
72. Such an illusion appeared also in T. Szentes, 1971. By contrast with the diagnosis outlined in that book, which still seems to be relevant, the "recipe" was based upon a vision of a democratic socialist alternative within single countries, more or less delinked from the dominant centre of the world economy, and assigning a decisive role to the state in development, but avoiding the trap of Stalinism, saved from those "distortions", "errors"

and anti-democratic practices that characterized the Stalinist régimes. Such a vision, no doubt, was influenced at that time by the promising start of an alternative development in post-Arusha Tanzania, and later by Allende's Chile for a while. Harsh reality, however, has totally dispelled such an illusion both in respect of "delinking", that is, escaping from the world system, and in respect of any tatist solution.

73. South Commission, 1990, p.285.
74. Ibid., p.225.
75. Ibid., p.264.
76. Ibid., p.267.
77. See Pronk, 1991, pp.9-10.
78. Ibid.
79. The Report correctly refers to the hypocritical distinction drawn between the labour services of the South as "immigration", to be controlled by national laws, and the technology-related services of the skilled labour of the North which should enjoy free international mobility just like capital.

Bibliography

Balogh, Thomas
    Unequal Partners, Vol. I-II, Blackwell, Oxford, 1963.
Leontieff, W.W.
    "Factor proportions and the structure of American trade: further proportions and empirical analysis", *Review of Economics and Statistics*, Vol. 38, November 1956.
Nerfin, Marc
    "Neither prince nor merchant: citizen: - an introduction to the third system", *Development Dialogue*, No. 1, 1987.
Pronk, Jan
    Towards a System of Responsible Global Governance for Development, Speeches delivered by Mr. Jan Pronk, Netherlands Minister for Development Co-operation, The Hague, 1991.
Singer, H.W.
    "Distribution of gains between investing and borrowing countries", *American Economic Review*, May 1960.
South Commission
    The Challenge to the South: The Report of the South Commission, Oxford University Press, Oxford and New York, 1990.
Szentes, T.
    The Political Economy of Underdevelopment, Akademiai, Budapest, 1971, 1973, 1976, 1983, 1988.
Szentes, T.
    Theories of World Capitalist Economy: A Critical Survey of Conventional, Reformist and Radical Views, Akademiai, Budapest, 1985.
Szentes, T.
"Radical transformation, democratization and re-opening in the East: Motives, implications and dilemmas", *Institute for East-West Security Studies*, East-West Task Force on Seeking Security in the 1990s, Washington, D.C., June 1989.
Szentes, T.
    Changes and Transformation in Eastern and Middle Europe
    Implications and Effects on the South and East-South Relations --A Study for the South Commission, Geneva, 1991.

13. WISE, BUT NOT TOUGH, OR IS IT CORRECT, BUT NOT WISE?

Immanuel Wallerstein

I must confess at the outset that the South Commission's Report, The Challenge to the South, is a disappointment. It is written by a stellar group of political and intellectual leaders of the South: former presidents, former or current secretaries-general of international organizations, a cardinal, world-renowned economists. It offers the reasoned view of the South after the "lost decade"[1] of the 1980s, in the light of the "deep pessimism in much of the Third World about the prospects for economic development".[2] It asserts that the countries of the South are in a "profound development crisis",[3] one that is exacerbated by the "general erosion of the political and economic effectiveness of state and government in the countries of the South".[4]

These premises seem to me unquestionably sound. They are wise statements, or at least correct ones. Furthermore, the Commission accepts one more basic premisse. The bases for North-South solidarity are all in place, the authors say: "However, the North, its governments and its decision-makers, by and large refuse to acknowledge them."[5] One could not state the current reality more clearly.

These premisses having been stated, the rest of the Report consists of a good deal of detailed (and once again correct) analysis of a long series of specific issues, and a series of basic recommendations. And therein lies the paradox. The "Six Point Global Programme of Immediate Action"[6] could have been written 20 years ago. Indeed it was. The call for making "the basic needs of the mass of the people"[7] a priority goal could have been written 20 years ago. Indeed it was. But if the world in general, and the North in particular, has totally ignored these proposals over the last 20 years, what is there in the current situation, or in the Report of the South Commission, that should lead one to expect the least change in attitudes or behaviour?

At the beginning of the "lost decade", in 1980, the Brandt Report (written by an international commission composed of persons from North and South, and including three persons who are also members of the South Commission)[8] recommended a programme not too different from that the South Commission now recommends. At the time, I wrote about the Brandt Report:

I believe myself that the next 20 years of North-South negotiations are not going to be more significant or efficacious than the last 20 years, and I believe the evidence for this belief lies in the very structure of the Report as I have analysed it. An appeal of the liberals among the powerful to their compeers to make reforms in the interest of equity, justice, and heading off worse has never had any significant effect in the past several hundred years except in the wake of direct and violent rumblings by the oppressed, and it will have no more effect now.[9]

I fear that the South Commission has also succumbed to the attractions of the rhetoric of global liberalism. What could epitomize such rhetoric more than what it calls "the vision: a rational and development-oriented international system"?[10] Proclaiming such a vision may be wise, but is it tough? Or perhaps one should say, proclaiming such a vision is certainly morally correct, but is it wise to offer such a patently politically improbable objective?

For all the political experience evidenced in the biographies of the members of the South Commission, the Report is strangely apolitical. Each issue is treated technically, and morally, but never politically. This is true not only when the Commission adjures the North to behave differently, but even when it adjures the South to do something. One small example will illustrate this apoliticism. On page 87, the South Commission asserts that "for food security to become a reality, the state's investment and promotional policies will also need to be reoriented in favour of small peasants and co-operatives". No doubt! But reorienting state policies in favour of small peasants is no minor task, and the history of the past 200 years gives ample evidence of the enormous resistance to such reorientations. There is, however, not a word on the real political obstacles to such a realignment nor any tough recommendations on what to do about it.

The reality is that it is most unlikely that the dominant forces of the world system will permit, let alone encourage, the creation of "a global rule-based system built on the principles of transparency, multilateralism, and non-discrimination",[11] the hope of the South Commission. If they did, it would mean the end of the functioning of the capitalist world economy as it has been known for the last 500 years. What the South Commission wants is a revolutionary transformation in the whole structure of the world system, and it asks for it very politely, almost timidly. Its wish will not be fulfilled.

The five principal political issues of the next decade (indeed the next three to four decades) are scarcely adumbrated in the Report. What one desperately needs to know is the views and recommendations of Mwalimu Nyerere and his colleagues on these five political issues and dilemmas.

Issue No. 1 is North-North differences. The emerging tripartite dispersion of power and wealth in the North (EC, Japan, the United States) is noted by the South Commission and some minor consequences are discussed. But this is to underplay a major shift in geopolitics. The period 1945-1990 was an era of US hegemony and a factitious Cold War, on whose pretensions, however, the South could occasionally play via the proclaimed tactic of non-alignment. Now this is history. The world has entered the post-American era, that of US decline, which is likely to witness a vicious, non-ideological struggle for capital accumulation among the powerful states of the North.

Is this good or bad for the South? Should the South take sides? Can the states of the South avoid being forced to be satellites to the one or to the other? Should they perhaps seek to be in one or the other orbit? Must the world wait until 2010 for a serious policy discussion of such an urgent issue?

Issue No. 2 is the ex-East as South. China, Eastern Europe and the USSR have always been economically a part of the South. But they refused to recognize this for political reasons while the communists were in power. And now, when the communist parties have been in most places evicted from power, they are for other reasons still refusing to recognize this.

The truth is known in the South. But the expression of the truth takes the complaining form that OECD countries are now redirecting aid and other efforts from "South" to "East". Is this the appropriate line of analysis? Would intellectuals in the South complain that there is too much aid going to the Middle East and therefore not enough to Latin America? This would not be a politically useful stance. Nor is it vis-à-vis Eastern Europe. Should not the South Commission be tackling more directly, and more politically, the political recognition of the East as South? Should not the Commission be suggesting what kinds of political alliances this shift portends for the future?

Issue No. 3 is South-South wars. Can the Commission afford to ignore this troublesome reality, which promises to become far more important, not less, in the decades to come? The Iran-Iraq war did more to set back the economic development of those two countries (at least) than the provisions of GATT. Not to speak of the Iraq-Kuwait war, or a Croatia-Serbia war. The increasing prospects of such wars are linked no doubt to the "deep pessimism ... about the prospects for economic development" of which the Commission speaks, as well as of the "erosion of the political and economic effectiveness" of states. But what are the implications?

Issue No. 4 is South to North migration, including now "East" to "West", migration that is heavily "illegal" or "unauthorized". It is like a tidal wave, and there seems to be little that governments (North or South) can do to slow it down significantly. In an economically and demographically polarizing world, South to North migration has enormous advantages at the level of individual households in the South as well as at the level of enterprises in the North.

But politically the consequences promise to be enormous, within the states of the South, and probably even more serious within the states of the North. Has the enlightened political leadership of the South no view on this issue? Is it a good or a bad thing, in terms of the evolution of the world system as a whole? What are its implications for concepts such as national identity and global solidarity? As the North clamours for more "human rights" in the South, should not the South be clamouring for "human rights" in the North?

And Issue No. 5, the prospect of North-South wars, is totally skirted. But the first of the deliberate North-South wars has taken place just recently, that of the Persian Gulf, and I doubt very much that it will be the last. However undesirable, actual warfare is being planned for in the defence ministries of the North, and at least contemplated in some of those of the South. Must 20 years elapse before political leaders begin to discuss North-South "security" issues with the same assiduity that East-West "security" issues were discussed from 1945 to 1990?

I write as someone sure that a long period of very difficult disintegration of the modern world system lies ahead, but also as someone who is far from certain what is the best strategy to pursue in order that such chaotic disintegration should be succeeded by a world that is more democratic and more egalitarian, one in which the very concept of a South as the worse-off partner in a North-South polarization will have become archaic.

I look to the persons on the South Commission, or if not these then to others in the South, to propose tough and realistic strategies in this transformation. I frankly believe that the illusions of "developmentalism" should be put aside -- that is, the illusion that, within the framework of a capitalist world economy, the underdeveloped South will ever disappear as a construct. The most serious anti-systemic movements of the last 100 years have all in the end failed, and failed badly, but they failed precisely because they never put that illusion behind them.

If we want a democratic, egalitarian world, we must all (persons of the South and of the North) put illusions behind us. We must recognize the social strengths of the capitalist world economy (which has enabled it to survive so many challenges so well). But we must also analyse its fatal flaws which are bringing it to an end amid disintegration. One of its fatal flaws is its inability to sustain illusions indefinitely. Those opposed to the system must not promote the very incrementalist illusions that have sustained it in the past. Rather they must prepare us for the crossing of the desert, and maximize the possibility (which can never be a certainty) that we shall thereby reach the promised land, or at least a land that is considerably different and considerably better than the one whose negative realities the South Commission knows so well.

Notes

1. South Commission, 1990, p.19.
2. Ibid., p.35.
3. Ibid., p.61.
4. Ibid., p.65.
5. Ibid., p.225.
6. Ibid., pp.268-270.
7. Ibid., p.273.
8. Brandt Commission, 1980.
9. Immanuel Wallerstein, 1981, pp.346-347.
10. South Commission, 1990, p.222.
11. Ibid., p.223.

Bibliography

Brandt Commission (Independent Commission on International Development Issues)
   North-South: A Programme for Survival, Pan Books, London, 1980.
South Commission
   The Challenge to the South: The Report of the South Commission, Oxford University Press, Oxford and New York, 1990.
Wallerstein, Immanuel
   Article in *Towards One World? International Responses to the Brandt Report*, Temple Smith, London, 1981.

III. NORTH AND SOUTH IN THE NEW WORLD ORDER

14. SOUTH-SOUTH CO-OPERATION: A HORIZON OF HOPE

Y. Seyyid Abdulai

The Report of the South Commission, a milestone in thinking on development issues, warmly welcomed by the OPEC Fund for International Development, should be required reading for all concerned with development.

The three years of study and contacts distilled in *The Challenge to the South* embodied the very principle of self-reliance, and the South's own intellectual and financial resources and some of its best minds combined to formulate a comprehensive and coherent body of analysis and proposals, far removed from the paternalism that so often suffuses prescriptions from the North.

The discussion initiated by the Commission must be continued, and words must be followed by deeds.

First, a few comments on the Report as a whole. The OPEC Fund is in full agreement with the South Commission's stress on the need for the countries of the South to learn from past failures and succeses, and we, too, accept that appropriate economic policies, social justice and the building of efficient institutions are prerequisites of effective development co-operation. For instance, the striking success of OPEC's most populous member, Indonesia, shows that, in time, consistent policies directed towards stability, economic efficiency and a high rate of internal savings and foreign investment do bring the desired results.

At the same time, we share the Commission's belief that development cannot be measured in economic terms alone. We strongly support the principle of "people-centred" development, and therefore welcome the Report's emphasis on the need for grassroots participation in development, and on the crucial importance of human resources. We, too, have noticed that projects embodying such popular participation often achieve the best results, if only because it leads to the quick correction of mistakes.

While fully endorsing the Commission's willingness to face up to "home truths" regarding the past weaknesses of the development models adopted by some nations of the South, we likewise concur with the Report's indictment of the havoc wrought by the external economic environment during the "lost decade of the 1980s". In international fora the OPEC Fund has repeatedly pointed out that the adjustment efforts of developing countries around the globe have been hampered, if not thrown into disarray, by the external shocks so ably analysed by the South Commission. I need only mention declining commodity prices, high interest rates, protectionism, negative net financial flows and the unresolved debt crisis. The North did, indeed, as the Commission states, shift the burden of its own adjustment needs to the South.

We are bound to accept that a fundamental change of heart is not in sight, and that therefore the South cannot expect any fundamental improvement in the external context; it must look to its own collective resources of strength and wisdom.

Nevertheless, we take the view that the North bears a heavy share of the responsibility for the desperate situation faced by much of the South, especially the Least Developed Countries (LDCs). While there have lately been a few hopeful signs in respect of private financial flows, there is no escaping the fact that, for such countries, official development assistance remains a matter, literally, of life and death.

The OPEC Fund

Much of the South Commission Report concerns the need to revitalize South-South co-operation, and it is this aspect that I wish to highlight. I need hardly stress that the establishment of OPEC represented a breakthrough in collective self-reliance and the replacement of neo-colonial economic structures. Today, the Organization stands as a symbol of the feasibility of long-term co-operation between developing countries. It proves that the community of interests and experience among the peoples of the South is capable of transcending regional, cultural, political and economic distinctions.

The Report gives due recognition to the part played by OPEC in the evolution of the concept of South-South co-operation, and to its role as the main source of intra-South development assistance. As OPEC assistance represents perhaps the outstanding example of successful South-South co-operation at a practical level, it seems appropriate to start by examining it.

The commitment embodied by the OPEC Fund and its sister institutions stems from OPEC members' strong sense of fellowship with other developing countries – itself a product of the Organization's traditions of internal solidarity. It is the fact that the donors are themselves developing countries that gives OPEC aid its special character. In the case of the OPEC Fund, this has manifested itself in stress on rapid, unbureaucratic delivery and sensitivity to beneficiaries' priorities, as well as the absence of ties in respect of acquisitions, and the preference given to competitive offers, of goods and services from enterprises in the developing world.

As at the end of December 1990, the OPEC Fund had committed a cumulative total of 3.7 billion US dollars in loans, grants and allocations to international institutions. It is important to note that this was only a fraction of an overall OPEC aid effort totalling approximately 100 billion US dollars to date. Despite the fact that most OPEC countries are far from prosperous, and all have suffered from the instability of the price of the commodity upon which their economies depend, this effort has continued. Thus, the amounts committed under the OPEC Fund's two-year lending programmes have been increased regularly.

At a time when cases of misdirection of development finance are in the public eye, the targets, as well as the volume of assistance, are understandably subject to scrutiny. Here, I can point to our reputation for efficient delivery, and to the fact that independent assessment has shown the vast majority of projects supported to have been successful. Being free of political motives -- it is accorded without regard to race, region, ideology or religious beliefs -- the Fund's assistance has been directed to those most in need. In consequence, historically over half of the lending commitments have been to LDCs.

As regards the Fund's priorities, there is a striking similarity to the reasoning of *The Challenge to the South*. Thus, the Fund, too, regards the development of human resources as the central issue, and therefore accords high priority to projects in the fields of education and public health. Likewise, its emphasis on reaching the poor inevitably places the promotion of modernized peasant agriculture, and related improvements in infrastructure, credit and extension services, in the forefront of operations. For the same reasons, OPEC members, acting through the Fund, played a crucial role in the establishment of the International Fund for Agricultural Development, and have made large contributions to the replenishments of its resources.

At the same time, we support projects of benefit to the urban poor, including programmes aimed at alleviating the social effects of adjustment policies. We are also aware that industrialization ultimately represents the path to self-reliance and dignity in the South, and we do not neglect projects that contribute towards it. Meanwhile, like the authors of the South Commission Report, we believe that development work must be supported by a wide range of intellectual and scientific activities, and these have thus been the object of numerous grant operations.

We share the concern of the South Commission regarding the global system of commodity trade. The instability of commodity prices threatens to nullify the best efforts towards economic reform of the majority of developing countries that depend on exports of primary products. The OPEC Fund was therefore active throughout the long and tortuous process that ultimately led to the creation of the Common Fund for Commodities, albeit in a truncated form. The OPEC Fund assumed responsibility for the subscriptions of 34 LDC members, and contributed the largest grants, as compared to other donors, to the Second Account which finances research and development, and measures aimed at improving the structural conditions in the markets and enhancing long-term competitiveness of particular commodities.

South–South Co-operation

Obviously, the OPEC Fund alone cannot bring about the revitalization of South-South co-operation for which the South Commission so rightly calls. Indeed, given the parlous state of many economies of the South, it would be unrealistic to expect them to become a major source of development finance at present. Other forms of co-operation are of significance, and I should also like to touch on these.

One aspect rightly emphasized by *The Challenge to the South* is the need for a stronger collective profile in international negotiations, which in turn requires stronger institutions of the South. The manner in which this may best be achieved is open to argument, but there is no question of the need to combat the trend towards marginalization of large parts of the developing world, which has perversely accompanied increasing economic globalization and the move towards regional integration in the North.

The stalled Uruguay Round negotiations clearly call for a strong collective stand on the part of the developing world, but the growth of intra-South trade need not depend on GATT. For instance, simple lack of knowledge is often an obstacle – importers do not know what can be bought elsewhere in the South – and this is addressed by the plan for a trade information network, recently endorsed by Chambers of Commerce and Industry of the Group of 77.

As the South Commission Report notes, countries in crisis or preoccupied with adjustment programmes were not best placed to further regional institutions, and a number of promising ventures virtually ground to a halt during the 1980s. However, the low priority assigned to such efforts reveals the deeply ingrained habit of looking to the North.

South-South exchanges are no longer a matter of idealism: they make good economic sense, now that the range of manufactures and services, available in the South at attractive terms, is infinitely wider than it was. In many cases technologies and services adapted to conditions in developing countries will be more appropriate than Northern counterparts. That such advantages are too seldom realized illustrates a deeper problem to which the South Commission has pointed – namely, the tendency to continue aping Western patterns of technology and consumption, regardless of their frequent irrelevance to the needs of the South.

The rapid growth of trade among OPEC members shows what is possible. Likewise, the fact that Brazil is already the leading trade partner of some Latin American countries indicates what can be achieved when a large and relatively powerful developing economy is present in a given region. On the other hand, we find that, within the ECOWAS (Economic Community of West African States) area, less than 5 per cent of all trade is carried on between member states. If Africa's economic problems are the most severe, this is surely not unconnected with the degree of dependence.

It is heartening to see that progress towards a strengthening of regional economic communities has now resumed. In Africa, for instance, the first steps have been taken towards placing the various regional groupings on a firmer footing, and ultimately integrating them in a single African Economic Community. In Latin America, we see the commitment to Mercosur – the Southern Cone Common Market – and an Andean free trade zone. Another type of organization is Fonplata (River Plate Basin Development Fund), which recently signed a memorandum of understanding with the OPEC Fund.

The Challenge to the South issues a warning to developing countries that both markets for primary commodities and hard-won success in diversification of their economies are at risk from technological developments in the North. The knowledge base required to retain competitive positions is expanding, yet, in many countries of the South, cuts in public expenditure have affected education and science budgets. Particularly for smaller countries, the case for co-operation in order to achieve better use of scarce intellectual and other resources is compelling – the more so for research and development activities that require a given critical mass.

As with trade, such exchanges are not a matter of mere replication of endeavours in the North. Scientists and technologists in the South will have different priorities, while their Northern counterparts will understandably tend to neglect problems that do not affect their societies. For instance, there is no substitute for the agricultural research conducted by the various centres of CGIAR (the Consultative Group on International Agricultural Research), which we have frequently supported with grants.

It is my belief that, at national level, sound macro-economic policies, combined with judicious privatization, provide the best framework for development. Hopes for recovery in developing countries are increasingly attached to the private sector. Yet this does not mean that the state has no role to play. On the contrary, by withdrawing from activities to which it is ill suited, it should become capable of doing a better job where it is most needed. Apart from ensuring a degree of social welfare, its tasks certainly include measures to foster an enabling environment for investments both domestic and foreign, large and small.

Small and medium enterprises are particularly dependent on a functioning infrastructure, efficient service industries, and a healthy, educated and properly trained workforce. They need reliable commercial, scientific and technological information, knowledge of standards and patents, and competence in handling trade and technology transfer negotiations. The well-founded selection of promising projects or technologies will not happen by itself. Neither will such competence automatically spread beyond large urban centres. As with agriculture, someone must see to it that extension services reach the entrepreneur. The same applies to credit, which has to be supplied at appropriate rates by responsive institutions. If the state does not assume such tasks, it must at least ensure that they are performed.

Another area of South-South co-operation is the settlement of regional conflicts, for which there is great scope. As shown by the fate of my own continent, Africa, such conflagrations do immeasurable damage to all forms of collaboration between states, and to development itself. The fear of warfare also costs many lives, for military budgets eat into productive spending. According to the United Nations Development Programme, in the 25 years up to 1986, military spending by developing countries grew by 7.5 per cent per year, to absorb 5.5 per cent of their gross national product. In many developing countries soldiers outnumber the teaching and medical staff, and military spending surpasses the combined education and health budgets, sometimes by factors of two or three.

The end of the Cold War should reduce both foreign intervention and the inducement to import outworn ideological models, leaving us freer to develop in our own way. Where bloodshed erupts, it is the countries of the affected region that should serve as the "fire brigade" – as, indeed, they often do.

In the long run, intensified co-operation between countries of the South at all levels is the best hope for removing the need for crisis management. And as common interests come to outweigh divisions, so, too, it should prove easier to beat swords into ploughshares.

All this being said, it is important to stress that South-South ties in no way conflict with or replace North-South co-operation. Rather, there are many ways in which the two can complement each other. To take an example from my own experience, there is everything to be gained from joint funding of multilateral institutions by both North and South, and, indeed, these play a crucial role in development assistance. The OPEC Fund not only welcomes the activities of national and multilateral development agencies and non-governmental organizations, but frequently works together with them, just as it seeks to co-ordinate its operations with those of fellow OPEC institutions. To the extent that South-South co-operation enhances the effectiveness of development assistance, it serves to further North-South co-operation as well.

I need hardly add that nothing could be further from the thinking of the South Commission than a wish for confrontation with the North. The most cursory reading of *The Challenge to the South* reveals that the current inadequacies of North-South co-operation are the object of criticism. These underline the necessity of stronger South-South ties, which are at all events a matter of simple common sense.

Unfortunately, as the history of OPEC demonstrates, South-South co-operation has often been the object of hostility, misrepresentation and disruption. There is no shortage of links between North and South, though they often rest on exploitation rather than equal partnership. It should not be necessary to point out that partnership between countries of the South does not, *per se*, constitute an "attack" on the North. Yet the wilful misconstruction of the South Commission Report by some Northern commentators indicates that such attitudes persist.

Even though no policy or programme can encompass the myriad actions required to accelerate flows of trade, finance, technology and skills in the South, the South Commission's proposals generally strike me as an excellent starting point. Perhaps the Commission's greatest contribution has been to infuse the debate on the next decade of development with renewed hope and urgency. These, as well as necessity, are the mothers of invention.

15. THE CHALLENGE OF GLOBALIZATION: DELINKING

Samir Amin

The double collapse in the latter half of the 1980s of the "socialist" systems of the East and of the aspirations for national independence of the countries of the South, bringing the "Bandung era" (1955-1975) to a close, ushered in a new period in history. The central feature of this new period is already visible: the attempt to reconstruct the unification of the world through and on a "market" (capitalist) base.

With regard to this far-reaching globalization, three options are theoretically possible: (a) Take up the challenge of capitalist globalization as it is, while trying to better the national position by joining in the game of international competition; (b) Act to change the world system in a direction favourable to a "better" (and even "fair") globalized development; (c) Stand aloof from such a world system ("delinking").

In this respect, the Report of the South Commission takes positions that are great improvements over those found in previous international reports. There are no pipe dreams about mitigating the harmful effects of capitalist globalization; instead it stresses the need for selective delinking and in particular, for South-South co-operation. I shall therefore adopt the viewpoint of the Report of the South Commission while putting forward my own reasons.

The law of globalized value – the foundation of the global system – is at the very origin of world polarization (contrast: centres/peripheries). Capitalism as a world system cannot be reduced to the capitalist mode of production, as the capitalist mode of production assumes an integrated three-dimensional market (goods, capital and labour).

This integration, effected in the context of the history of the formation of central bourgeois nation states, was never extended to world capitalism. The world market is exclusively two-dimensional in its growth, progressively integrating exchanges of products and the flow of capital – to the exclusion of labour, for which the market remains compartmentalized. This very fact is enough to bring about unavoidable polarization.

The modern form of polarization appeared in the nineteenth century in consequence of the division of the world into industrialized countries versus those not engaged in industrialization, though this contrast was not the eternal, definitive form of capitalist polarization. Dominant from 1800 to 1945, this contrast gradually became less marked after the Second World War, with the industrialization of the peripheries, whereas the criterion of polarization shifted to new ground.

The rise of the concept of world capitalist polarization has its own history. In the beginning, analysis had put the emphasis quite naturally on the industry/no-industry contrast, since polarization was in effect expressed through this dichotomy. Industrialization thus became the means of "development" whose historic objective was taken to be the ending of polarization ("underdevelopment"). In direct relation with this contrast, analysis focused on unequal exchange. Actually, unequal exchange – involving products embodying efforts for which the remuneration is more unequal than the difference of productivity suggests – is but the tip of the iceberg. Four polarization mechanisms operate outside any exchange: (a) capital flight from the peripheries to the centres; (b) selective migration of workers in the same direction (even though such migration, precisely because it is selective, excludes the formation of a world labour market); (c) control by the centres of access to the natural resources of the entire Earth; (d) the various monopoly positions held by the companies of the centre in the world division of labour.

The industrialization of the periphery does not put an end to capitalist polarization, but it does move the centre of gravity of the forces giving rise to the phenomenon to the control of technology, international finance, and of course the media (and through them political control), armaments (the monopoly of the means of genocide), or the discourse on the environment. In this context, peripheral industrialization can become a sort of modern putting-out system, controlled by the financial and technological centres. The newly industrializing countries of the South (and of the East?) are already the very core of tomorrow's periphery.

Yet it is said that the Third World is becoming increasingly marginal in the world system, whether as a supplier of raw materials or as a market for exports from the centres and for the investment of their capital. True, the revolution of technology, on the one hand, and the quantity of mineral resources of the North American and Australian continents, on the other, have diminished for the time being the importance of the contributions of the Third World. But this does not mean that the Third World is now marginal. This fashionable idea is simply wrong. The relative decrease in its contribution is largely due to the depression – prevailing since 1970 – but there would be a revival in a new, sustained and long expansion. And though – thanks to the enormous strategic stockpiles of raw materials built up by the United States – there is no danger of serious shortages in case of localized conflicts, it is by no means evident that this situation can continue once a new strong expansion is under way. There is every chance of an all-out race for raw materials once again. This is all the more likely as these resources may very well become scarce, not only because of the exponential cancer of waste in Western consumption, but also because of new industrialization in the peripheries. Hence, conflicts for access to these resources have certainly not lost their raison d'tre. For that matter, the Gulf War proves that the control of the planet's natural resources is still the overriding concern of the Western states.

The reason why peripheries are always referred to in the plural, is – as I have argued – that they can only be described in negative terms, as the regions of the world system which have not transformed themselves into centres. The diversity of the functions they fulfil in the world system is the rule and not the exception. The concept of polarization means that the centres produce this system as a whole by shaping the subordinate modernization of the peripheries; of course, this world expansion is synonymous not only with the hierarchical development involved in modernization, but also with the process of destruction of the parts that have become dysfunctional to its global logic. Relegation to the periphery and devastation therefore go hand in hand and account for the permanent differentiation of the peripheries, reproduced in continuously evolving forms.

Polarization creates social, political and cultural conditions unbearable for the vast majority of the peoples of the peripheries: worsening poverty for most, frustration, flouted national feelings, bloody dictatorships imposed by the logic of unequal accumulation.

The repeated attempts in the history of capitalism to build world unity still remain a reactionary utopia which has only been realized for very short periods, because it inevitably tends to intensify the revolt by the majority of the world's peoples who are its victims. Generally associated with the aspirations of the principal centre to impose its hegemony, this utopia also brings in its wake, by the force of circumstances, the intensification of inter-centre conflicts.

Actually, the unification of the world by capitalism is a recent phenomenon. British hegemony was achieved quite late, after China and the Ottoman Empire had been "opened" up (from 1840), after the Indian Mutiny had been quelled (1857). Britain's industrial lead and financial monopoly, real at the time, did not lead to true hegemony. This so-called world hegemony had to reckon with the European balance of power, which was not dominated by Britain. In fact, no sooner had Britain's hegemony been established (from 1850 to 1860) than it was challenged industrially and militarily by the rise of her competitors,

Germany and the United States, as from 1880, even though London did hold on to its strong financial position for much longer. The 20 or 30 years of the relatively integrated capitalist world market (1850-1880) were followed by over 60 years of inter-imperialist rivalries (1880-1945), so violent that they led to two world wars; and, as from 1917, by 70 years of effective delinking by the Soviet Union, then by China. Unification of the world through the market and hegemony, far from being the rule in the history of capitalist world expansion, is the exception, and both short-lasting and fragile. The law of the system is continuing rivalry and delinking.

Have things changed since then? Or are they really changing? In some aspects the hegemony of the United States since 1945 is truly new in character. The United States, for the first time in history, has the military means to intervene (in an extreme hypothesis by destruction and genocide) on a planetary scale. Limited from 1945 to 1990 by the military bipolarity shared with the USSR, the United States has perhaps become – or is becoming – what no other country before it had been, except in Hitler's imagination: the (military) master of the world ... but for how long?

Talk about hegemony is fashionable today, as was to be expected: hegemony would ensure stability through respect for the "rules of the game" it imposes. This is an ideological legitimation. The "new world order" that the Gulf War ushered in, following quickly upon the beginning of the Soviet break-up, is quite different. It is a new empire of chaos, of the utmost instability, due to be afflicted by violent contradictions, renewal of inter-centre rivalries and upheavals in the peripheries in the South and tomorrow in the East.

In these circumstances the future structures of globalization are not the factors (determined in turn by technological constraints and their economic expression) which define the context in which competition between Europe, Japan, and the United States will unfold. On the contrary, it is the evolution of this competition that will determine the structure of globalization or its possible partial negation by the construction of regional groupings and/or by the delinking of regions in the periphery.

As one looks at the trends characterizing the exchanges between the EC, Japan, the United States and between these poles and regions of the Third World, one can see how – in the context of transnationalization – regional sub-poles crystallize around each of those three major poles, whose respective peripheries have, none the less, very different potentials. There is the vast American region, dominated by the United States. There is the vast region of East and South-East Asia, dominated by Japan, integrating the semi-industrialized Asian South-East, but whose frontiers remain blurred. There is no assurance that Korea can be considered as integrated in this ensemble, and even less does the prospect of including China make any sense. India itself, despite all its weaknesses, remains autonomous vis-à-vis the Japanese pole.

The cluster of countries attached to the EC has its own configuration, formalized by the EC-ACP association, strengthened partly by the rigid framework of the franc zone. But the African peripheries in question include precisely the group of the poorest countries whose potential – under the present system – is still weak.

It is premature, therefore, to speak of reorganization within transnationalization. The peripheries remain largely open worldwide to competition of the rival poles within their commercial and also financial markets. Besides, the competitiveness of these poles varies considerably from one type of product to another.

In any event, globalization – with or without regionalization – is unacceptable to the peoples of the periphery. Whereas in the central countries the transnational option is clear and opinions differ only as to its modalities, the question arises in very different terms in the Third World and in the East.

The argument that no society can escape the permanent challenge of (capitalist) globalization, that development is nothing other than development within this system, and that no autonomous development is possible outside it, is tied to the reality of the facts alone – that is, that this is how capitalist development works – but immediately forswears the idea that it may be possible to "change the world". Because the two have to be kept distinct, I suggest that the two concepts of capitalist expansion and development should not be mixed up even if in current usage they are frequently confused. Capitalist expansion is by nature polarizing. Development should, by definition, be different in nature so as to overcome this polarization. The development concept is in essence a concept critical of capitalism.

The development ideology that prevailed after the Second World War did not make this distinction clear. For some – the national bourgeoisies of the Third World of the Bandung era (1955-1975) – the objective of development was "to catch up", while staying in the world system, through appropriate state policies (nationalization, industrialization, etcetera). For others, the "socialist" states, this same objective ("to catch up", which implies evident similarities) was mixed with some shreds of the contradictory objective of building "another society".

Moreover, the uncontrollable exponential growth that follows from the logic of the capitalist mode of production is, as was rediscovered by ecologists, suicidal. Capitalism both as a mode of production and as a world system is therefore simultaneously suicidal and criminal, with possible implications of massive genocide in the potentially rebellious peripheries.

During the three post-war decades (1945-1975) the capitalist system underwent a remarkable expansion. Because of this, the dominant ideology was that of "development", offering the countries of the centre the possibility of virtually boundless and crisis-free growth, and for those of the periphery the possibility of overcoming their "underdevelopment". Those days are gone. The failure of the "development", incapable of reducing the gap, led to an ideological crisis. In its place a series of new initiatives appeared, replacing the political responses and stressing the democratization of power, sacrificed until then for the sake of the illusion of accelerated development. Democracy, in this spirit, was advanced as the condition for development and no longer as its delayed product.

The Western powers themselves stood at the forefront of the movement, mobilizing the powerful resources of their media and their ability to intervene economically, financially, politically and even militarily At the same time the idea was put forward that interdependence at all levels (the theme of environment naturally falls into this context) is such that only "world development" is henceforth conceivable (national development is described as a myth); that this development, founded on political democracy and the market, could be "something else" (and better) than that known up to now in the history of capitalist expansion. Put otherwise, social-democracy could become the solution to the problems on a world level as it has been for the Western countries.

Are these theses credible, and do they offer anything but yet another illusion?

Respect for the rights of the human being, democratization of politics and society, the guarantee of the collective rights of the different communities (religious, linguistic, cultural, and so on) are, in and by themselves, positive requirements; their entry into the awareness of people always represents an indisputable step forward. This progress cannot be "brought in from the outside", but must be won by the people concerned. I would even say that in this conquest the peoples of the periphery are blocked by the objectives of the Western powers, for these are preoccupied exclusively with the maintenance of the *status quo* of which they are the beneficiaries. The postulate affirming the identity of capitalism and democracy, which is the underlying theme in the orchestration of the North's interventions in the South, is a deceitful trick. On the contrary, and this is particularly clear in all the peripheries, the progress of democracy implies social measures that clash with the logic of capitalist expansion.

Endless examples could be given to show that this new "humanist and universalist" discourse is not credible. For five centuries absolutely no

Western intervention in Asia, Africa and Latin America has been favourable to the interests of the peoples of these regions. There are no signs that the logic of the system is changing. True "globalized development", favourable from the viewpoint of the peoples of the periphery, will be possible only when the West itself has evolved in a much more radical way than the best of its social-democrat régimes have allowed. Meanwhile the only possible progressive intervention by the West in the affairs of the Third World is non-intervention. The democratic forces in the West have to realize this and to take their fight into this field. Attempts at reforming the international order have so far not received any favourable response from the dominant powers in the centres of world capitalism, be it for the "New International Economic Order" proposed by the ruling classes of the Third World in 1975 (in an unreal attempt, as I said at the time, to define the rules of a non-polarizing interdependent development) or by sheer rhetoric (as in the Brandt Report[1]).

The only meaningful strategy on a world scale for progressive forces, in which the internationalism of the peoples of the three regions (West, East, South) could be given a fresh start, should come within the perspective of a polycentric world bringing together the different regions that make it up, in a flexible way which would make possible the implementation of the specific policies required by the diversity of the objective situations. "General interdependence" and the legitimate concern for self-reliance must be reconciled; the logic of mutual and reciprocal adjustment must replace the logic of unilateral adjustment on the part of the weakest in the pursuit of expansion for the exclusive benefit of the strongest. This is precisely my definition of delinking: the submission of external relationships to the needs of internal development. This concept is therefore exactly the opposite of the concept of unilateral adjustment advanced today in theory and practice.

Notes

1. Brandt Commission, 1983.

Bibliography

Brandt Commission (Independent Commission on International Development Issues) *Common Crisis. North South: Co-operation for World Recovery*, Pan Books, London, 1983.

16. WORLD ORDERS, OLD AND NEW

Noam Chomsky

The South Commission study *The Challenge to the South* closes with a call for a "new world order" that will respond to "the South's plea for justice, equity, and democracy in the global society".[1] The rulers of that society, however, adhere to quite a different conception of world order, expressed by Winston Churchill: "the government of the world must be entrusted to the satisfied nations", the "rich men dwelling at peace within their habitations" whose power places them "above the rest", not the "hungry nations" who "seek more" and hence endanger tranquillity. The global rulers can hardly be expected to heed the pleas of the South, any more than rights were granted to the general population, as a gift from above, within the rich societies themselves. Those assigned the status of spectators from below can afford no illusions on these matters.

The realities are illustrated in the South Commission's study. For instance, it observes that gestures to Third World concerns in the 1970s were "undoubtedly spurred" by worry about "the newly found assertiveness of the South after the rise in oil prices in 1973".[2] As the threat abated, the rich lost interest and turned to "a new form of neo-colonialism", monopolizing control over the world economy, undermining the more democratic elements of the United Nations, and in general proceeding to institutionalize "the South's second-class status". The pattern is consistent; it would be remarkable if it were otherwise.

It is Churchill's vision that has always inspired the rich rulers, who, needless to say, did not achieve that status by "dwelling at peace within their habitations". Nor do they take lightly any threat to that status.

A few years before Churchill's forthright articulation of the vision of the powerful, a War Department study transmitted by Secretary Henry Stimson to the State Department warned of the "rising tide all over the world wherein the common man aspires to higher and wider horizons" (July 1945).[3] It was in this context that a potential Soviet threat to the post-war order was perceived. There is no proof that Russia has "flirted with the thought" of supporting the rising tide of aspirations of the common man, the study observed, but it might do so. Taking no chances, the United States must therefore defend itself by surrounding the potential criminal with military force aimed at its heartland. The common man's aspirations posed a particularly severe threat because, as director of the Office of Strategic Services, William Donovan had informed the President the United States had "no political or social philosophy equally dynamic or alluring" to counter the "strong drawing card in the proletarian philosophy of Communism", particularly attractive at that historical moment, when empires were in disarray, the traditional conservative order was discredited by its fascist associations, and the resistance, popular-based and exhibiting radical democratic tendencies, was enjoying much prestige. The threat was countered by a worldwide campaign to destroy the anti-fascist resistance and restore the conservative business-ruled order. This was chapter one of post-1945 history.

The threat, however, did not vanish. A decade later, President Eisenhower complained that, unlike "us", the communists could "appeal directly to the masses". His Secretary of State, John Foster Dulles, deplored their "ability to get control of mass movements", "something we have no capacity to duplicate". ... "The poor people are the ones they appeal to and they have always wanted to plunder the rich", he observed to his brother, CIA director Allen Dulles, in 1958. The "social philosophy" that the rich should plunder the poor lacks popular appeal, a public relations problem that the rich rulers have never been able to overcome. The same concerns extended to "the preferential option for the poor" of the Latin American bishops and other commitments to social justice or democracy in more than form. The basic threat is the possibility of loss of control. Accordingly, similar concerns extend to such traditional friends as Mussolini, Trujillo or Saddam Hussein when they disobey orders.

Much the same was true of the relations of the United States with the USSR. It was not Stalin's crimes that troubled Western leaders. Truman noted in his diary that "I can deal with Stalin", agreeing with Eisenhower and others: what went on in Russia was not his concern, Truman declared. Stalin's death would be a "real catastrophe", he felt. But co-operation was contingent on the United States getting its way 85 per cent of the time, as Truman made clear. In a leading scholarly study of United States security planning in the early post-war period, Melvyn Leffler observes that "rarely does a sense of real compassion and/or moral fervor emerge from the documents and diaries of high officials. These men were concerned primarily with power and self-interest, not with real people facing real problems in the world that had just gone through fifteen years of economic strife, Stalinist terror, and Nazi genocide".[4]

The West's concern was not with Stalin's enormous crimes, but with the apparent successes in development and the appeal of the "proletarian philosophy" to the "common man" in the West and to subjugated and oppressed people everywhere. The failure of Eastern Europe to return to its traditional role as a supplier of food and raw materials to the West compounded these concerns. The West is not disturbed by crimes, but by insubordination, as was shown once again in the case of Saddam Hussein, a favoured friend and trading partner of the United States and its allies right through the period of his worst atrocities. As the Berlin Wall fell in 1989, the White House intervened directly, in a highly secret meeting, to ensure that Iraq would receive another 1 billion US dollars in loan guarantees, overcoming the Treasury's and the Commerce Department's objections that Iraq was not creditworthy. The reason, the State Department explained, was that Iraq was "very important to US interests in the Middle East"; it was "influential in the peace process" and was "a key to maintaining stability in the region, offering great trade opportunities for US companies". As in the case of Stalin, Saddam Hussein's crimes were of no account, until he committed the crime of disobedience on 2 August 1990.

Whatever its political colour, an independent course is unacceptable; successes that might provide a model to others are still more so. The miscreant is then termed a "rotten apple" that is spoiling the barrel, a "virus" that must be exterminated It is a "threat to stability". When a successful CIA operation overturned the democratic capitalist government of Guatemala in 1954, an internal State Department report explained that Guatemala had "become an increasing threat to the stability of Honduras and El Salvador. Its agrarian reform is a powerful propaganda weapon; its broad social program of aiding the workers and peasants in a victorious struggle against the upper classes and large foreign enterprises has a strong appeal to the populations of Central American neighbors where similar conditions prevail."[5] In the operative sense of the term, "stability" means security for "the upper classes and large foreign enterprises", and it must naturally be preserved. These are crucial features of the old world order, well-documented in the internal record, regularly illustrated in historical practice, bound to persist as contingencies change.

Writing on the world order in 1992, one can hardly ignore the approaching end of the first 500 years of a world order in which the major theme has been Europe's conquest of most of the world. The cast of characters has changed somewhat: a European-settled colony leads the crusade, and Japan, one of the few regions of the South to escape subjugation, was able to join the club of the rich. In contrast, parts of Western Europe that were colonized retain Third World features. One notable example is Ireland, violently conquered, then barred from development by the standard "free trade" doctrines selectively applied to ensure subordination of the South – today called "structural adjustment", "neo-liberalism", or "our noble ideals", from which the rich, to be sure, are exempt.

Throughout the Colombian era, the South has been assigned a service role: to provide resources, cheap labour, markets, opportunities for investment and for the export of pollution. For the past half-century, the United States has been the global enforcer, protecting the interests of the rich. Accordingly, the primary threat to US interests is depicted in high-level planning documents as "radical and nationalistic regimes" that are responsive to popular pressures for "immediate improvement in the low living standards of the masses" and for diversification of the economies, tendencies that conflict with the need to protect US control of raw materials and "a political and economic climate conducive to private investment". The basic themes of internal planning sometimes reach the public record, as when the editors of the *New York Times*, applauding the overthrow of the parliamentary Mossadegh rgime in Iran, observed that "underdeveloped countries with rich resources now have an object lesson in the heavy cost that must be paid by one of their number which goes berserk with fanatical nationalism". Most important, the historical record conforms to this understanding of the role of the South.

Within the rich men's club, order must also reign. The lesser members are to pursue their "regional interests" within the "overall framework of order" managed by the United States, the only power with "global interests and responsibilities", as Kissinger admonished Europe in 1973. In the early post-1945 years, a European third force could not be tolerated. Neutralism would be "a shortcut to suicide", Dean Acheson held. The formation of NATO was in large part motivated by the need "to integrate Western Europe and England into an orbit amenable to American leadership", Leffler observes.[6] With US economic domination in decline, those strictures might become harder to enforce. For the moment, they remain fairly valid in the loose framework of world government (Group of Seven, the IMF and World Bank, etcetera).

Standard reasoning is developed in a secret February 1992 Pentagon draft of Defense Planning Guidance, which describes itself as "definitive guidance from the Secretary of Defense" for budgetary policy to the year 2000. The United States must hold "global power" and a monopoly of force. It will then "protect" the "new order" while allowing others to pursue "their legitimate interests", as the United States defines them. The United States "must account sufficiently for the interests of the advanced industrial nations to discourage them from challenging our leadership or seeking to overturn the established political and economic order", or even "aspiring to a larger regional or global role". There must be no independent European security system; rather, US-dominated NATO must remain the "primary instrument of Western defense and security, as well as the channel for US influence and participation in European security affairs". ... "We will retain the pre-eminent responsibility for addressing selectively those wrongs which threaten not only our interests, but also those of our allies or friends"; the United States alone will determine what are "wrongs" and when they are to be selectively "righted". As in the past, the Middle East is a particular concern. Here "our overall objective is to remain the predominant outside power in the region and preserve US and Western access to the region's oil" while deterring aggression (selectively), maintaining strategic control and "regional stability" (in the technical sense), and protecting "US nationals and property". In Latin America, a crucial threat is Cuban "military provocation against the US or an American ally" – the standard Orwellian reference to the escalating US war against Cuban independence.[7]

The case of Cuba well illustrates the persistence of traditional themes and the basic logic of the North-South conflict. One hundred and seventy years ago, the United States was unsympathetic to the liberation of Latin America, adopting Thomas Jefferson's precept that it is best for Spain to rule until "our population can be sufficiently advanced to gain it from them piece by piece". Opposition to Cuban independence was particularly strong. Secretary of State John Quincy Adams, the author of the Monroe Doctrine, described Cuba as "an object of transcendent importance to the commercial and political interests of our Union". Expressing the dominant lite view, he urged Spanish sovereignty until Cuba would fall into US hands by "the laws of political ... gravitation", a "ripe fruit" for harvest. One prime concern was the democratic tendencies in the Cuban independence movement, which advocated abolition of slavery and equal rights for all. In the rhetoric of contemporary planners, there was a threat that "the rot might spread", even to US shores.

By the end of the nineteenth century, the British deterrent was gone and the United States was powerful enough to conquer Cuba, just in time to prevent the success of the indigenous liberation struggle. Cuba was effectively placed under the rule of the white propertied classes and US firms. In the 1930s, President Roosevelt revoked the "good neighbor policy" to overturn a civilian government regarded as a threat to US commercial interests. The Batista dictatorship served those interests loyally, thus enjoying full support.

Castro's overthrow of the dictatorship in January 1959 soon elicited US hostility. By late 1959, Washington had concluded that Castro was unacceptable. One reason, State Department liberals explained, was that "our business interests in Cuba have been seriously affected". A second was the threat to "stability":

The United States cannot hope to encourage and support sound economic policies in other Latin American countries and promote necessary private investments in Latin America if it is or appears to be simultaneously cooperating with the Castro program.

Studies of Cuban opinion provided to the White House concluded that most Cubans were optimistic about the future and supported Castro, while only 7 per cent expressed concern about communism. The Soviet presence was nil. "The liberals, like the conservatives, saw Castro as a threat to the hemisphere," historian Jules Benjamin comments, "but without the world communist conspiracy component."[8]

By October 1959, US-based planes were attacking Cuba. CIA subversion included supply of arms to guerrilla bands and sabotage of sugar mills and other economic targets. In March 1960, the Eisenhower administration formally adopted a plan to overthrow Castro in favour of a rgime "more devoted to the true interests of the Cuban people and more acceptable to the US", though it must be done "in such a manner as to avoid any appearance of US intervention". As always, the United States is the arbiter of "true interests".

Sabotage, terror and aggression were escalated further by the Kennedy administration, along with the kind of economic warfare that no small country within the US sphere can long endure. Kennedy also sought a cultural quarantine to block the free flow of ideas and information about Cuba to the Latin American countries, whose excessive liberalism was considered a problem, particularly their unwillingness to emulate US controls on travel and cultural interchange and their legal systems, which insisted upon evidence for crimes by alleged "subversives".

After the Bay of Pigs failure, Kennedy's international terrorist campaign escalated further, reaching quite remarkable dimensions. This is largely dismissed in the West, apart from some notice given to the assassination attempts, one of them carried out on the day of Kennedy's assassination. The operations were formally called off by President Lyndon Johnson. They continued, however, and escalated during the Nixon administration. Subsequent terrorist actions arc attributed to renegades beyond CIA control, whether accurately or not; one high Pentagon official in the 1960s, Roswell Gilpatric, has expressed his doubts. The Carter administration, with the support of US courts, condoned hijacking of Cuban ships in violation of the anti-hijacking convention that Castro was respecting. The Reaganites rejected Cuban initiatives for diplomatic settlement and imposed new sanctions against Cuba on the most outlandish pretexts, a record reviewed by Wayne Smith, who resigned as head of the US Interests Section in Havana in protest.

The embargo against Cuba was tightened in the 1980s, and again in mid-1991, while the United States resumed Caribbean military manoeuvres, a standard technique of intimidation. As in the 1820s, such policies are supported across the spectrum of articulate opinion. Washington makes no effort to conceal that it is exploiting the disappearance of the Soviet deterrent and the decline of the East bloc's economic relations with Cuba to achieve its longstanding aims, through economic warfare or other means. Similarly, throughout the 1980s, the liberal press scoffed at Gorbachev's "New Thinking" because he had not yet offered the United States a free hand to attain its objectives in Central America. The right of the United States to demolish those who stand in its way is beyond debate: ergo, those who attempt to defend themselves are criminals, and anyone who assists them is engaged in a criminal conspiracy. The power and uniformity of these doctrines in a country that is unusually free, by world standards, constitute a most illuminating phenomenon.

The Cuban record demonstrates with great clarity that the Cold War framework was scarcely more than a pretext for concealing the standard refusal of the United States to tolerate Third World independence, whatever its political cast From 1917 through the 1980s, virtually every US act of subversion, violence or economic warfare in the Third World was justified on grounds of defence from the Russians. Woodrow Wilson needed other pretexts when US troops invaded Haiti and the Dominican Republic, just as George Bush needed to seek new ones. But the basic realities do not change.

The Cold War itself had many of the features of North-South conflict. The Third World first appeared in Eastern Europe, which began to supply raw materials for workshops of the West as far back as the fourteenth century, and then followed the (now familiar) path towards underdevelopment as trade and investment patterns took their natural course. For reasons of scale, Russia's economic subordination to the West was delayed, but by the nineteenth century the process was well under way. The Bolshevik takeover in October 1917, which quickly aborted incipient socialist tendencies and destroyed any semblance of working-class or other popular organization, extricated the USSR from the Western-dominated periphery, setting off the inevitable reaction, beginning with immediate military intervention. These were, from the outset, some of the basic contours of the Cold War.

The logic was not fundamentally different from the case of Grenada or Guatemala, but the scale of the problem was. It had been enhanced after Russia's leading role in defeating Hitler had enabled it to isolate Eastern and parts of Central Europe from Western control. A tiny departure from subordination is intolerable, a huge one far less so, particularly when it threatens "stability" through the "rotten apple" effect. No less ominous was the ability of the Soviet Union to lend support to targets of US subversion or destruction, and its military capacity so enormous as to deter US intervention elsewhere. Under such circumstances, "coexistence" was even more out of the question than in the cases of Chile, Grenada, Guatemala, Nicaragua, etcetera. Though far from the whole story of the Cold War, this was a major theme, and a very familiar one.

The USSR reached the peak of its power by the late 1950s, always far behind the West. The Cuban missile crisis, revealing extreme Soviet vulnerability, led to a huge increase in military spending, levelling off by the late 1970s. The economy was then stagnating and the autocracy unable to control internal dissidence. The command economy had carried out basic industrial development but was unable to proceed to more advanced stages, and also suffered from the global recession that devastated much of the South. By the 1980s, the system had collapsed, and the core countries, always far richer and more powerful, "won the Cold War". Much of the Soviet empire will probably return to its traditional Third World status, and the ex-*nomenklatura* will be taking on the role of the Third World élites linked to international business and financial interests. But the United States is deeply in debt at every level (federal, state, corporate, household) after a decade of Reagan-Bush economic mismanagement. It is not well placed, therefore, to compete with its rivals for domination of these restored Third World domains, one of the sources of tension within the rich men's club.

A further consequence of the Soviet collapse is that a new framework is needed for intervention. The problem arose through the 1980s, requiring a propaganda shift to international terrorists, Hispanic narcotraffickers, crazed Arabs and other chimeras. Yet another consequence is that the collapse of the Soviet deterrent "makes military power more useful as a United States foreign policy instrument ... against those who contemplate challenging important American interests" (Dimitri Simes of the Carnegie Endowment for International Peace). This insight was echoed by Elliot Abrams, the Reaganite planner of policy towards Latin America, during the invasion of Panama and by commentators throughout the Gulf crisis, who noted that the United States and the United Kingdom could now use force without limit against a defenceless enemy.

Other factors, however, are likely to inhibit the US recourse to force in order to control the South. Among them are the successes of the past years in crushing popular nationalist and reform tendencies, the elimination of the "communist" appeal to those who hope to "plunder the rich", and the economic catastrophes of the last decade. In the light of these developments, limited forms of diversity and independence can be tolerated with less concern that they will lead to a challenge to ruling business interests. Control can be exercised by economic measures: structural adjustment, the IMF regimen, selective use of free-trade measures, and so forth. Needless to say, the successful industrial powers do not accept these rules for themselves, and never have done. But for the purposes of domination and exploitation, there is great merit in imposing them on the Third World. Quite generally, democratic forms are tolerable as long as "stability" is ensured. If this dominant value is threatened – by popular uprisings in Iraq, the electoral victory of a radical priest in Haiti, an Islamic movement in Algeria, or any uncontrolled popular force – then the iron fist must strike.

Another inhibiting factor in the United States is that the domestic base for foreign adventures has been eroded. A leaked fragment of an early Bush administration national security review observes that "much weaker enemies" must be defeated "decisively and rapidly"; any other outcome might "undercut political support". The Reagan administration was compelled to resort to clandestine terror and proxy forces because political support for violent intervention was so thin. And it has been necessary to whip up impressive propaganda campaigns to portray "much weaker enemies" as threats to the country's very existence, so as to mobilize a frightened population to give at least temporary support for decisive and rapid action.

Still another problem is that the other two centres of economic power – German-led Europe and Japan – have their own interests, though the Defense Planning study cited earlier is correct in noting that basic interests are shared, notably, the concern that the Third World should fulfil its service function. Furthermore, the internationalization of capital that has accelerated since Nixon dismantled the Bretton Woods system gives a somewhat new cast to competition among states. Merely to cite one indication, while the US share in world manufactured exports declined by 3.5 per cent from 1966 to 1984, the share of US-based transnational corporations (TNCs) increased slightly. And international trade patterns yield a very different picture if imports from overseas subsidiaries are counted as domestic production. These are factors of growing importance in the new world order.

Furthermore, the United States no longer has the economic base for intervention. Recognition of this fact has led to proposals in the business press that the United States should become a "mercenary" state, using its "monopoly power" in the "security market" to maintain its "control over the world economic system", selling "protection" to other wealthy powers who will pay a "war premium" (*Chicago Tribune*, financial editor William Neikirk).[9] Foreign financing of Washington's war in the Gulf in 1991 provided the United States with "$33 billion more than the war cost it, temporarily easing the budget deficit and balance of payment", *New York Times* economic analyst Leonard Silk concluded. Nearly half of a substantial decline in the US current account deficit for 1991 is attributed to foreign payments towards the cost of the Gulf War, much of the rest by exports to Middle East oil producers, including billions of dollars' worth of weapons exports. The profits of Gulf oil production, in particular, must continue to be available to support the economies of the United States and its British associate, who are to carry out the enforcer role. These developments are foreshadowed in US-UK internal documents after the Iraqi military coup of 1958, which emphasize that Kuwaiti oil and investment must be used to prop up the ailing British economy, a concern that extended to the United States by the 1970s and remains a significant factor in Middle East policy.

The use of force to control the Third World is a last resort. Economic weapons are more efficient. Some of the newer mechanisms can be seen in the GATT negotiations. One major US concern relates to the "new themes": guarantees for "intellectual property rights," such as patents and software, that will enable TNCs to monopolize new technology; and removal of constraints on services and investment, which will undermine national development programmes in the Third World and effectively place investment decisions in the hands of TNCs and the financial institutions of the North. These are "issues of greater magnitude" than the more publicized conflict over agricultural subsidies, according to William Brock, head of the Multilateral Trade Negotiations Coalition of major US corporations. In the latter sphere, the United States objects to a GATT provision that allows countries to restrict food exports in times of need, demanding that US agribusiness must control raw materials no matter what the human cost. In general, each of the wealthy industrial powers advocates a mixture of liberalization and protection designed for the interests of dominant domestic forces, and particularly for the TNCs that are to dominate the world economy.

The effects would be to reduce the role of Third World governments to a police function, to control their own working classes and superfluous population, while TNCs gain free access to their resources and control new technology and global investment – and, of course, are granted the central planning and management functions denied to governments, which are unacceptable agents because they might fall under the influence of popular pressures reflecting domestic needs, the "radical nationalism" of the internal planning record. The outcome is called "free trade", but some have more accurately described it as a kind of "corporate mercantilism", with managed commercial interactions among corporate groupings and continuing state intervention in the North to subsidize and protect domestically based corporations and financial institutions.

The Latin Americanization of the East follows the familiar course. Poland, adopting the doctrines professed by the rich, liberalized its economy. In reaction, the European Community (EC) raised import barriers to protect its own industry and agriculture. EC chemical and steel industries warned that "restructuring" must not harm Western industry. The World Bank estimates that the protectionist measures of the industrial countries – keeping pace with free market bombast – reduce the national income of the "developing societies" by about twice the value of official "development assistance", much of it a form of export promotion.

The situation is reminiscent of the 1920s, when Japan followed the rules officially proclaimed, but so successfully that Britain abandoned its liberal doctrines and effectively closed the empire to Japanese exports (as did the United States and the Netherlands, in their lesser domains). Similarly, the Reagan-Bush Caribbean Basin Initiative encourages open export-oriented economies while maintaining US protectionist barriers. The patterns are as pervasive as they are understandable, on Churchillian grounds.

There are many familiar reasons why wealth and power tend to reproduce. It should, then, come as little surprise that the Third World continues to fall behind the North. United Nations statistics indicate that as a per cent of the GDP of developed countries, Africa's GDP per capita (minus South Africa) declined by about 50 per cent from 1960 to 1987. The decline was almost as great in Latin America. For similar reasons, within the rich societies themselves large sectors of the population are becoming superfluous by the reigning values and must be marginalized or suppressed, increasingly so in the past 20-year period of economic stagnation and pressures on corporate profit. Societies of the North – notably the United States – are taking on certain Third World aspects, as wealth and power are increasingly concentrated among investors and professionals who benefit from the internationalization of capital flows and communication.

Like the domestic poor in the developed societies, the South has little bargaining power in its dealings with the club of the rich. The prospects for "justice, equity and democracy" (in a meaningful sense) are not auspicious. But they are not hopeless. The South Commission mentions several directions that should be pursued, though I think the analysis is too optimistic in expecting these to influence the policies and attitudes of the rulers. One direction is internal change leading to meaningful democracy, social justice and improvement of conditions of life, and popular control over capital and investment so that such resources as are available will be used for constructive development rather than for investment abroad or for enriching TNCs and small wealthy sectors linked to them. If, for example, Latin America could control its own wealthy classes, preventing capital flight, much of the region's foreign debt would be wiped out. A related need is South-South co-operation to address common economic, social and cultural needs.

But the crucial factor can only be internal changes in the core countries. The possibility that such changes may take place is not to be dismissed. Throughout the North, notably in the United States, there have been significant changes in the past 30 years, at least at the cultural if not the institutional level. Had the quincentennial of the old world order occurred in 1962, it would have been celebrated as the liberation of the hemisphere. In 1992 large sectors will demand recognition of the fact that the "liberation" set off the two worst demographic catastrophes in human history, in the Western hemisphere and Africa. The domestic constraints on state violence, noted earlier, are another case in point. Perhaps the most striking example is the Third World solidarity movements that developed through the 1980s in the United States, to a large extent based in churches and with broad social roots. This process of democratization and concern for social justice threatens power, and is therefore minimized or dismissed in the doctrinal system, but it has large significance, I believe.

Democratization and social reform in the South are values in themselves. But there is little reason to suppose that steps towards internal freedom and justice will appeal to lite opinion in the West; on the contrary, they will be no less frightening than the so-called "crisis of democracy" within the rich societies (that is, the efforts of large parts of the population, since the 1960s, to enter the political arena). But in this way, the South can move towards mutually supportive relations with liberatory tendencies within Western societies. Such developments will naturally be regarded by the powerful as dangerous and subversive. However, they offer the only real hope for the great mass of people, even for the survival of the human species in an era of environmental and other global problems that cannot be dealt with by primitive social and cultural structures which are driven by short-term material gain, and which consider human beings to be instruments, not ends.

Notes

1. South Commission, 1990, p.287.
2. Ibid., p.216.
3. Expanded Draft of Letter from SecWar to SecState, "U.S. Position re Soviet Proposals on Kiel Canal and Dardanelles", 8 July 1945. Cited by Melvyn Leffler, 1992, p.78 (see note 87, p.540, for fuller citation).
4. Leffler, 1992.
5. Internal State Department report of 1953 (prior to 1954 CIA-backed invasion). Burrows to Cabot (Assistant Secretary of State for Interamerican Affairs), 23 December 1953, cited by Piero Gleijeses, 1991, p.365.

6. Leffler.

7. Defense Planning Guide, 1992 (draft). The draft has never been released. The only information is from press citations, which include leaked excerpts and comment; a sample is given in Excerpts from draft, *New York Times*, 9 March 1992. Patrick Tyler, *New York Times*, 10 March 1992.

8. Jules Benjamin, 1990.

9. William Neikirk, 1990.

Bibliography

Benjamin, Jules
  The United States and the Origins of the Cuban Revolution, Princeton University Press, Princeton, 1990.
Gleijeses, Piero
  Shattered Hope: the Guatemalan Revolution and the United States, 1944-1954, Princeton University Press, Princeton, 1991.
Government of the United States
  USG, NSC 5432/1, 3 September 1954, *Foreign Relations of the United States*, 1952- 4, vol. IV, 81ff.
Leffler, Melvyn
  A Preponderance of Power, Stanford University Press, Stanford, CA, 1992.
South Commission
  The Challenge to the South: The Report of the South Commission, Oxford University Press, Oxford and New York, 1990.

Newspapers and journals

Neikirk, William
  "We are the world's guardian angels", *Chicago Tribune* business section, 9 September 1990.
New York Times, 9 and 10 March 1992, New York.

17. PROSPECTS FOR SOUTH–SOUTH CO-OPERATION[1]

Abdul Aziz Jalloh

Any assessment of the prospects for South-South co-operation in the 1990s and beyond must re-examine the underlying ideas, the strategy and the approach which have served as the foundation for this co-operation thus far, with a view to determining their continued relevance and efficacy in the future. Only after such exercises would it be possible to chart a new course for South-South co-operation.

Either myth or ideology may generate the ideas forming a basis for co-operation. Myth refers to widely held beliefs and values, whereas ideology is a systematically articulated set of ideas which criticizes the *status quo* and postulates a new, more desirable and attainable future state, with some suggestion as to how this future state of affairs could be brought about. Myths and ideologies are important in that they provide a sense of direction, mobilize individuals and, above all, justify present sacrifices for future rewards. They also facilitate compromise in the name of a higher good among groups of actors. Myths and ideologies are therefore important to efforts to co-operate in that they help in resolving disputes, encourage sacrifice and reinforce perseverance, despite failures to achieve immediate gains.

Three strands of thought have served as the basis of South-South co-operation since the 1950s. These were the claim to moral superiority of the South, the conviction that new and better – both materially and spiritually – societies could be developed by the countries of the South, and the allegation that poverty in the South was to a large extent the result of exploitation by the North.

The first assertion, that of the moral superiority of the South, was loudly proclaimed by the founding fathers of the Non-Aligned Movement, notably Tito, Nehru, Sukarno, Nasser, Nkrumah and others. These leaders depicted the North, particularly the West, as aggressive, exploitative, materialistic, decadent and racist. While views about the East were not as harsh, it was still seen as spiritually bankrupt. In contrast, the South was characterized as free of all sin and as innocent as a new-born baby. In the South, idealism prevailed and humankind was truly the centre of all things and the end of all developmental efforts.

Humankind was therefore truly free, with unlimited and unfettered possibilities of realizing its true self, which perfectly balanced both the material and the spiritual. The new being was emerging in the South, and the future belonged to the South.

Following from this view was the rejection of both Western and Eastern models of society as the basis for organizing societies in the South. Both Western and Eastern societies, but more so Western ones, were depicted as anti humanistic, fundamentally flawed, and therefore incapable of being reformed. They were a throw-back to an earlier epoch. Radically new societies superior to anything in the West or East were emerging in the South and were the wave of the future. Thus the advocacy of developing "African socialism" and its many variants and similar notions in other parts of the South, all of which attested to the fact that, in many ways, concepts of socialism which originated in the West constituted the foundations of these new societies which it was alleged were being created in the South.

The third major element in the ideational basis of South-South co-operation was the accusation that poverty and economic development in the South were essentially the result of domination and exploitation of the South by the North, specifically the West. This conviction was embodied in various theories of imperialism, notably the Marxist and New Left theories of imperialism which were current in Western intellectual circles from the 1960s onwards, as well as in various theories of dependency and underdevelopment. In its extreme form, this view held that the development and riches of the North, especially the West, were the result of the underdevelopment and poverty of the South and vice versa. The transfer of resources from the South to the North started with the slave trade and colonialism, and continued under neo-colonialism and an unjust international economic order. The only way out for the South lay in rupture from the existing international economic order, in South-South co-operation and in the establishment of a new international economic order.

Our concern with the formative ideas on which South-South co-operation is based is not whether the assertions were true or not. Rather, it is to spell out the body of ideas which led the leaders and people of the South to believe that they were different from others, that they were better than others, that they should therefore co-operate with each other, and that co-operation would be in their best interest. The question is how relevant this body of beliefs is today and how likely it is to serve as a rallying cry for South-South co-operation in the future.

Regrettably, one is forced to admit that, in light of the political and economic history of the South during the past 30 odd years, especially the record of these countries in the area of human rights, the claim to Southern moral superiority is now devoid of all credibility. Tangible evidence in support of this conclusion is that there is virtually no Third World political leader or intellectual of any stature who is presently making this claim. Similarly, the objective of creating new and better societies different from those in the North, especially in the West, has been all but abandoned. Indeed, what we have been witnessing in recent years is the near stampede of countries of the South to introduce free market economies and Western-style democracy and to proclaim their adherence to this form of organizing societies. Lastly, while there is still criticism of the existing international economic order and external exploitation, Third World countries now openly admit that mismanagement accounts for a large part of their economic plight.

This comes out clearly in the Declaration on the Economic Situation in Africa adopted by the 21st Ordinary Session of the Assembly of Heads of State and Government of the Organization of African Unity, which was held in Addis Ababa, Ethiopia, from 18 to 20 July 1985, and in which it was stated that "some domestic policy shortcomings" are partly responsible for bringing "most of our countries near to economic collapse", that "shortcomings in development policies have contributed to the present debt crisis", and that "we reaffirm that the development of our continent is the primary responsibility of our Governments and peoples".

What all this adds up to is that the conceptual basis of South-South co-operation which existed for nearly three decades now no longer exists. The question then is what is the myth and/or ideology on which South-South co-operation could be built? Until this question is satisfactorily answered it is difficult to see what could sustain the efforts of the South in working towards co-operation, an enterprise which, under the best of circumstances, is protracted and inherently difficult.

The Report of the South Commission develops what it calls "a strengthened rationale" for South-South co-operation which aims at promoting development and safeguarding economic independence. The key components of this "strengthened rationale" are several: the emergence of new complementarities among countries of the South; the existence of surplus capital in a few countries of the South which could be profitably invested in other countries of the South; the need for joint management of natural resources and to deal with common problems such as the environment, illicit drug trafficking and harnessing science and technology; the fact that the North could no longer be counted on to promote growth and development in the South because of the reduced need for raw materials produced by the South; the shift in attention from the South to the East; and the challenge to the South of larger economic groupings in the North.

Again, what is crucial in this "strengthened rationale" is not so much its validity as the extent to which it could serve as the political rallying cry, provide the vision, inspire and be effective in mobilizing the efforts of the South in promoting co-operation and sustaining these efforts over the hurdles and difficulties they would inevitably encounter. It does not take much reflection to conclude that the "strengthened rationale" supplied by the South Commission fails to meet this test. The ideas are too technical and lack the power to inspire and move people in the way that the earlier motivating ideas for South-South co-operation did.

The South Commission itself notes that "the political factor, while not sufficient by itself, is of immense importance to the fortunes of most regional groupings and other programmes of co-operation, particularly during their take-off phase".[2] This political factor has still to be provided and, until it is, South-South co-operation will face a very uncertain future.

Another vital task to be accomplished before one could assess the prospects and map out the strategy for future South-South co-operation is to re-evaluate the strategy of co-operation pursued up to the present.

The example of the only really very successful contemporary effort at economic co-operation, that of the European Community, demonstrates the importance of a self-conscious – at least to the leaders guiding the co-operation effort – strategy firmly grounded in the political and economic structures of the countries participating in the co-operation effort. In contrast, the efforts at co-operation in the South have operated thus far without the benefit of any clear-cut strategy of co-operation. Worse yet, these efforts have merely copied the programmatic elements of co-operation in the North, especially in the West. Accordingly, these efforts have tried to expand trade and promote the movement of factors of production, establish common services, and harmonize policies towards third parties. In pursuing these objectives, co-operation efforts in the South have selected tasks and activities on an *ad hoc* basis without any thought of how they relate to each other and in what sequence they should be undertaken so that, taking into account the political and economic structures of the countries concerned, the successful implementation of these tasks and activities would enhance the overall level of co-operation.

The Report of the South Commission concludes that "one of the chief shortcomings of South-South co-operation has been weak organization and lack of institutionalized technical support, both at the international level and within most countries".[3] This conclusion is true, but it is superficial and does not go far enough. Besides the issue concerning the ideas or notions underlying South-South co-operation, which was addressed earlier, the other main factor responsible for the failure thus far of South-South co-operation is that there has been no strategy of co-operation based on the economic and political structures of these countries. The whole objective of co-operation has been pursued in a haphazard, catch-as-catch-can manner, or by emulating practices that have succeeded in radically different environments. In sum, the efforts at co-operation in the South have functioned without any viable and effective strategy to guide them. No wonder these efforts have not succeeded.

This conclusion leads one to ask whether co-operation is essentially an act of will or determination and could be successfully pursued anywhere, regardless of the structural conditions. This is a difficult question to answer. There are very few cases of successful co-operation which could serve as the basis for this type of generalization. None the less, the question must be raised if only to force the advocates of South-South co-operation to examine carefully the structure of developing countries and point out the compatibility of this structure with their strategy, approach or proposals for South-South co-operation.

In its Report, the South Commission observes that "clearly, the developing countries will need to agree on a global strategy for South-South co-operation. Such a strategy should serve as a basis for elaborating more specific regional, sub-regional, and national programmes of co-operation".[4] Paradoxically, after this assertion, and after noting that this strategy should identify broad fields of co-operation, indicate long-term goals, propose activities to be undertaken in the short and medium term, hold out the promise of success and wider and deeper co-operation, and list the steps to be taken in implementing both the short- and the medium-term programmes,[5] the Report proceeds to give a long list of activities to be undertaken within the framework of South-South co-operation. In doing so, the South Commission commits the error of substituting a checklist of what should ideally be done for a systematically articulated strategy of South-South co-operation. Despite the claim that the proposals of the South Commission are merely intended as "a contribution to the formulation of such a strategy", there is no escaping the conclusion that idealism and wishful thinking have again triumphed and the *ad hoc* approach has won out against strategic thinking and planning.

The "Programme of Priority Action for South-South co-operation"[6] described in the Report embraces many areas, notably the establishment of a South Secretariat; regular and institutionalized consultation among heads of State and Government; internal policies; co-ordinating mechanisms and public mobilization efforts in support of South-South co-operation; development of Centres of Educational Excellence; formation of a debtors' forum; creation of a South Bank; strengthening and expanding producers' associations; establishment of an Association of Third World Chambers of Commerce and Industry; co-operation in the areas of food security and science and technology; and reinforcing existing subregional and regional co-operation efforts. This listing of desirable activities does not amount to, nor is it a substitute for, a strategy for South-South co-operation.

In addition, while some new elements are contained in the list, for example a South Secretariat, South Bank, the list is not radically different from the activities pursued in the 1960s and 1970s. The South Commission itself concludes that "while moves to promote South-South co operation have involved much effort and produced many initiatives and schemes, the practical results have been rather limited".[7] There is no reason to expect that the initiative of the South Commission would yield better results. This is because it makes no attempt to link its proposals with the structure of societies in developing countries, the contemporary international environment, and the desired end goal. In fact, not even the broad features of what the terminal state of South-South co-operation would look like is depicted.

The South Commission is right. Idealism alone is not enough. Rather, it must be "tempered by a degree of practicality or matched by commitment to action".[8] In this spirit, it must be acknowledged that the prospect for South-South co-operation does not seem to be too bright for several reasons.

The first two factors that make South-South co-operation difficult have already been addressed. These are the absence of any credible and force-ful myth or ideology to sustain this co-operation and the lack of a comprehensive and viable strategy to guide it. The third factor is that the failure thus far of efforts at South-South co-operation has led to a great deal of pessimism and a growing belief that South-South co-operation might be inherently impossible, given the structure of these societies.

This sentiment must be overcome and a new confidence in the prospects for, and optimism in, the potential gain from South-South co-operation instilled. This will not be an easy task, especially since the few cases of economic success by developing countries, notably the newly industrializing countries of Hong Kong, Singapore, South Korea and Taiwan and other developing countries following in their footsteps – Malaysia and Thailand – owe nothing to South-South co-operation, while developing countries which have invested heavily in this co-operation have little to show for it.

Heterogeneity and economic inequality are also increasing among developing countries. Some, even though only a few, developing countries have transformed their economies, made significant progress in harnessing science and technology to production, and are poised to compete effectively in the world economy. Most others remain backward and have registered virtually no progress since the 1960s. If the past is any guide, this trend towards greater diversity will not facilitate co-operation among countries of the South.

Lastly, the implications of the shift from a bipolar to a unipolar or imperial international system for South-South co-operation need close examination. In a bipolar world, it was easier for the countries of the South to position and differentiate themselves from the East and the West, while feeling closer to each other. This is much more difficult in a unipolar or imperial system.

The South Commission should be congratulated on its bold and ambitious effort at trying to provide a sense of direction to South-South co-operation in the 1990s and beyond. However, this effort would seem still to be at a very preliminary and rudimentary stage. An "ideational" basis and a strategy for this co-operation must be articulated and the implications for future South-South co-operation of the failure of past efforts, growing differentiation among developing countries, and the passing of the bipolar world must be carefully examined. Only then would it be possible to launch South-South co-operation on a practical, viable and promising basis. Hopefully, the South Centre will concentrate its efforts and energies on these tasks in the foreseeable future.

Notes

1. The ideas expressed in this paper are those of the author and do not necessarily reflect those of the Islamic Development Bank.
2. South Commission, 1990, p.150.
3. Ibid., p.149.
4. Ibid., p.157.
5. Ibid., p.158.
6. Ibid., pp.206-210.
7. Ibid., p.149.
8. Ibid.

Bibliography

South Commission
   The Challenge to the South: The Report of the South Commission, Oxford University Press, Oxford and New York, 1990.

18. TRANSFORMING THE NORTH-SOUTH RELATIONSHIP: THE POLITICAL CHALLENGE OF THE 1990s

John W. Sewell and Nicole Melcher

The momentous political and economic changes that have taken place around the world in recent years have created a new opportunity to address long-standing global development problems. The South Commission correctly identifies the political challenge: "The issue for the South is not whether to cut its links with the North, but how to transform them. The relationship must be changed from exploitation to shared benefit, from subordination to partnership."[1] The question, then, is how to transform the North-South framework.

The South Commission wisely chose to focus its Report on "ways of rekindling hope in the South through a self-reliant and people-centred development effort, through intensified South-South co-operation and, through a restructuring of international economic relations".[2] Its recommendations, however, assume a continuation of the North-South world of the 1960s and 1970s.

If the Commission's proposals are to be implemented successfully in the rapidly changing political environment of the 1990s, the traditional North-South context will either have to be adapted to new realities or abandoned. In its place, policy-makers will need to devise a new policy framework different from the North-South, East-West setting that dominated the post-1945 world. This new framework will have to be designed to improve massively the well-being of men, women and children throughout the world over the next decades.

Although development remains a critical issue, the world in which development will have to be fostered has undergone cataclysmic changes since the "North-South" framework took shape in the late 1950s. The end of the Cold War, the convergence of thinking on economic policy in the North and South, the diffusion of economic strength among the United States and other major powers, and, above all, the growing differentiation within the South have profoundly changed the international political and economic landscapes. Moreover, the end of the East-West conflict with the August 1991 revolution in the Soviet Union has removed one of the major defining elements of the North-South divide as well as of American foreign policy. The nations of Eastern Europe and the Commonwealth of Independent States are now requesting aid, investment and technical assistance, and are seen by many as competing with the South for financial and other help.

By now, the lines that divided the First, Second and Third Worlds have blurred to the point where the tripartite division of the globe has become largely meaningless. In the 1990s and beyond, the key differences will not be between East and West or between North and South, but between those countries that manage their economic, political and social development well and those that do not.

One reason why the international environment has changed so profoundly is that North and South have come to depend more and more upon each other. The dependence of the South on the North has always been palpable. The South relies upon the North for export markets, supplies of imports for production and consumption, technology and capital. Now, however, the reverse is increasingly true. As the South Commission Report pointed out, the North values the South's export markets and realizes that "faster growth in the South will spur international flows of trade and investment, foster growth and employment in the North, and help to reduce payments imbalances among industrial countries".

This conclusion was underscored during the 1980s when the slow growth attributable to the debt crisis hurt nations both in the South and in the North. In the United States, for example, global recession and the developing countries' debt crisis in the early 1980s combined to throw US exports to those countries off the growth path of the 1970s. In 1986, the value of US exports to developing countries was only half of what it might have been had the growth trend of the 1970s continued. This translated into a loss of 1.8 million US jobs. Although US exports have increased since 1986, the gap between actual and potential exports has not narrowed significantly. In the absence of the recession and debt crisis, US exports to developing countries in 1990 might have exceeded 200 billion US dollars, whereas the actual figure was 132 billion US dollars.

Over the years, development has worked. The developing world has achieved remarkable economic progress overall since the 1940s. In many countries, incomes have increased, savings and investment rates have risen, and trade has expanded so rapidly that some countries have moved out of the aid category. Whereas Britain took nearly 60 years to double per capita income in the 18th century, Brazil recently achieved the same result in only 18 years, and China more recently in 10! Developing countries are now not only important markets for the United States and other exporters, but are also growing competitors in a wide range of manufactures. Between 1965 and 1988, manufactured goods jumped from 16 per cent to 64 per cent of total developing country exports.

Also, the human condition has improved measurably. Over the past 30 years, average life expectancy in the developing countries increased from 46 to 63 years. (The average life span in those countries is longer than that in the United States in the 1930s.) The adult literacy rate jumped from 20 to 60 per cent, and the infant mortality rate dropped in many countries.

Political openness has increased. The last decade brought a welcome wave of political liberalization to the developing world and Eastern Europe. In Latin America, the trend has been away from military régimes and towards democratically elected governments. In Asia, the Republic of Korea, the Philippines, Singapore, Taiwan and Thailand all seem to be moving to more open political systems. And in Eastern Europe and the Commonwealth of Independent States, one-party Marxist governments have disappeared in response to popular movements. More than ever, competitive political systems are seen as the desired norm.

Political reform has been matched by economic liberalization in Eastern Europe, the Commonwealth of Independent States and the developing world. Mexico's economic reforms are among the most remarkable in the Western hemisphere, but even in Africa the dominant economic role of the state is being de-emphasized in a large number of sub-Saharan countries. As a result, there is now a convergence of views on the respective roles of the state and market, the value of international trade and investment, and the importance of pluralism and democracy in both North and South.

The South has a long-standing common goal – to escape poverty and underdevelopment – but the South itself is now marked by increasing divergence. The developing countries have become more and more differentiated, as some (notably in East Asia) forge ahead with rapid industrialization, competitive agriculture, and explosive export growth, whereas others (notably in Africa and in zones of prolonged regional conflict) have actually lost ground in the last two decades. In fact, rates of progress have varied to such an extent that discerning the commonalities between an industrial power, such as Mexico, and a poor landlocked agricultural country, such as Mali, is now much more difficult than in the past.

Widely divergent growth rates have resulted in incomes that differ dramatically. In 1950, countries such as South Korea and Ghana had roughly the same levels of income, but now one is rich, the other poor. The average annual per capita income of the industrialized countries exceeds 17,000 US dollars. The 17 better-off (upper-middle income) developing countries have a per capita GNP of 3,240 US dollars, whereas the 42 lowest income countries have a per capita GNP of 320 US dollars.

Developing countries also have had very different experiences with improving human well-being. People in East and South-East Asia now live on average a decade and half longer and are nearly twice as likely to be literate as those in sub-Saharan Africa. Yet, in spite of the remarkable progress that has been made, more than one billion men, women and children still live in absolute poverty.

At the same time, the gap between rich and poor within some developing countries has been expanding. When pursuing high-growth policies, developing nations tend to favour economic goals above social objectives. This preference often benefits middle and upper income groups rather than the poorest (particularly women and children). Unless greater attention is given to the distribution effects of growth, this trend could continue and could further fragment the South.

South-South fissures may be deepened by the impact of the so-called "Third Industrial Revolution". The world economy is on the threshold of a series of innovations in science and technology that rival in magnitude the introduction of the steam engine and the discovery of electricity.

These new technologies will have varied impacts on the developing world and will tend to benefit the more industrial economies. To utilize these technologies, a nation will need a strong research and development capacity, which in turn requires the capital and technological skills that a number of developing countries lack. In addition, many of these new technologies require fewer workers. A country like Mexico faces the difficult choice between investing in these technologies in order to remain globally competitive and addressing the need to create a million new jobs a year for its growing population. Furthermore, developing countries that do not have a significant industrial base and that do not already export to industrialized countries will not be equipped to assimilate the new technologies. Consequently, as the South Commission Report rightly highlighted, the Third Industrial Revolution threatens to leave behind countries that do not have the capacity to utilize new technology, while enhancing the potential for sustainable development for those that do.

At the same time, the "North" now also is a far less meaningful concept. The First World of the industrial countries has been reshaped, and there are now three relatively co-equal global power centres – Europe, Japan and the United States. They are no longer unified – if they ever were – particularly in terms of interests in the developing world. Divergences in the North will be intensified by the end of the Cold War. Japan has yet to come to grips with the policy implications of its global power; Europe will remain preoccupied with its internal consolidation and with absorbing Eastern Europe for much of this decade. And for its part, the United States faces serious domestic economic problems and has not yet redefined its role in a world where it is a major but not dominant power. The differences concerning external policies have already become noticeable – in the Gulf, towards Eastern Europe, and over issues like agricultural policy, migration and global warming.

Paradoxically, a world with no clear North-South or East-West boundaries may provide new opportunities for increased multilateralism and renewed attention to global co-operation. The decades of the 1990s and beyond are not likely to be a period of grand, comprehensive global bargains, whether a "New International Economic Order" or a "new Bretton Woods". They may, however, be marked by an increasing emphasis on "functional multilateralism" – the negotiation of a series of agreements or "compacts" on a number of pressing global issues common to both North and South.

This flexible pattern of decision-making is multilateral in that it involves many players coming to the bargaining table at the same time, and functional in that the actors at the table will shift according to the issue under consideration and over time. New international agreements will be driven by a growing realization that certain domestic problems can only be dealt with through international action and multilateral co-operation. These new functional "compacts" may be explicit or implicit, formal or informal, partial or comprehensive. Each, however, will have to enlist the participation of groups of developed and developing nations. And many will have to engage the countries of the former Second World. Functional multilateralism responds to the growing heterogeneity that marks both the North and the South.

Recently, functional multilateralism has been used for tackling specific issues and regional needs. The Cairns Group and Asia Pacific Economic Co-operation (APEC) are two examples. Fourteen nations, including Argentina, Brazil, the Philippines and Thailand from the South and Australia and Canada of the North, formed the Cairns Group to foster more market-oriented policies for agriculture. APEC, which includes the ASEAN nations and China as well as Australia, Japan and the United States, was established in 1989 as a consultative mechanism for addressing Asia Pacific issues.

The Global Coalition for Africa is another form of functional multilateralism. Designed specifically for the least developed countries of sub-Saharan Africa, the Global Coalition for Africa encourages a broad policy dialogue between African governments, private sectors, non-governmental organizations and the international donor community. These groups support efforts by African nations in designing and implementing their economic and social policies, improving governance, promoting popular participation, and discouraging unprincipled business practices by local firms. Also, technical assistance approaches will be re-evaluated so as to match African capacities more realistically, and donors will be encouraged to co-ordinate their efforts more effectively.

The US-sponsored Enterprise for the Americas Initiative (EAI), which calls for the promotion of free trade, debt reduction, private investment and the creation of environmental funds in a region stretching from Alaska to Argentina, is another example of functional multilateralism in action. The EAI seeks to engage not only governments and multilateral agencies but also the private sector and grassroots organizations. Multilateral organizations, including the IMF and the World Bank, will work on debt reduction, the Inter-American Development Bank will manage private investment, and governments will set the agenda and negotiate the rules for the environment in which firms will trade and invest. Local environmental, community development and scientific groups will serve on the boards of the national environment funds. Who are to be the actors and what strategies are to be applied for functional multilateralism will be determined from case to case, in the light of the particularism involved.

A multilateralism organized on functional lines, however, will have flaws. Some issues (for example, poverty, drugs, migration) and some countries (especially smaller, poorer ones that might not be critical to the solution of particular problems) may be left out. Indeed, the number of countries that will be crucial for the purpose of addressing specific global problems will vary considerably according to the subject, and will not be confined by either of the traditional North-South and East-West demarcations. Also, the dominance of the powerful may continue but, rather than North versus South, the powerful may be from both the North and the South. Functional multilateralism will be beneficial to people only if pressure is put on governments to change to more equitable development strategies. Otherwise business will continue as usual.

The South Commission's view that the South needs a greater role in the international arena supports the increased application of functional multilateralism. Southern governments will be on a more equal footing with larger nations because their participation in agreements will be seen as essential. Ultimately, this change of status may lead to more meaningful arrangements between North and South.

Transforming the North-South relationship would facilitate tackling this decade's global agenda of new and old interrelated problems, in the interest of both rich and poor countries. That agenda includes restarting economic growth, eliminating the absolute poverty that still scars the lives of over one fifth of the world's population, protecting the earth's physical environment and sustaining the political openness that has spread throughout the developing world, Eastern Europe and the Commonwealth of Independent States.

Restarting economic growth in the developing countries will first require crucial policy choices by their governments. One of the clear lessons of the past 40 years is that economic growth will not occur unless leadership emphasizes economic efficiency. Fortunately, a growing number of leaders in the South have learned the lesson, and are committing themselves to implement what the World Bank's *World Development Report 1991*[3] refers to as "market friendly" policies.

To apply these policies successfully, developing countries will need both adequate investment capital (whether from public or from private sources) and an open world trading system for those that can and choose to export. The successful completion of the multilateral trade negotiations is essential, but barriers to developing country exports will have to be further reduced in the years ahead. Surplus countries and industrializing developing nations will have to open their markets to promote efficiency, and a major assault on existing barriers to trade in agricultural products and textiles – sectors where many developing countries have a natural advantage – is needed.

Debt reduction will also be important for economic progress. During the 1980s, developing nations that managed to avoid debt-servicing difficulties experienced more rapid growth than the industrial countries, but in those with debt-servicing difficulties per capita income actually declined. Because of their undeniable interdependence, both North and South must work together to find functional multilateral approaches for revitalizing economic growth.

Global poverty remains as serious as ever, despite the progress that has been made. More than one billion people in the developing world are living in absolute poverty – literally on the margin of life – at a time when the planet is richer than ever. Progress is, however, quite possible with the appropriate internal strategies and aid from the industrialized countries. Economic growth, combined with policies designed to enhance the productivity of the poorest people (their labour is their biggest asset) and targeted social programmes could reduce the number of the absolute poor by more than 300 million by the end of this decade. Establishing the Global Coalition for Africa clearly is a step in the right direction.

Rising economic activity has caused increasing stress, at both the global and local levels, on the very environment on which both rich and poor countries depend. Global climate change is a real possibility, and fragile lands throughout the developing world – forest, hilly and arid areas – are deteriorating at an alarming rate. If future growth in the developing world is based on the same patterns of economic activity (particularly energy use) as were followed in the past by rich and poor countries alike, the impact on the global environment could be disastrous.

Although action to alleviate poverty will incidentally also contribute to the protection of the environment, for at the local level much of the environmental damage in the developing world is caused by poor people who have no choice but to use available resources to eke out a meagre livelihood, unchecked population growth will further aggravate both poverty and environmental stress. The United Nations Population Fund estimates that the world's population (over 5 billion in 1990) will increase by 90 to 100 million people each year, mostly in the developing world. The consequence will be additional consumption of limited resources as developing nations attempt to combat poverty and environmental deterioration (while also working to achieve economic growth).

Maintaining and promoting political openness will be difficult. Vested interests of all kinds will resist change, and popular demands for early material improvements will compete with the need for investment and increased efficiency. Economic pressures on newly democratic régimes in the developing world, Eastern Europe and the Commonwealth of Independent States will remain severe throughout the decade. Most of the countries will have to maintain strict economic austerity if they want to make the adjustment to an open, highly competitive world economy and, no less importantly, to satisfy the conditions that the international financial institutions, notably the World Bank and the International Monetary Fund, attach to continued, urgently needed financial support.

It is critically important that newly democratic governments which are implementing economic reforms should have access to sufficient external financial support to satisfy pent-up political and social demands. New governments in the post-socialist nations as well as the developing world are being asked to undertake economic and political reform simultaneously, a trick that has been tried successfully by few, if any, governments in recent history. The success or failure of these reforms will hinge not only on the skills of the leadership groups and the discipline and cohesion of their compatriots, but also on how much financial breathing space they can expect. Co-operation between developing and industrialized nations will be essential for safeguarding political freedoms.

The South's vision of a new world order is well described in the Report: "The South seeks an undivided world in which there would be no 'South' and no 'North'; in which there would not be one part developed, rich, and dominating, and the other underdeveloped, poor, and dominated."[4]

South-South co-operation is critical for achieving development goals, and the way in which these issues are addressed is very important. Now is the time for serious thought about a new more realistic and meaningful framework to replace the anachronistic North–South dichotomy.

Notes

1. South Commission, 1990, p .211.
2. Ibid., p .31.
3. World Bank, 1991.
4. South Commission, 1990, p.9.

Bibliography

South Commission
    The Challenge to the South: The Report of the South Commission, Oxford University Press, Oxford and New York, 1990.
World Bank
    World Development Report, Oxford University Press, New York, 1991.

19. ECONOMIC RELATIONS BETWEEN NORTH AND SOUTH IN A NEW WORLD ORDER

Percy S. Mistry

Southern Realism in a Changing Global Landscape

In its Report *The Challenge to the South* in 1990, the South Commission took a sober view about prospects facing the developing world in the decade ahead. It recognized that the global environment had shifted firmly in favour of spreading democracy and market economics as two essential ingredients in a successful recipe for broadly based, durable economic and social development; the two being seen as inseparable sides of the same coin. Belief in *markets* has been reinforced by the economic success of several newly industrialized Asian countries and the collapse of communism.[1] Support for *democracy* has been reinforced largely by the unfolding of events in Eastern Europe and Latin America; most of the successful developing economies in Asia developed in the shadow of distinctly undemocratic régimes – giving rise to the superficial but long popular view that premature democracy was antithetical to rapid development. Till 1990 the main donors of the North were not particular about the types of political régimes they supported in the South as long as those régimes were aligned to accommodate their own economic and security interests. The end of the Cold War has transformed the scene with democratization assuming more importance as a specific policy objective in the North's agenda for the South.

To its credit, the South Commission Report took a critical look at how the South had let itself down over the years through sustained domestic mismanagement. The plight of too many developing societies indicated that the promise of independence, and the simple aspirations for sufficient food and shelter to which four fifths of humanity subscribes, have yet to be fulfilled. Egregious spending on armaments throughout the Third World showed at least as much disregard for genuine development priorities and multilateralism by the South as by the North. Self-indulgence with the public purse for coronations, basilicas and new capitals to reflect illusions of success and delusions of grandeur, along with the accumulation of personal bank balances in offshore financial centres by leaders whose avarice stretched belief, were hardly the images to impress the North about the South's commitment to improving its material circumstances. The breach of faith between the South's disconnected and imperious political leaders and the societies they cavalierly impoverished was pointed to by the Report as being at least as large a cause of development failure as the oft-repeated (but no less true for that reason) charge that rapid development in the evolving global environment remained a Sisyphean endeavour under a loaded international economic system in which the strong kept entrenching and increasing their advantage over the weak.

All of these strands of argument (except the last) are now becoming crucial determinants in governing flows of aid, trade and capital between the developed and developing world. For precisely that reason they constitute the new (and still being extruded) filaments of dialogue between North and South, though neither bloc is as monolithic or unified as the terms might once have suggested. In one sense the North-South divide has taken on a new significance with the former East-West conflict having disappeared – at least in terms of Cold War rivalry. Much of the old East has temporarily become a part of the South in terms of its reduced economic circumstances. Nevertheless, it regards itself as part of the North in a geopolitical and multilateral context. Possibly the old East (or large parts of it) will, before too long, become an integral part of a larger and economically even more successful North; one strengthened by the economic opportunities offered by reconstruction in Eastern Europe and the former Soviet republics and by their eventual absorption into the production-consumption structures of Europe. Even so, another more ominous East-West divide is emerging with more profound implications for North-South relationships. It represents increasingly contentious economic competition between Japan (and its emulators in Asia) and its less successful (and less efficient) trade partners in Europe and North America. In this new economic war the South will be affected in ways that are not yet fully clear – apart, of course, from being immediately and adversely influenced by the general sense of threat (countered by increasing trade protectionism) on the part of the West about being dominated by an economically resurgent but different East.

The North–South Dialogue

In a literal sense, the North-South dialogue (NSD) has been an ever-present feature of international relations. Covering mainly issues of aid, trade and capital flows, NSD has embraced several different, if sometimes interrelated, discussions between developed and developing countries on these issues.

Increasingly, NSD has come to include inter alia exchanges on refugees, the environment, as well as global social problems such as the growing immigration problem worldwide, the interdiction of illicit drugs and associated money laundering, the global regulation of banks and financial markets, countering the spread of AIDS and so on. Such discussions take place bilaterally and multilaterally (most visibly in the joint Development Committee of the World Bank and IMF, UNCTAD, GATT, the United Nations General Assembly and in several other multilateral institutions, global and regional). The 1970s offered a moment when the South believed that its interests could best be served by formalizing these discussions within an overarching structure for "global negotiation". In those turbulent years NSD came to represent a structured process of bargaining on global economic issues which affected the conflicting interests of the "haves" and "have-nots" in a world which successive oil and commodity shocks had turned upside down. But that moment passed. In the 1980s NSD became less a dialogue and more an ideologically driven monologue. It appeared to be taking place largely between the conveniently deaf. In the 1990s it is clearly in need of revival; and not – as contemporary idiom would have it – on a voluntary, case-by-case basis.

A feature which has put the South at a disadvantage in pursuing NSD is that the substantive aspects of the "dialogue" are now being conducted mainly in the World Bank, IMF and GATT. In the first two of these fora the inconvenience of unweighted voting does not have to be suffered by the North. Though it may continue for diplomatic reasons to pretend otherwise, the North now has less incentive than before to resuscitate a substantive agenda for wide-ranging NSD with the dramatic changes that have occurred in the post-1989 world. Vast differences in their respective fortunes, and consequently in their geopolitical interests, have emerged among nations of the South over the last decade. Coupled with the unfolding of events in Eastern Europe, they have strengthened conviction in much of the North that time is on its side in influencing the future trajectory of global development. The implication is that the South must acquiesce, however reluctantly, to the North's views on how (and at what pace) the South should develop, politically and economically. A second corollary is that the South must accept and live with the intellectual and economic terms of trade established by the North in the distribution of gains or losses emanating from global economic transactions. It must accommodate deliberate Northern-induced distortions in global markets for agriculture, minerals, labour, textiles and other manufactures in which the South might demonstrate greater comparative advantage and productive efficiency. Yet it must correct distortions in Southern markets for services in which the North might have an advantage (such as financial services) with insufficient offsetting compensation by way of aid, debt relief and new capital flows and with new demands for respecting (and paying heavily for) intellectual property rights.

For precisely those reasons, the South now has a much greater stake in reviving NSD with urgency and conducting it on a different basis to its former pursuit of a New International Economic Order (NIEO). In those days its fortunes were buoyed by commodity price windfalls and the North seemed weak and rudderless. Those advantages have been lost through reckless borrowing and mismanagement by the South of its internal politics and its relationships with the North. The South therefore stands disadvantaged to pursue an effective NSD at this juncture. But it has little choice, especially if its legitimate interests and concerns are to avoid being drowned in a sea churning with global and regional geopolitical ferment or, even worse, ignored as not being sufficiently threatening to the security and prosperity of the North.

Though the Second World has now disappeared as a distinct economic and socio-political entity, the real estate that it occupied remains immutable. Chauvinistic ethnic claims over that property will result in kaleidoscopic redivisions with attendant changes in East European political/economic structures and borders. These developments leave no room for optimism that emerging instability in Eastern Europe and the increasingly fragmented Soviet republics will be a short, transient phenomenon. They introduce considerable uncertainty about what shapes will eventually crystallize in the form of independent nation states in that region and what kind of regional economic and trade arrangements will emerge to govern the obvious interdependence among them. It is perhaps easier to define the destination of the painful transition which these economies are now making from plan to market than to anticipate the pitfalls and disruptions which will inevitably feature in their uncharted journeys.

The demise of the Second World on which the South relied for pursuing what once appeared to be an attractive alternative model (to market-based capitalism) for development is likely to affect the South's psyche and politics in more profound and disturbing ways than is immediately apparent. The failure of a paradigm, in which so much faith had been invested by several Southern régimes, could not be accommodated within their own political systems without traumatic dislocations. Too many nations of the South relied on Eastern European or Western financing and preferential trade arrangements for playing either the wrong end, or both ends, of the East-West game during the Cold War. For them the demise of the Second World as a globally influential partner and financial sponsor is a serious blow. Apart from depriving large parts of the South of a source of development assistance and subsidized trade, the Eastern European and

Soviet republics have now become impoverished competitors in attracting aid and Western capital. The eclipse of the Second World has also deprived the South of a source of "moral" and political support in international fora where NSD was earlier conducted. That is certain to make the South much weaker in representing its own interests vis-à-vis the North in the United Nations system (in which the weight of the Second World was once seen, somewhat myopically, by the South as an asset rather than a liability) and is likely to lead to a refocusing of the United Nations as a vehicle for closing the East-West rather than the North-South divide for the rest of this decade.

Dominance of a conservative political ethos throughout the industrial world in the 1980s clearly took its toll of North-South relations. The North's hectoring exhortations to the South in this Reagan-Thatcher era became a form of ideological harassment. But it was not the principal cause of the desultory state to which NSD has now been reduced. The malaise is more deeply rooted. It may reside in the reality that the premises on which NSD has been based over the last two decades are contradictory and self-defeating. It is questionable whether the familiar NSD agenda for the South, framed in the 1970s and not much changed despite the realism of the South Commission Report, remains relevant to the developing world's interests in the 1990s. Though the present political leaderships in Britain and the United States (two countries which still determine the Northern agenda) have adopted more amicable and pragmatic tones for their dealings with the South in the 1990s, the underlying philosophy and principles which have underpinned NSD in the past no longer seem sufficiently compelling to command the same kind of attention or response as hitherto on the part of a North which now sees its own interests, and interdependence with the South, quite differently from earlier eras.

The Dominance of the United States in Shaping the Northern Agenda on NSD

History suggests that NSD has so far been more a matter of US-South relations than of wider North-South relations.[2] Other members of the North (particularly the ex-colonial powers, France and Britain) may see events differently, with themselves cast in larger and more favourable light in shaping NSD. That view is not supported by evidence. In the 1970s Europe and Japan, in alliance with newly enriched OPEC members, did attempt to compensate for the vacuum in NSD caused by US drift. But they did not permanently change the basic post-1945 nexus. In the 1980s, European countries and Japan provided either a moderating influence when the United States seemed prone to excess or stepped on the accelerator when the United States seemed uninterested. But they have not done much more than that.[3] Continued US domination of the North-South agenda has been possible largely because of fragmentation on the part of individual European countries in the conduct of multilateral affairs. European leadership in NSD during the 1980s was there for the taking. Japan had neither the experience nor the desire to play a frontline role. But Europe abdicated, with Britain toeing the US line throughout the 1980s. Building on the trends of the 1970s and acting collectively, Europe could have achieved much more in changing the tenor of the North-South dialogue and assuming a leadership role which, arguably, it might naturally deserve.

Collectively, Europe pays far more than either Japan or the United States to maintain the "North-South system of interdependence" if military expenditures are excluded. It has a much greater stake in the health and welfare of that system than Japan or the United States. It trades more with the South and is more dependent on the South for its commodities. Europe is more vulnerable to political and economic disruptions in the South than either Japan or the United States. Yet it has ceded leadership to the United States on NSD in the last decade and may have to cede to Japan in the next one. On North-South issues, Europe remains internally divided; not on substance but in being unable to decide who should do what. National governments are unwilling to cede sovereignty to Brussels in dealing with NSD, though on the trade front (and in matters of finance and capital flow) the EC is already in the driver's seat. That anomaly will need to be cured in the 1990s if bargaining between the North and the South is to be undertaken on the basis of a better balance of interests within both blocs. It makes little sense for Europe to deal with the South *en bloc* on virtually all economic interactions except for aid flows (in which bilateralism prevails).

Between 1945 and 1967 the United States was a benign and powerful influence in shaping the destiny of the South. Between 1968 and 1979 – preoccupied by Viet Nam, Watergate and Iran – a loss of confidence disabled the United States from continuing in that vein. Its priorities changed and it adopted a less idealistic, more cynical view of the South. None the less, NSD prospered because Europe, Japan and OPEC members provided the impetus and means to maintain North-South relationships in the face of US default. Through collective European default in the 1980s the United States reasserted its dominance over the agenda for NSD; but this time it was for the worse. That period has been detrimental to the South but, as time will probably reveal, it is likely to be no less so for the longer-term interests of the North. The trend-shift which occurred in NSD during the 1970s could have been consolidated rather than dissipated during the

1980s. It has to be reversed yet again in the 1990s for NSD to yield productive outcomes.

Revisiting Principles and Premises on which NSD Has Been Conducted

With NSD shaped by shifting forces over the last 45 years, it is difficult to adumbrate concisely the principles on which it has been founded or the premisses which have influenced views and negotiating positions on either side. These are best discerned through: the interpretation of behaviour; the changing objectives and perceptions of each side; the demands each bloc has made on the other; and the way in which objectives and demands have been accommodated or dismissed by the other side. Principles and premisses are rarely subscribed to by every member of each bloc nor are they immutable. They have been influenced by bilateral relationships, prevailing political climate and global economic circumstances. For the sake of argument, these principles and premisses can be divided roughly into three categories, that is, those that: (a) North and South subscribe to jointly in having a dialogue in the first place; (b) shape the position of the North in this dialogue; and, correspondingly, (c) influence the positions of the South.

Principles and premisses subscribed to by North and South

Without attempting to define each of the arguments employed by individual members of the two blocs in supporting NSD, and concentrating only on the common principles broadly subscribed to by the blocs as a whole, the following are important:

- North (that is, the OECD countries) and South perceive a mutual interest in ensuring global economic security and prosperity in order to avert prospects of: (a) human degradation (famine, starvation, dis-ease, natural disasters, etc.) in a world increasingly seen as a global common rather than as the parcelled property of sovereign nations; and/or (b) violent conflict within or between these blocs.[4]

- North and South share the desire to narrow, not widen, the large gap in income and wealth between them. Such narrowing cannot be achieved within a framework which impoverishes the North in order to transfer wealth to the South. North and South accept, implicitly, that the gap can only be narrowed by a faster rate of growth in the South than in the North; but *growth* in both places none the less.[5]

- The North is the principal repository of the capital and technology required by the South to develop. The North is obliged to transfer both capital and technology on commercial as well as non-commercial terms, though there is no clear understanding about the basis on which the non-commercial proportion is to be determined.

- The North provides the principal markets for the South's exports. To permit development in the South – particularly if it is to be at a faster rate than in the North – these markets must be open and accessible if the South is to acquire the capital and technology it needs on commercial terms. Closure of such markets results either in the South not developing fast enough or in placing greater pressure on the North to provide more of what the South needs on non-commercial terms.[6]

- For the four principles enunciated above to be realized in practice, bloc-to-bloc dialogue between North and South is needed to cover bilateral, regional or other forms of arrangement/negotiation between various parts of the North and South.[7]

- Government-to-government dialogue as well as publicly administered flows of capital and technology are necessary as the main channels of North-South interaction.[8]

There many other principles and premisses which have come to be shared between North and South over time but they do not all require cataloguing and elaboration. Areas of broad consensus aside, the areas of disagreement on other principles and issues are equally important in comprehending the nuances of NSD and in explaining why it often makes so little progress. Some of these are covered in the paragraphs below. But, before getting into them, it is worth digressing to note one striking aspect of the points enumerated above. These principles ring hollow when measured against actual accomplishments. On the whole, little progress has been made over the last 45 years in achieving their underlying promise or aim. Since 1945, all parts of the North but only a few parts of the South have grown more prosperous. The relative income and wealth gaps between the two blocs have increased, not diminished. Though large parts of the South are better off than before, even larger parts have remained static or retrogressed in absolute terms. That is not true of the North. While relative changes have taken place between individual countries of the North, none is worse off in absolute terms than it was before.

The fundamental thrust of the North-South dialogue has therefore hardly been realized yet. Is that because the North has not done enough in living up to its part of the bargain? Or is it because the South has simply dissipated its own resources as well as those provided by the North? Is the dialogue faulty? Are the specific means to translate vague and general goals and principles into specific, concrete actions missing? Unfortunately, the answer to all these questions is in the affirmative. Assuming that those conditions are likely to persist, can NSD achieve a meaningful change over the next 45 years? Is it worth continuing it in its present form? Or should it be abandoned, leaving it to each country to achieve the best deal it can for itself without relying on a bloc-to-bloc framework? Is that practicable? Those questions are much more difficult to answer except to suggest that, if NSD is to continue, it will need to do so on a different basis to that of the past.

Premises which influence the North's views on NSD

For the relative failure of NSD to be fully appreciated, a broad perspective on the premises which shape the separate views of North and South needs to be established. This is difficult to do dispassionately. Indeed the premisses of each side are rarely explicated. When they are, they seem to be the opposite of what their behaviour actually suggests. They can only be realistically deduced from patterns of behaviour apparent over the years. Of the premisses employed, implicitly or otherwise, by the North in conducting its part of NSD (and, again, allowing for the reality that while these may not be universally shared they may none the less influence bloc behaviour), the following seem the most significant (at least as seen by the South):

- Jointly subscribed principles notwithstanding there are clear limits (budgetary, institutional and political) to what the North can do in tangibly fostering development in the South. These limits govern both the pace and magnitude of Northern effort and are related to the political, economic and security exigencies which the North faces at any particular time.

- Target limits agreed in public fora such as the United Nations (for example the 0.7 per cent of GNP as annual ODA transfers and similar targets) are not binding. Nor is disregard for them a source of embarrassment. Development assistance effort is a matter of individual choice among North bloc members. Trade relationships between North and South are less a matter of individual choice and more a matter of collective bargaining. Commercial capital flows to the South from the North are neither; they are a function of policies employed by the South, not by the North.

- The raison d'tre for fostering Southern development en bloc is to forestall the prospect of "losing" the South, or any part of it, to a competing ideology. If parts were lost then they lost the right to participate fully in the North-South system as it is currently configured (for example Cuba, Nicaragua, Viet Nam – but there are also exceptions such as Ethiopia). A (variable) degree of tolerance was permissible in how far any Southern country could drift from market principles in its own domestic economic and political configuration (short of outright alignment with the former

Eastern bloc) before losing its rights to participate. Direction of movement was a critical factor. If countries formerly aligned with the Eastern European bloc drifted towards market economics, they could participate fully in the North-South system even if on the economic spectrum they were less market oriented than others (for example China and Yugoslavia).

- Fostering development in the South is important for expanding markets for the North's exports of goods, services and, frequently, skilled management and labour. Individual members of the North are free to compete aggressively in these Southern markets and to use development assistance as a means to acquire competitive advantage.

- Development assistance and NSD are useful for securing stable sources of supply for essential commodities, particularly minerals, non-food agricultural commodities and tropical beverages.

- Promulgating reliance on market economics is of key importance to the North in the context of NSD, at least since 1980. But there are limits. The North is not prepared to accept market discipline being carried to its logical conclusion in all economic interactions with the South. For example, it is out of the question to free international markets for agricultural produce, manufactures (textiles), labour or services in which the South might have a comparative advantage (for example transportation, tourism). In short, market discipline is to be forced on the South by the North except in those areas where it could result in social or political dislocations in the North.

- Southern national borders should be permeable to movements of capital, technology and physical output, and to one kind of ideology but not the other. They should be relatively more permeable to the movement of labour from the North than from the South.

- The South offers a vast opportunity for the development and sale of military hardware regardless of affordability or of other political or economic consequences. The market principle of caveat emptor applies in the South's purchases of weaponry or indeed of other capital goods which may prove totally inappropriate to its needs.

- Till the end of the Cold War in 1989, as long as the South pursued economic régimes consonant with the interests of the North, the North was inclined to be indifferent to the domestic political régimes which countries of the South adopted.[9]

- Southern élites dominating the machinery of government have little interest in widespread prosperity or power sharing (economic or political). Their interest lies primarily in concentrating political power and ensuring longevity. Such circumstances diminish the likelihood that resources provided by the North will be satisfactorily used to promote genuine widely based development.

- The South adheres tenaciously to discredited theories about the merits of government intervention in promoting equitable development and growth. After 40 years of experimentation, the North and the Second World have abandoned reliance on "socialist" and "social market" dogma. The South must be coaxed to apply the same lessons more swiftly than it seems inclined to.

- The South cannot be trusted to employ global bargaining power in a wise, temperate manner. Power sharing in international institutions must therefore be resisted until the South displays greater capacity for moderation and greater regard for mutual (rather than self-) interest. The North is inherently more responsible and the South should accept that, for the foreseeable future, the world is safer in its hands.

- The South looks too much to the North for earning its livelihood and not enough to itself for greater trading, investment and development opportunities. With different levels of development emerging within the South, there is ample opportunity for greater South-South inter-action which could relieve North-South circuits from overload. Responsibility for expanding South–South interaction lies in the South not in the North.

Though these points emerge provocatively, they are not intended to. They are meant instead to highlight the inherent misconceptions and anomalies which characterize North-South relationships. Those are to be expected. Many are inevitable consequences of political structures and the public-private nexus within the North (and to some extent within the South). But these anomalies ought not to overwhelm the thrust and direction of NSD, nor to govern the basic presumptions of the North (or for that matter the South) which, all too often, they do.

Premisses which influence the views of the South

In the South, there has been more conscious effort to articulate the objectives and expectations of NSD. That is not surprising. The South wants a transfer of various kinds of resources (financial, human and technological) from the North through NSD; and sooner rather than later.

The North feels no urgency in relinquishing these resources or making the concessions which the South claims in the name of global equity. The North's efforts to make NSD productive has understandably, therefore, been more casual. NSD has thus been characterized throughout its life by the South being aggressively proactive and the North passively reactive. For that reason it is less difficult to be clear about the premisses which shape the South's views. Even so, the approach adopted in discerning the South's premisses is similar to that for the North with judgement based more on interpretation of behaviour than on formal explication.

Bearing in mind that the South has become in the 1980s and 1990s a less cohesive bloc than it once was, and much less cohesive than the North still is, the premisses which individual members of the South may operate upon could be different to those outlined below. None the less, to the extent that the South still attempts to maintain a front of solidarity in its dealings with the North, some premisses do determine common positions even if they are not universally subscribed to. The most significant ones seem to be the following:

- The North owes the South a living. Despite protests and qualifications that this is not a premiss on which the South bases its calls for a more productive NSD, the specific features of the South's "demands" return, inescapably, to its underlying logic.

- The current state of the South's dispossession from claim to an equitable share of global wealth results from past Northern policies and actions. Redress is essential and must be an in-built feature of NSD.

- Reliance on market economics permits the North to continue exploiting the South -- by rigged pricing for resources, labour, natural endowments and now for debt owed. Market power is too heavily loaded in favour of the North. Markets cannot be relied on to give the South a fair share. Public intervention/regulation is therefore needed to compensate for in-built biases toward market failure.

- The South is excessively vulnerable to exogenous shocks caused by the North or by other forces, for example oil shocks, interest rate shocks, exchange rate instability, droughts, natural disasters and so on. It has no control over these factors and little capacity to adapt or adjust swiftly to their effects. The more capable North is under a moral and economic obligation to provide grant assistance or satisfactory compensatory mechanisms to buffer the South against such shocks or to ameliorate their effects.

- The information and financial revolutions of the 1970s and 1980s have largely by-passed the South, leaving it even further behind in competing with the North for products and markets of the future. Because of the South's minimal indigenous capacity to keep up, the North has an obligation to share knowledge and investment on the basis of global comparative advantage. It has an equal obligation to weave the South into the emerging global production-consumption structure, but on terms amenable to the South.

- Private investment (particularly foreign) is intrinsically inimical to the social and political development interests of the South; it is exploitative and anti-social. It must be heavily regulated and taxed to prevent private sector activity and reliance on free markets from worsening problems of income distribution and relative political power. The North's insistence that the South rely increasingly on private resources, both domestic and foreign, is therefore fundamentally misplaced and counterproductive. In many instances (particularly in Africa) the basic prerequisites for competitive private sector activity simply do not exist; reliance on the private sector is thus a recipe for social disruption and unequal, unjust development.

• The North is uninterested in giving the South a greater say in matters of mutual economic interest. It is more interested in dividing the South and having individual Southern members join Northern ranks at a controlled pace thus continually weakening the South's bargaining position. The North systematically diminishes any forum in which the South has an equal voice while diverting dialogue through the allegedly neutral and dispassionate multilateral institutions over which the North has total control.

• The suspicions of the South about the motives of the North are borne out by the North's indifference to the consequences for the South of the debt crisis. The North has been prepared throughout the 1980s to accept a reverse transfer of real resources from South to North of a magnitude far greater than the cumulative positive transfers which took place from North to South in the previous two decades. Debtor-creditor relations, shaped by excessive reliance on private financing, have worked in much the same way as colonization in draining the South of real resources; the only difference being that this outcome has been achieved more effectively and in a legally acceptable fashion. Under those circumstances, the basic shared principles underlying NSD have little practical validity.

• Continual Northern criticism about the inadequacy of the South's policies being the real constraint to development is merely a deflecting tactic to evade the North's responsibilities and obligations. The South was pursuing much the same policies when it developed quite fast and more equitably in the 1960s and 1970s, when it did not have the burdens of debt and rigged commodity prices. Moreover, the policies pursued by the North have created global uncertainties and imbalances in the South which have had a far more deleterious effect on their economies than Southern domestic policies.

• The North is impatient, fickle and prone to instant gratification. It sets unrealistic objectives for the economic, social and political development of the South and reaches premature conclusions about failure. The North's expectations of quick development results ignore the real progress which the South has made in a much shorter time-span than the North did at a similar stage of economic and social evolution.

- Southern development is too vulnerable to shifts in fashion in Northern political thinking. Northern institutions seem to have a vested interest in continually changing their prescriptions about the type of political economy most conducive to rapid, equitable development. The South is thus continually detribalized by being discouraged from staying on a particular development path long enough to succeed.

- The political machinery of the South is not as well equipped as that of the North, nor are its economic structures as resilient at accommodating shifts in political preferences of the kind which regularly take place in the North. The South cannot afford the resource-dissipating effects of such shifts; nor are its populations sufficiently sophisticated to cope with their meaning and implications.

- The North does not understand that there is little choice in the South but for élites to rule (as they did for long periods in the North even under democracy) until social mobility widens their ranks sufficiently for proper democracy to operate. The North's expectations of political standards in the South, acceptable by its own benchmarks, are not consistent with its expectations of rapid economic development. Hence, while financing and supporting Southern development, the North should keep out of its internal political affairs – or not use them as an excuse for not doing what the North morally must to assist development – unless specifically invited to intervene.

Enumerating the different broad premisses which lurk behind the attitudes and perceptions of the two blocs engaged in NSD would highlight, at the risk of caricaturing, the chasm which exists in the fundamental perceptions of both sides. To the extent that these premisses, or their subtler variants, continue to influence the attitudes of those at the front line of NSD it is difficult to see any substantive, durable break- throughs emerging in the foreseeable future. What is surprising is not that NSD has been relatively unproductive but that, in the face of these conflicting presumptions, which have hardened over the years, so much has actually been achieved. Though the South does not see it that way, practical progress, particularly through incremental steps taken by the United Nations machinery and the Bretton Woods institutions, has been considerable. It must be acknowledged though that relative to the 1970s, the 1980s have seen a series of reversals for the South. The roles of the IMF and the World Bank have been seriously distorted in coping with the strains of the debt crisis – a reality which has influenced the outlook and programmatic orientation of these institutions. They are becoming increasingly dysfunctional for the South and are, indeed, in danger of becoming vestigial in the absence of a framework to replace the Bretton Woods Agreement, which redefines more clearly their charters (in a way which addresses the political and economic realities of 1990, not 1945) and the rules under which they operate. By contrast, the United Nations system has been more sensitive and responsive to the crisis faced by the South, at considerable risk to its standing in the North. It is likely to emerge the stronger and more credible for it in the 1990s.

The Future of NSD

If little were to change in the current global nexus, the basic orientation of NSD would still require alteration if only to bring the respective presumptions of the North and South more in line with each other for progress to be made. But, much is likely to change in the global system of interdependence which has so far bounded North-South interaction. These changes fall into three categories: (a) changes occurring in the North; (b) changes occurring in the South; and (c) changes outside of North and South (as these two blocs are generally conceived) which are likely to impinge on the mutual interests of both.

Changes within the North

These might perhaps be enumerated as follows:

- The era of hardline right-wing ideological proselytizing is over in the leading nations of the North. Pragmatic leadership has taken hold. Earlier international excesses are likely to be blunted as urgent domestic and social issues press on Northern governments for resolution.

- Prospective reductions in the US twin deficits are likely to pose both a threat and an opportunity for the South. As long as the correction of the trade deficit is through an expansion of US exports and not a contraction of its imports, the South is likely to gain in two ways. First, expansion of US exports will necessarily require the United States to bolster the financial capacity of the South to absorb more imports. Second, the South is likely to increase its competitive edge in US markets with greater product penetration and efficiency and because of major trade differences likely to emerge between the United States, Europe and Japan respectively.

- The confrontational approach taken by the US vis-à-vis the South during the 1980s has been replaced with a genuine, if cautious, approach aimed at co-operation and accommodation, centred around its immediate neighbourhood, the Caribbean, Central and South America. The realization has set in that a different debt strategy must be pursued to reduce the massive reverse net transfers taking place. The connection between debt and the disintegration of governments in Bolivia, Colombia and Peru is becoming clearer. So is a similar connection between debt and social disintegration in Argentina, Brazil and Mexico. Equally the realization is taking hold in the United States that focus must shift from military to economic intervention if the explosive potential of social problems in Central and Latin America is not to spill over further to the detriment of US society.

- European economic dealings with the South are likely to come increasingly within the ambit of the EC and will be influenced by the unification of the European market. It is generally expected that the 1990s will see Europe increasingly preoccupied with its own new problems and relatively less interested in those of others, including the South. That view is coupled with a foreboding that single Europe will become fortress Europe reluctant to open its borders to Southern exports and more inclined to concentrate on preferential trading arrangements with: (a) its own "South" (the economies of Greece, Portugal, Spain, and possibly Turkey); (b) Eastern Europe, which holds considerable economic and political promise for Western Europeans; (c) the contiguous economies of the southern Mediterranean and (d) the ACP (African, Caribbean and Pacific) states covered by the Lom Agreement. Though trade between Europe and the remainder of the South (particularly the Asian and Latin American economies) may well suffer some hiccups, an overall European view of dealings with the South is likely to be beneficial in the context of NSD, especially in making multilateral institutions more responsive to the South's interests and, possibly, in increasing overall volumes of financial flow, commercial and concessional.

- Japan will become a much more influential and constructive force in North-South relations, veering away from the strictly commercial interests which have characterized its approach towards the South till now and developing a more holistic interest in Southern development. The benefits are likely to be felt most directly by Asian economies, perhaps less so by those in Africa and Latin America. Obviously Japan's backyard economies have much to gain by working out more clearly and in advance what they expect from Japan and what they are prepared to give in order to get it. The reticence of China and India in attracting much greater Japanese involvement will need to give way to more pragmatic positions which ensure that they benefit from interaction with Japan at least as much as Japan does. It is likely that the more advanced economies of Asia will benefit the most and the less developed ones the least, unless they give special attention to attracting and retaining Japan's interest in their welfare.

- The like-minded OECD countries (Canada, the Netherlands, the Nordic Group and, increasingly, Australia) which have through the 1970s and 1980s championed the cause of the South and fought to get its voice heard in Northern fora are likely to step up that role as the prospects of what they have been advocating actually   begin to materialize. These countries, however, are likely to focus more of their own efforts and assistance towards sub-Saharan Africa and countries in Asia which exhibit similar characteristics (Afghanistan, Bangladesh, Cambodia, Laos, Myanmar and Viet Nam).

- The ageing of the North is likely to alter consumption and saving patterns, increase the demand for services in which the South may have a comparative advantage, and create serious pressures in particular Northern labour markets which may exacerbate the Southern brain drain problem.

- Public enthusiasm in the United States for high levels of defence expenditure may diminish, though this is likely to affect the North in different ways. Europe and Japan may find themselves under pressure to increase their own defence expenditures to allow room for the United States to reduce its own. Hopefully, these adjustments will still result in fewer net resources being devoted to defence in the North as a whole.

Changes in the South

The changes already in train within the South are likely to have an even more profound effect on NSD. These include:

- Accelerated diversification and fragmentation of different economic interests within the South. This process began in the 1970s and picked up steam in the 1980s. It is likely to continue at an even faster pace in the 1990s. This will probably make it more difficult for the South to maintain common positions across the board in NSD. This view is predicated on the following assumptions:

    (a) Assuming that unexpected reversals do not deflect them from their current trajectory, the sovereign Asian NICs (Korea, Singapore, Taiwan and possibly Thailand), along with Turkey, will probably enter the ranks of "developed" countries during the 1990s.

    (b) Other smaller ASEAN, Middle Eastern, North African (except Egypt) and Latin American economies could, if internal political disturbances do not derail them, reach the living standards that Korea reached in the late '1970s and early 1980s. All of the Latin and some North African economies will have little option but to put their debt problems behind them (through debtor cartel formation if that proves unavoidable) and resume growth if their growing social problems are to be contained.

(c) The smaller, poorer economies of Asia (Afghanistan, Bangladesh, Indochina and Myanmar) and Africa will remain poor with economic growth barely keeping pace with population growth. The 1990s are likely to bring more hope than the 1980s and consolidate the upturn in output trend that is now emerging in Africa. But these economies will confront the problems of massive infrastructure reconstruction and continued food insecurity. They will remain vulnerable to external influences and to their debilitating shortage of human capital.

(d) The biggest question facing the South in the 1990s concerns large influential economies such as China, Egypt, India, Indonesia, Iran, Iraq, Nigeria and Pakistan. Though very different in character and size, they share certain characteristics. They are all littoral powers; some are becoming affected by crippling debt burdens (for example India). And they are all much poorer than their resources and human capabilities warrant. If these countries are able to surmount their current political difficulties (which in the short term will probably worsen before they improve) and unleash the energies of their private sectors, they could transform the Southern scene. But that hope has been dashed before. Whether the 1990s will be different remains an open question though a few portents do justify optimism.

(e) Realization on the part of the island economies of the Caribbean and Pacific that they need to formulate totally different strategies for economic survival. They will not be able to rely only on privileged access to traditional markets (Australian, EC or North American) for commodity exports in order to maintain artificially high standards of living.

* Growing recognition throughout the South that dirigisme and excessive government intervention in economic life have not delivered sufficiently rapid progress. They have drained scarce resources and have overstrained, if not corrupted, the administrative infrastructure of several countries with little to show for it.[10]

* The inexorable pressures for greater democratization and enfranchisement on the part of a growing vocal minority – the middle classes in several developing countries.

* Growing realization that the arguments for NSD based on global equity and justice and forged in the 1970s no longer influence the behaviour of the North (if indeed they ever did except by way of winning debating points). The South's economic failures and political

excesses have damaged the credibility of what the North perceives to be its sanctimoniously hollow positions in NSD. The South now recognizes that: its economic wounds are not always externally inflicted but often due to internal development efforts being inadequate and ineffective; and that, in the absence of more committed internal effort, external resources are unlikely to be available in any appreciable quantity or to have more than a marginal effect.

● Mounting concern that global revolutions in finance, information and management technology, which have transformed economic activity in the North, have largely by-passed the South. The South is only just beginning to become aware of the self-inflicted damage caused by closing its economies in the name of independence and sovereignty. In the mistaken belief that its labour surpluses did not make it necessary for the South to employ technology or organization to the same extent as the North (in manufacturing, banking, transportation, etc.), the South has, in effect, shut itself off from precisely those technological impulses which are key to the restoration of its competitive advantage in manufacturing and services.

● Peace is breaking out with the end of Cold War rivalry resulting in sharply reduced proclivities on the part of the United States and the former USSR to continue financing client régimes (or their opponents); this holds the prospect of significant diminution in levels of South-South border conflict.

● Hard-headed realization that South-South co-operation, about which so much has been said, still remains an unrealized dream. [11]

Changes elsewhere

The shifts in political orientation, awareness of internal deficiencies and greater appreciation of the benefits/costs of interdependence now occurring within the North and South blocs are likely to have a profound influence on the direction, content and tone of NSD in the 1990s. But, these factors apart, the change which may have the most profound impact on the nexus between North and South in the 1990s concerns the radically changed domestic circumstances and global stance of the former Soviet Union and its former satellites. Part of the problem is that, from the North's viewpoint, Eastern Europe and the former Soviet republics have become, economically at least, a part of the South – indeed less developed than many parts of the South. From the South's viewpoint, the perspective is the opposite; the East bloc was till now a part of the North as a competing source of aid (mostly military), trade, technology and investment (though to a much lesser extent than the OECD in aggregate terms).

Republics in the former Soviet Union and Eastern European countries will become fully fledged members of the global financial, monetary and trading rgime by the mid-1990s. The South will probably pay lip service to the merits of including the Eastern Europeans within the global system but with profound concern about whether the entry of these countries will compete with Southern claims on finite resources. To the South it must by now be painfully clear that the erstwhile Eastern bloc wishes to join the global monetary and trading system to promote its own development and not to be a champion of, or net contributor to, the needs of developing countries. For the South, the crucial question is whether Eastern European entry into the global system is likely to be of benefit. In some ways it will be. To the extent that tensions are eased between East and West, the South is less likely to waste its own resources on counter-productive internal and regional conflict. If the North's acceptance of a sharply reduced security threat from its Cold War adversaries can eventually be translated into lower levels of defence spending, the pool of resources available for investment in Southern development might be expanded – but perhaps not till well into the late 1990s. Expanding Eastern European markets may well provide increased trading opportunity for the South. As many other richer developing countries already do, the Eastern Europeans may eventually begin to again contribute aid through multilateral concessional resource pools (such as IDA) once their own efforts at economic transformation and recovery are successful.

In other ways, Eastern European entry into the multilateral economic system may conflict or compete with the immediate interests of the South. First, Eastern Europe and the former Soviet republics are likely to be major takers from the IBRD's and IMF's hard loan windows during the 1990s despite the creation of the new European Bank for Reconstruction and Development (EBRD) to meet their special needs. As these countries face harsher pressures to invest in their own modernization and development, their domestic resources will be absorbed internally. Former levels of CMEA assistance to the Third World have disappeared altogether. It is difficult to see these levels being replaced by aid from traditional Western donors, whose purses will be stretched in meeting the new demands of Eastern Europe and addressing some of their own neglected social problems. The former Soviet republics and Eastern Europe urgently need access to global trade and to international capital markets. They will therefore compete for the world's common pool of financial savings; not just with the United States (which will remain a net debtor throughout the 1990s and beyond) and other net borrowers in the North, but with the South for resources which are available from private markets on commercial terms. They will need greater access immediately to hard currency export markets, particularly to the single European market. Europe (particularly Germany) for its own economic, security and political reasons is likely to provide preferential access to Eastern European countries possibly at the expense of the more advanced developing countries. Initially, at least, Eastern European entry is unlikely to expand global trade sufficiently to offset fully a competitive loss for the South in Northern markets, although later on it might. And, finally, the countries of Eastern Europe could easily emulate the Latin countries in becoming too heavily indebted for their economic capacities to cope with (they are more than halfway there already), thus further damaging the interests of the South. The recent debt deal for Poland demonstrates how political perceptions in the West could result in preferential economic treatment for Eastern Europe over the countries of the South.

What is unclear is whether the former Soviet republics and Eastern European countries will align themselves with the South in the major multilateral institutions or whether they will play a more neutral role, lending weight to the small but influential "like-minded" countries which play a pivotal role in bridging the chasm between the hard-core North and the South. The South may well believe that Eastern European entry into GATT and the Bretton Woods institutions will strengthen its bargaining position in the North-South dialogue. That may prove a mistaken assumption. The North would be understandably concerned about CIS and Eastern European entry resulting in a loss of absolute majority control and a tilt towards the South. If that happened, the Bretton Woods institutions and GATT face the prospect of suffering the same loss of credibility as the United Nations throughout the 1970s and 1980s. If, on the other hand, the former Soviet republics and Eastern Europe align themselves with the North, will that result in an increase of the enlarged North's responsiveness to the South's legitimate concerns and needs? Answers to these questions are unclear and cloud the prospects for NSD in the 1990s.

These opportunities and risks, which the promise of greater involvement by the former Eastern bloc countries in the global economic system holds out, need to be as carefully assessed by the South as by the North – and not just in the limited context of NSD. Clearly, involvement by these countries in the multilateral economic system is to be welcomed as a positive development in its own right. But that involvement must be carefully "managed" in its transitional phase by both North and South to ensure that the stability of the system is not disrupted before necessary evolutionary changes can occur. Unless the South's positions and objectives are much more realistic and clear, and its affairs much more astutely managed than they have been in the past, it may become a net loser in a new North-East-South triangle. And that may well happen if the North perceives its economic and security interests to be better served by consolidating its much stronger position vis-à-vis the emerging CIS republics and Eastern European countries through economic means than by catering to the needs of the South.

Revising the South's Priorities for NSD

Taking into account both the history of NSD and the realignments presently taking place, what should the South's agenda for NSD be? Should it still pursue an impractically over-ambitious agenda aimed at reviving NIEO? Or should it confine itself to a few well-thought-out initiatives which represent step-by-step progress on foundations already established? Should the South sanguinely believe that the winds of political conservatism have blown their course in the North and the cycle is now, inexorably, turning back to more benign times for the South? Or should it frame an agenda which endures and can be pursued irrespective of the periodic fashions which afflict political thinking in the North? The way in which the questions are phrased clearly suggest what the answers ought to be. Though the common principles underlying NSD (outlined above) should remain largely intact, it is clear that the premises on which both North and South have based their respective positions need to be reconsidered and better aligned. Indeed, it is a peculiar shortcoming of NSD that the premises of either side are rarely discussed or explicated – as if both North and South have decided that game theory precludes either revealing to the other what its premises and preferences are. The unfortunate inference is that both have already concluded that NSD is a zero or negative sum game, that is, both sides are convinced that whatever one side gains from NSD the other one loses. Neither fully accepts that NSD could be a positive sum game, of benefit to both sides with both gaining from mutually acceptable initiatives and compromises. The South too often argues that the imperatives of development supersede other considerations reflective of normalcy in its relations with the North, though that argument is rarely correct or acceptable.

Assuming that the North maintains the view that its global interests require any concessions or expenditures for accelerated Southern development to be made grudgingly, it remains for the South to change the course of NSD for the better. How might it do so? The following suggestions are offered for consideration and debate as starting points:

- The South should frame its NSD agenda on the premisse that it has not yet done enough, economically or politically, to help itself. Until it does, dialogue with the North is unlikely to yield much. Though incapacity is a basic condition of underdevelopment, there is sufficient knowledge and expertise within the South to do much better than it has.

What is needed is the will and the institutional structure to organize its own efforts. The South can hardly expect the North to do politically difficult things if it is unwilling to, or cannot, make the same effort itself.

- Apart from the poorest, most deserving of its members (not often the ones to whom resources always go) the South ought to focus less on demanding aid and focus much more on issues of trade and capital flows on commercial terms, on which there is more "give" in the North. For most of the South this should be looked at more from the viewpoint of "offsetting compensation" for the North's distortions of markets in particular areas of international trade which deprive the South of a fair chance to earn a living. The principle underlying this stance is no different to that which underpins agricultural and other price support systems which the North has devised for its own special interest groups. The North is trying to restore market rules gradually in these instances. Till it manages to accommodate the South in the same way, "compensatory offsets" for putative income losses to the South ought to provide a more useful framework for looking at aid flows.

- If the South believes that resource scarcity is the critical constraint to development it should exert far greater effort to stop wasting resources – its own as well as those obtained externally. Governments in the South should bow to experience and change course, relying more heavily on non-public investment resources and initiatives to stimulate development, encouraging different types of private enterprise to flourish. Given their limited capacities, they should focus on: the fundamental processes of governance; providing an "enabling environment" through infrastructural and utility investment; minimum levels of social income support expenditure; and not on much else. Public investments should be undertaken through capable enterprises protected from political and other corrupting (often market-based) influences. Government investment in production should be undertaken only when no other option is available. On the other hand Southern governments should avoid misplaced faith in the alleged magic of the market-place. Markets are not particularly magical; left entirely to themselves, they are often not even efficient vehicles for promoting development. But, administrative intervention (particularly in the South) in the name of development has, contrary to hope, proved to be even less so. Southern governments should rely instead on sensible regulation to foster healthy competition and using price signals along with market forces to encourage deconcentration of wealth and privilege in societies where these qualities are too heavily skewed in the wrong direction. Regulation and licensing should be aimed at making private enterprise and markets work, not at encouraging them to be inefficient or strangulating them.

- If it is to stand on moral ground of any worth, the South should be far less tolerant, in the 1990s, than it has been up to now of the rapacity and brutality of too many Southern leaderships. It cannot hide behind concepts of sovereignty to permit or condone excesses on the part of Southern leaders. It cannot justify a moral position based on "equity and justice" in its dialogue with the North if it defends, condones ignores or fails to condemn unacceptable behaviour in any part of the South. If the South, collectively, feels unable to exert the necessary moral suasion in available multilateral fora, or exercise other forms of sanction within its own ranks, it should give up the pretence of representing its interests en bloc vis-à-vis the North and let dialogue descend to bilateral levels. The South cannot afford more Amins, Marcoses and Duvaliers to diminish its case and yet too many such leaders remain in power. It has lost enough credibility with Northern publics who provide the mandate for constructive NSD; it cannot afford to lose more. The South's cleaning up of its own act should not be conditional upon reciprocity from the North. Blind opinion aside, the North's record in these areas, though hardly pristine, is much cleaner. But regardless of that, it is in the interests of the South to do so irrespective of other considerations.

An Agenda for the South in the 1990s

What might a specific NSD agenda incorporate for the 1990s? The wish list approach employed all too often in the past is unproductive. To make progress, the South must concentrate on a few, digestible measures and pursue them relentlessly. Recommendations can be grouped into three broad areas: aid, trade and capital flows. For reasons of space, only broad lines of recommendations are set out below.

Development Aid

NSD should continue to remind the North about the findings of several regional and global taskforces and expert groups set up under various multilateral auspices on the need for increasing concessional ODA flows. The South might consider more practical, achievable targets for DAC-ODA as a whole between 1990-1994 and 1995-1999. The 0.7 per cent target should remain intact as an incentive to those donors whose governments and legislatures are influenced by them. The arrangement should recognize that compromise measures are needed till that target is met. Shifting focus, in the interim, from globally applicable percentage targets it might try getting the North to agree to aggregate dollar targets. The North should decide how that aggregate figure might be shared among key donors. It should also secure formal agreement on the North's assurances that increases in DAC-ODA will not be diverted to Eastern Europe and the former Soviet republics. Any assistance provided to the former Eastern bloc should be additional to DAC-ODA. Politically motivated and militarily associated aid, which is often used to retard rather than foster development, should be excluded from ODA contributions simply because it is not development assistance in any commonly accepted sense. This shift should not be taken as abandoning the 0.7 per cent target even though these aggregate targets would keep ODA increases just slightly ahead of projected long-term OECD GNP growth rates during the 1990s.

The South should focus more than it has on the distribution of ODA – too much of which is currently allocated to upper- and middle-income developing countries. So far the South has been unwilling to discipline its own members who exacerbate entrenched tendencies towards misallocation, remaining content instead to criticize the North for misplacing its priorities.

A collective Southern effort is required to: (a) get the IMF to disengage from a permanent role as long-term aid provider to the South; (b) shift a greater proportion of concessional resources through the regional multi-lateral development banks (RMDBs) in which the South has a little more influence than in the Bretton Woods twins; and (c) increase bilateral aid flows substantially for projects and programme funding. To encourage flows through regional institutions the South should exert maximum effort to improve the quality and capability of the RMDBs.

Emulating the practices of some of its more experienced and astute members, the South should develop the capacity and the will to refuse aid which is not in its own long-term interests. Inappropriate aid has been the unfortunate experience of much of the 1970s and 1980s. Greater use of impartial, independent expertise by the South to assess (*ex ante*) the quality of aid projects and programmes is necessary. The North should be engaged in assisting the South to establish appropriate arrangements (which will prove of mutual advantage) for ensuring that such expertise is available in the right way at the right time.

With particular reference to technical assistance, the South should gear up the capacity to participate in its design and use. Too much technical assistance is wasted and too much aid money is spent on it without the South deriving any lasting advantages. With particular reference to Africa and the poorest countries in Asia, the South should initiate a major undertaking to devise innovative and acceptable multilateral arrangements which would permit continuity in the sustained, ·long-term delivery of external assistance aimed at bridging shortfalls in Africa's own endowments in public administration capacity as well as in its productive sectors.

Trade

The agenda pursued by developing countries on trade issues was not as carefully crafted in preparation for the Uruguay Round as it might have been. The South Commission has since tried to rectify that shortcoming with a comprehensive statement outlining the position of developing countries in August 1988. The South is right to press to extract whatever concessions it can from the North for (a) the unjustifiable retention of the MFA (multi-fibre agreement) and (b) the reticence of Europe and Japan in particular to reduce domestic agricultural price supports which damage the South's trading interests. It should press for trade-offs to protect its interests as best as it can recognizing the tendency on the part of the North to contravene GATT rules with its preferences for devices such as voluntary export restraints and orderly marketing arrangements. On manufactured exports, the South remains too divided in the competitive posture taken by its different members (individual and regional blocs) for preferred access to Northern markets recognizing the differences in capacity which characterize them. Nevertheless these disparities are counterproductive and self-defeating in the long term; they weaken the South considerably in extracting concessions which are vital collectively as well as for individual developing countries.

The South's position on restrictive barriers to services does not seem to be as well thought out as it might be. In several services sectors the South could develop competitive capabilities in the intermediate term if its markets were open to the entry of foreign service firms. The South might adopt a much more positive negotiating stance on services and focus on reciprocal concessions (such as greater labour mobility for its own nationals in those Northern markets whose services firms are permitted entry into Southern markets) which would enable the South to develop its own services capabilities (as it already has in sectors such as hotels and airlines). The South's fear that opening foreign entry to the services sector will stunt the development of indigenous capability is as mistaken as the approach taken earlier to protect domestic markets in goods, which led to only a few developing countries being able to compete efficiently. The whole argument about exemptions from normal rules to accommodate legitimate objectives of "development policy" needs to be reviewed, since it has all too often resulted in "development policy" achieving the opposite of its intended aim.

Typically, the South has focused too much on its differences with the North in the Uruguay Round and not sufficiently on how South-South trading interests might be better organized and accommodated. That is an omission which requires urgent correction.

The South's concerns about the protection of intellectual property rights are well founded but its arguments are not. Intellectual property (especially in the information and communications technologies) is generally the product of massive research and development expenditures by Northern private sectors. The expectation of returns on these expenditures is not unreasonable. To argue that knowledge is a global resource which should be freely available, especially to developing countries, is not particularly realistic in current circumstances, unless means to ensure adequate returns on knowledge-based investments are put in place. This issue impinges on trade as well as aid policy and needs to be treated in fora relating to both. The South needs to undertake considerably more thinking on this issue rather than base its position on ex cathedra assertions and obduracy in circumstances which require that the South increase, not decrease (as its present position is likely to), access to technology.

Capital flows

The South's most urgent priority for the 1990s should be to reverse the net outflow of capital and real resources that has been a persistent feature of the 1980s. The South must, therefore, apply greater collective leverage for the establishment of a multilaterally supported debt-relief facility along lines already proposed in several forms.

As part of the overall objective of reversing negative capital transfers, the South's agenda should include negotiating a reorientation of official (non-concessional) financing. As with aid, the South should first prevent the inadvertent consequence of present efforts by the North which would result in the permanent enshrinement of the IMF's role in long-term development financing through adjustment-orientated facilities. Its role should be redirected to short-term balance-of-payments equilibration and management of the global monetary system. Second, the South should exert efforts to discourage the World Bank from continued emphasis on structural and sectoral adjustment lending, which the Bank has demonstrated no ability to do well. The Bank should in the 1990s revert to project and sectoral investment lending, which is its traditional forte. Third, the South should make the 1990s the decade of the *regional banks* putting its weight resolutely behind increases in the capital and non-concessional lending of the RMDBs.[12] Fourth, the South needs to reactivate the interest of the North in large-scale officially supported export credit financing but on a much more prudent basis than in the 1970s when that activity was driven more by banks, exporters and the anxiety of Northern governments to export their way out of the oil shocks, than by the legitimate needs of developing countries.

The onset of the debt problem and the reluctance of Northern governments to expand official capital flows to the South sufficiently (in effect repeating the mistakes of the 1970s) requires the South to reconsider carefully its access to private foreign equity capital. A knee-jerk reaction to the debt crisis had been that the South must now attract foreign equity flows to a much greater degree. This has been the underlying principle behind the current fashion of debt-equity swaps; the establishment of indirect portfolio funds for emerging developing country capital markets; the emergence of interest in private financing of infrastructural projects through build-own-operate-transfer (BOOT) techniques; and a renewal of interest in direct foreign investment. None of these developments are panaceas, though they are all likely to be helpful at the margin. None are likely to address the problem of large-scale steady capital transfers to the South on a sustainable basis for the foreseeable future. Yet, the South needs to establish the foundations now for gradually acquiring access to such funds and increasing it over time. The South needs to approach this issue more sensibly than it seems to be doing or indeed than the North wants it to. It must be recognized at the outset that equity financing is, in a steady state and over the long run, the most expensive form of financing that can be raised by corporations (in terms of returns that must be provided). Equity has its advantages, the most impressive being its ability to share in risks and losses. But for equity financing to be attracted in any quantity on a sustained basis the incidence of risk and loss has to be tolerably small. The three specific types of flow that the South needs to focus on are: increased direct foreign investment; attraction of portfolio investment; and repatriation of flight capital and remittances.

These points constitute a sufficiently long revised agenda for the South to pursue in the 1990s. It is a practical NSD agenda framed in an evolutionary rather than revolutionary context. It requires careful consideration and more fleshing out as each of the broader objectives is translated into key tasks and negotiating processes. Hopefully, a sufficiently clear indication of strategic thrust is provided such as to require no further elaboration. Much work needs to be done in bringing the views and objectives of the North and South in closer accord as they conduct NSD in the 1990s. It is unlikely that much will be accomplished if the underlying tone of NSD continues to be regarded (by the North) as complaining on the part of the South and (by the South) as an arrogant unwillingness to contemplate overdue changes in the world order on the part of the North. There is too much mutual advantage at stake for NSD to be relegated to the low ranks of global priority that it was through most of the 1980s. The current US and European leaderships seem to sense that reality. NSD needs to be encouraged by the increasingly stronger Eastern European and Japanese partners in the North and, above all, by more realistic and pragmatic interim goals for NSD on the part of the South.

Notes

1. This has, of course, resulted in the effective disappearance of the Second World; thus the term "Third World" has now lost the Cartesian logic which has supported its popular usage up to now though it remains in vernacular vogue. Throughout this chapter the loose terms "Western" and "Northern" are used synonymously to refer mainly to the OECD group of developed countries while the terms "South" or "Southern" will refer largely to the developing world. Of course, the former use of the term "North" also used to include the erstwhile East bloc which, for the time being, must be excused from its membership in any serious sense.

2. It has been influenced more by the vagaries of changing US administrations (and the prejudices of their key officials) than by any other single factor. To a large degree that impression reflects reality. The South benefited immensely from US confidence and munificence in the immediate post-1945 era. It is arguable whether developing countries would have fared as well in the 1950s and 1960s had their fates in the international arena been left to dealings with their ex-colonial governments. The US created and underpinned a global order in which the world -- including the South -- prospered for a quarter of a century. It is unlikely that, without US pressure on European powers, much of the South would even have achieved independence as soon as it did. It is equally true, however, that when the United States became less benign and turned inward, after the failures of the late 1960s and 1970s, that is, when it began perceiving its largesse toward the South to have been largely wasted (measured in terms of alliances and political gratitude) North-South relations, taken as a whole, deteriorated.

3. No doubt countries such as France, in their limited zones of influence, have taken a different path to the benefit of those few members of the South associated with it. So have other Northern countries, particularly the Nordic ones, which attempted to insulate individual developing countries from wider North-South rifts with their "programmes of concentration". Britain (despite its unique attachment to a large, diverse Commonwealth) has been much less influential and, together with Germany and Japan, has tended to reinforce US positions during the 1980s for better or for worse at crucial times (such as during the IDA 7 replenishment). These three countries, despite all the will in the world, have not made a crucial difference. They hid behind arcane burden-sharing principles when circumstances demanded that they take a different stance.

4. This "principle" has been honoured more in the breach than in the keeping. Several dozen human disasters and violent conflicts -- civil as well as cross-border -- have erupted since 1944, all confined to the South on each of its continents. Many have involved, directly or indirectly, the North as sponsor of one side in the dispute.

5. Here the global principle is different to what has been attempted within a national context. Most governments, in the North and South, have explicitly intended to impoverish their rich (through punitive income and wealth taxes) in absolute, not merely relative terms, and transfer wealth to their poor (through welfare support payments and subsidies). The 1980s have shaken that premiss even in the national context by acknowledging that former policies have tended to kill, or encourage the migration of, those of their geese that laid golden eggs.

6. There was no corresponding understanding, in principle, that the South should reciprocally keep its markets open to the North. Indeed for a long time it was accepted wisdom that the South would need to protect its markets for some considerable time in order to develop. That wisdom, earlier shared, has undergone a sea change in the North both on grounds of theoretical belief in the advantages of global competition and, more expediently, as it faces intense trade competition from certain parts of the South. The same change has not yet been fully accepted by the South.

7. Bilateral and regional arrangements and preference areas were not seen as less desirable. Indeed quite the opposite as the American, Lom, and Commonwealth arrangements clearly suggest. It was felt though that these arrangements should subscribe to and reinforce a bloc-to-bloc framework rather than diminish or replace it.

8. This is specifically said because, in the North, government-to-government actions of any sort have fallen into disrepute, at least rhetorically if not in practice. Private sector and people-to-people interaction is seen as much healthier and promising. The South clearly has no such delusions and is disinclined to leave its fortunes to the mercy of transnationals, well-intentioned individuals and private voluntary organizations. But, even that reaction is seen as the natural knee-jerk response of "government élites" in the South bent on continuing their régimes of oppression. Sadly, the South has provided more than enough ammunition to justify that view.

9. In other words, human rights violations by rightist governments were formerly acceptable; those of leftist governments were not. To put it crudely, the Ida Amins, Duvaliers, Marcoses, Somoza-Sacasas and Bokassas were acceptable partners for doing North-South business as long as they maintained a choke-hold over their domains. They became dispensable only when they lost their grip or when the end of the Cold War permitted the North to exercise its political preferences more visibly. Conversely, more humane political régimes were unacceptable to the North if their economies were not applying market principles. In the North's thinking, the concept of a humane political rgime applying non-market economic principles was a non sequitur in practice: no "market freedom" automatically translated into "no human freedom".

10. The South is learning, if all too reluctantly that, of its own durable successes, none has been achieved through a socialist model of development. But, nor have these successes relied on the private sector to the degree that current ideology presupposes. All have been based on successful mixed economy recipes in which government has let the private sector undertake most of the responsibility for physical goods production and services. Government has concentrated on: investment in infrastructure and public utilities; governing, that is, ensuring law and order (often brutally at the expense of human rights) along with relatively efficient administration; being concerned about income distribution; permitting trade unions to function sensibly; and ensuring sufficient competition to let market economics work. Occasionally successful governments have undertaken strategic investments or indulged in private sector bailouts to underpin confidence. But none of these governments have been dirigiste in the commonly accepted sense.

11. The South has simply not applied itself to forging those alliances and welding those institutions which permit South-South trade, development and capital flows to grow rapidly and durably. South-South interaction is still too often mediated by the North. The preoccupation with "hard currency" earnings and intense competition among the countries of the South for privileged access to the markets of the North causes many of these countries to ignore prospects for export market development or technology transfer within the South. Nor are the egregious surpluses of many Southern economies being recycled to meet the South's financial needs, even where worthwhile investment opportunities seem available. In short, despite its pretence at solidarity, when it comes to substantive economic issues, the South-South divide is wider and deeper (and characterized by greater mutual mistrust) than the North-South divide.

12. As noted earlier, the South should not leave its fortunes vulnerable to the management of any one institution. The 1980s saw too much faith being misplaced, and concentrated, earlier in the IMF and later in the World Bank. Nor should it encourage concentration of portfolio risk in any one institution. A regional focus on capital mobilization is timely for other reasons as well. The 1990s may enable greater quantities of officially supported capital flows to be mobilized for regionally focused development especially when the North is undergoing a significant shift in the balance of financial power among its three major constituents, that is, Europe, Japan and the United States. With the IBRD's third general capital increase out of the way, it is opportune for the South to reorient its own emphasis towards strengthening the capability and capital structure of the RMDBs.

20. THE EMERGING NEW INTERNATIONAL FRAMEWORK: IMPLICATIONS FOR THE SOUTH

Carlos Pérez del Castillo

The Emerging New World Order

In the 1970s, when the bargaining power of the developing countries was temporarily strengthened by the creation of OPEC and the increase in oil prices, the concept of a "New International Economic Order" took shape. Its bases, which had been formulated in Latin America and enriched by major contributions from Africa, Asia and some Eastern European countries, became a negotiating platform and a programme of work that embodied the main aspirations of the developing world.

In the 20 years that have elapsed since then, the hopes of the developing countries have, one by one, failed to bear fruit. Meanwhile, the developed countries, which compensated for the limited redistribution of power that followed the creation of OPEC by introducing policies to conserve energy and the generation of new technologies, succeeded in rapidly consolidating their pre-eminent position.

The far-reaching changes that took place in the area of scientific and technological innovation and in the transformation of productive systems, which were concentrated, for the most part, in the industrialized countries, led, among other things, to a marked differentiation of products and prices between goods manufactured in these countries and in the Third World that was distinctly unfavourable to the latter. Faced by increasing imbalances, the developing countries were unable to come to an agreement that was satisfactory in either form or extent on view-points, actions and specific negotiating positions vis-à-vis the developed world.

At the strategic level, the East-West conflict, which had divided the world into two politico-military blocs on the basis of the post-Second World War agreements, intensified to a certain extent in the early 1980s. The result was an increased strategic alignment – resisted for more than three decades by most of the Third World countries – and the use of coercive measures to maintain bloc discipline.

Subsequently, after the meeting between the United States and the USSR in Malta – one of the landmarks in the abandonment of the Cold War – a process of détente and rapprochement began between the two sides, preceded by the increasing mobilization of social forces in all parts of the world, which led to the establishment of democratic régimes and the introduction of economic and social reforms.

At the beginning of the 1990s, after the war in the Persian Gulf, the characteristics of a new international order, which had little in common with the concept viewed as desirable in the South Commission Report, began to become clearly discernible. These features bore out the fears and suspicions felt in Latin America and the Caribbean, since the plan generates a strong impetus towards the marginalization of a large number of developing countries, where solidarity and co-operation, as the principles of harmonious coexistence, are under severe constraint.

The world that is taking shape is thus one that is ruled, with differing degrees of influence, by certain countries and regions where the bulk of the world's wealth and the main flows of trade, investment and knowledge are concentrated. The model of political, economic and social organization is, or tends to resemble, that of Western representative democracy, based on a market economy, but, in many cases, it lacks the minimum resources and conditions necessary to go beyond outward appearances and to become a practical reality.

The leaders of this world order form a triad: Europe, Japan and the United States. Each of them has its own sphere of influence and is attempting to build up a bloc that will increase its power and enhance its negotiating capability. The United States seems to have achieved some of its central post-1945 objectives in foreign policy: the retreat of Marxism, the strengthening of pluralist, participatory democracy and, above all, the predominance of market-based economic policies. Nevertheless, its political and military leadership is disputed in the economic field by the development and plans of the European bloc and by Japan.

The European Community is consolidating its integration process by the Single Act, plans to enlarge its membership and looks forward over the long term to creating a united Europe, aided by the changes that are taking place in Eastern Europe and the former USSR. Japan, for its part, continues to drive ahead, establishing close ties with the other South-East Asian nations and occupying a steadily increasing area and position of influence in the global community.

Meanwhile, the United States is taking decisive steps to form its own bloc through the negotiation of NAFTA – the free trade agreements with Canada and Mexico, and the launching by President Bush of the "Initiative for the Americas" addressed to the other Latin American and the Caribbean countries.

The importance of a project for the South

In reviewing the current evolution of the international system, with the South in mind, it is necessary to take into account a multiple and complex group of factors that interact on the socio-political, economic, techn-ological, strategic and cultural levels. In this respect, the South Commission's Report wisely adopts a multidimensional approach, taking as its guide the viewpoint of the South and incorporating all the existing interrelations among the various processes.

The Report assumes a concept of the international structure that is consistent with the common interests of humanity, not merely of privileged groups, the object being that, through agreements with the developed countries, this concept can become a reality. This is one of the Report's major accomplishments: it takes a stand on the future problems of global society with a view to achieving the equitable generation and distribution of development through economically viable measures and actions. But it is also its most vulnerable point: how is the plan to be made viable when the North systematically rejects any proposal that is not compatible with its own schemes and interests and the South is in such a weakened position?

The outlook offered by this new international framework for the multilateral exercise of economic relations is bleak indeed, narrowing still further the developing countries' scope for changing the system so as to lessen the existing asymmetries and arrive at a fairer and more mutually supportive order. The emergence of a structure of the kind described, which concentrates power in a relatively small number of countries has, among other things, a negative effect on the scenarios for dialogue and negotiation between the developed and the developing nations.

For Latin America and the Caribbean, a highly sensitive region that is vulnerable to changes in the world economy because of its trade, financial and technological dependence, the establishment of an international order of such a nature presents a new challenge and the certainty of extremely serious difficulties, unless the region manages to identify the appropriate response and to put it into effect without delay. To be viable, however, this response will require the support of the other developing regions and the co-ordination of efforts with theirs.

It follows, therefore, that a prerequisite for dialogue and negotiation between the developing countries and the North is the existence of a minimum intra-South common denominator on a broad, flexible and realistic basis. Here again, the South Commission Report reveals its importance, since it offers a comprehensive project for the development of the South, prepared by its own people for a world in which our countries must come to share the responsibility for solving its problems.

The imperative need for a South-based and regional union
An examination of the trends followed by the industrialized countries yields an unequivocal and very important message for us. These countries, with stronger economic structures than those of the South and with vast accumulated wealth, feel obliged, in view of the evolution of the world economy and the intensification of competition of every order, to set aside traditional rivalries, and to subordinate individual actions to collective endeavours that will give them a springboard towards positions of greater economic and political power. If this is true of those countries, how much more so must it be for Africa, Asia and Latin America. In this respect, the South Commission Report serves as a valuable political guide, in the light of which the developing countries could reach agreement on the formulation of common strategies and objectives for their international action that would effectively inspire them with driving force and strength.

Thus, the Report identifies interrelations not only among areas presenting major obstacles but also between the national policy options open to the developing countries and the adverse working of the system of international economic relations. In indicating the solutions, the Report correctly identifies the measures, both national and international, that are indispensable, if policy changes leading to the achievement of the development targets are to be introduced.

In this sense, the South Commission considers that some aspects of the world situation give grounds for hope, and also points out that there are possibilities of influencing public opinion in the North.

However, the Report introduces a note of realism in warning that the South's aspirations will not be realized without a difficult and prolonged struggle, since the North will not easily yield its positions, given that the basis of North-South interaction is essentially a power relationship. The developing countries must therefore acquire the greatest possible bargaining power by fuller exploitation of the collective resources of the South. This is perhaps the fundamental reason – though not the only one – for the need to forge a strong base for unity among the developing countries.

The Report as a basis for balanced negotiation
The third positive factor to be emphasized in the Report is the judicious and finely tuned balance of its opinions and assessments. The South Commission offers a balanced Report that is constructive in its criticism of both North and South and tries to convey messages that are appropriate

to both groups. It is founded on logic, and on the lessons learned from the practical experience of development problems.

In this context, the interests of North and South are not presented as inherently antagonistic but as basically complementary in an interdependent world, although the vision held out shows that the present behaviour of the North is prejudicial to the interests of the whole of humanity and to those of the developing countries in particular. The Report consequently seeks to appeal to the good sense of a resurgent North in the hope of establishing a useful dialogue in order to solve global problems and to remedy the inequalities of the international economic system. It also endeavours to consolidate the political will of the South.

A plan of action for South-South co-operation

One of the Report's valuable aspects is its identification of the links that should be forged between national strategies and strategies at the world, interregional, regional and subregional levels, in order to increase the chances of achieving the desired national objectives. In this sense it represents an important plan of action, which should be studied by every country or country grouping in the South, whether defined geographically or by some other criterion, so as to establish areas for co-operation and set priorities.

The Report also highlights the potential to be tapped in South-South co-operation, whether for limited or for wider purposes. This area lost most of its appeal during the crisis in the 1980s, when the case-by-case policy approach applied by the North restricted the South's possibilities ever more stringently. By revealing the numerous shortcomings, weaknesses and limitations of the approaches and policies adopted by the North and the body of interests shared by the developing countries, the Report is instrumental, to some extent, in drawing attention to the divisive message conveyed by an overemphasis on the differences separating the countries of the South because of the growing disparities in their development.

To my mind, these asymmetries, which admittedly exist, represent a new challenge, and they have to be taken into account in the diagnosis and formulation of strategies for co-operation. In this respect, I believe that the Report's analysis and proposals should be further elaborated, possibly incorporating more heterodox points of view.

The evolution of the global system increases intra-South differentiation without invalidating co-operation among the developing countries

As an integral part of the complex process of globalization, the formation of economic blocs, together with many other factors that point in the same direction, seems to be destroying – and has already destroyed up to a point – the underlying logic of the North-South divide and of the confrontation and co-operation that follow the same lines. The new economic areas that are taking shape around the European Community, Japan and the United States comprise both developed and developing countries. Similarly, the ongoing trade negotiations show clearly that common interests bring together under the same banner – by sectors, cases and specific situations – both industrialized and developing countries.

What has been described here is indicative of a movement towards more complex configurations in the global system and the disappearance on many occasions of a clear dividing-line between North and South. This confronts the developing countries with a new and more formidable challenge in their policy-making, which generates potential areas for specific co-operation with the North but does not remove the basic asymmetry between North and South in the distribution of resources and of costs and benefits. This still exists and is in urgent need of attention.

The inclusion of these concepts in external policy formulation thus become an essential condition for conferring legitimacy on the exchange of ideas and giving practical viability to action. In this respect, we see a basic line of thinking to be pursued in the studies and discussions to which the Report of the South Commission gives rise.

The cases now arising in the Asian area of the Pacific Basin, as well as the sudden proliferation of proposals for economic integration among the developing countries of those subregions, and the Initiative for the Americas launched by the President of the United States, are processes that should be studied closely. Experience has shown that agreements negotiated between North and South may or may not provide the elements necessary for promoting South–South co-operation. Whether they do so will continue to depend very largely on the position adopted by the developing countries participating in these groupings.

Latin America and the Caribbean vis-à-vis the South Commission Report

The contribution made by the Report of the South Commission to the treatment of the problems of Latin America and the Caribbean is multifaceted and cannot be appreciated at its full value in these pages. Accordingly, in the passages below I discuss only what I consider to be some of its main points and then add a few suggestions to facilitate the application of the initiatives proposed in the Report.

The role of regional integration and of South-South co-operation

Like the other developing regions, Latin America and the Caribbean share many vital interests which are more important than their differences. Nevertheless, the fact is that they are not fully aware of this reality. Despite the great progress made in this respect, they continue to apply approaches that are essentially unilateral and to accept interpretations of the problems and their solutions that have a large foreign content. Moreover, the perception of the international system and of its obstacles and advantages that still prevails relegates the concerted or collective actions that could be more beneficial to the entire region to a relatively minor role in practice.

As SELA (Sistema Económico Latinoamericano) has tirelessly pointed out, the answer to the problems of the developing countries and, more specifically, of the region, should be given by these countries themselves in the light of their own conditions and potentialities. A clear statement on the positive impact to be expected from promoting regional integration and co-operation efforts in order to remedy the structural problems and constraints on the development of our countries should constitute the guide and framework for action and for the links to be established not only among the countries of the South but also between these and the industrialized North.

In this respect one cannot expect the developing countries to be prepared to choose between North-South relations and South-South relations, any more than the developed countries themselves have done. At the same time, it is undeniable that in some sectors of the South there is a feeling, possibly encouraged by the North, that South-South solidarity is tantamount to anti-North solidarity.

This attitude, which can be found in some segments of Latin American society, has to be eradicated, while interest groups and the general public should be made aware of the need to promote regional and interregional co-operation. As the Report recommends, the South must take the initiative in seeking the political endorsement of the North as regards the vital need to promote South-South co-operation; we would nevertheless insist that the South must first be convinced of the desirability of such co-operation.

Domestic problems of the Latin American and Caribbean countries

One of the contributions made by the Report of the South Commission is that it provides an opportunity to reconsider the realities of the situation in Latin America and the Caribbean. The areas singled out in the Report (poverty, the development of human capital, science and technology, regionalism, etcetera) are of direct relevance for each country in the region, whatever its size and level of development. For instance, the concept of people-centred development, which gives special attention to the social dimension and to equity, has become an imperative for the region.

The role of Latin America and the Caribbean in consolidating the efforts of the South

The region has gradually stepped up its efforts in the directions proposed by the Report. It has become more aware of the need to introduce reforms at the national level and to intensify co-operation. It has strengthened and invigorated the processes of subregional integration and regional co-operation itself. Moreover, the region has succeeded in taking up co-ordinated positions, in a consistent manner, on key international subjects such as external debt and the Uruguay Round, thereby positioning itself in the vanguard in the South. Several countries have also forged close ties with other nations of the South in promoting and implementing important international initiatives such as OPEC, the Lom Conventions and the Summit Group on South-South Consultation and Co-operation.

All these advances do not, of course, compensate for the vast deficiencies in a number of important areas, but it does seem that, by comparison with other developing regions, the greater relative homogeneity of Latin America's and the Caribbean's interests and positions, coupled with their institutional experience, offers promising opportunities for making substantive contributions to the movement advocated in the Report.

As regards the deficiencies, it is evident, first, that the regional and subregional institutions have to be strengthened and given the necessary political support for the full achievement of their objectives.

Second, although institutional co-ordination at the regional level is an activity that has made great progress in recent years, interregional co-ordination among the governmental institutions of Latin America and the Caribbean and their counterparts in other regions of the South is virtually non existent. In order to contribute to remedying this problem, the Latin American Council of SELA has recently given the Permanent Secretariat a mandate to develop an extensive exchange of information and experiences with the subregional economic groupings and groups in the Asian area of the Pacific Basin; contacts already exist – and now require strengthening – with some African integration bodies.

Third, it is necessary to revitalize various mechanisms for regional and interregional co-operation. The possibilities afforded by technical co-operation among developing countries are still relatively little used in Latin America and for South-South co-operation. The Action Committees, a flexible arm of SELA, could play a much more important part in regional and interregional co-operation than they have done so far. They might perhaps be used as mechanisms for co-operation among the countries in different regions of the South. The South needs to develop its capacity to sustain an adequate growth rate, even if the driving force of the North slows down or is restricted in practice.

The South, in general, has enough markets and resources to make South-South co-operation into an effective instrument for adding to its economic options. Such co-operation is also a strategic necessity for ensuring the equitable management of world interdependence and the search for new models for international relations.

What must be recognized above all is that there is no magic recipe for relieving the developing countries of the present crisis. The only possible prescription demands effort, perseverance and a vision of the future that at times may seem incompatible with the urgent political and social demands of our countries. The realization of the need to act in concert is the nucleus of a possible solution, and a challenge to our maturity as sovereign states.

IV. GLOBAL DEVELOPMENT POLICIES

21. EFFECTIVE DEVELOPMENT STRATEGIES

Michel Camdessus

The task of the 28 eminent members of the South Commission was a daunting one: to distil lessons about effective development strategies from the varied experience of the developing countries. The quality and coherence of their Report marks yet another step toward a broad consensus on the essential elements of successful economic policies. My comments will focus on the need for further elaboration of that growing consensus and on its implications for policies in all countries, North as well as South, and for global economic institutions, especially the one I have the honour to head.

The South Commission's vision of a world united, not divided, on issues related to international economic development could not be more timely. The end of the Cold War offers a chance to shift resources from unproductive military expenditure to productive ends, but also to enlarge the scope for global collaboration to address a wide range of challenges, especially the challenge of economic development. International dialogue need no longer be constrained by narrow premises; the lessons of experience can be viewed pragmatically, without ideological blinkers. In fact, a "silent revolution" in thinking about appropriate economic policies has been under way for some time; the South Commission has given voice to views generally consistent with the new thinking.

The South Commission emphasizes that achieving high and sustainable rates of economic growth in developing countries is essential in order to create the resources than can provide people with a better life, but growth alone will not ensure that all sectors, including the poor, share in its benefits. The Report states that "the process of growth has to be oriented so as to raise the income and productivity of the poor and to promote a sustainable use of the scarce natural resources and the environment".[1] I share the Commission's concern for the quality of growth. As I have said on other occasions, "high-quality growth" must be both sustainable, in that it is based upon domestic and external financial stability, but also dynamic and equitable, in that it creates the conditions for future expansion by enhancing investment – in human capital in particular – by preserving the environmental base of the economy, and by raising the level of savings on a sustainable basis. High-quality growth is concerned, therefore, with the poor, the weak and the vulnerable, with the atmosphere, the rivers, the forests, the oceans, or with any part of human-kind's common heritage, as well as with the self-sustaining process of growth.

The New Role of the State in the Economy

The convergence of views extends as well to the types of economic policies most likely to lead to high-quality growth, or what the South Commission terms "people-centred development". Generally speaking, such policies entail quite a different role for the state from that which has been the prevailing pattern in many countries. The South Commission has noted that "most governments in the South tended to overcentralize administration and planning", which in turn led to "snail-pace decision-making and to inefficiency, and that it had particularly harmful consequences for the management of public enterprises and financial systems".

What the Commission appears to be calling for is a more pragmatic approach to defining the role of government in economic matters – a revision, not necessarily a diminution, of the role of the state: "The aim should be to modernize the state apparatus, as well as to create a stable and development-oriented macro-economic framework, encourage entrepreneurship, initiative, and innovation, and make the public sector more efficient." In addition to modernizing the state apparatus it is important that the role of the state be reduced through privatization, and that the state's interventions in the economic life of the nation must become more selective, more supportive of than competitive with the private sector and less costly. This is the essence of the new role for the state in the economy to bring about sustainable growth with equity.

The state has three key economic responsibilities: sound macro-economic management, providing an appropriate institutional and legislative framework for the market economy, and strengthening human and physical infrastructure. Simply put, governments can increase their chances of economic success if they aim at: firm macro-economic policies that establish a framework of financial stability and are conducive to steady, sustainable growth; structural reforms that establish an appropriately decentralized system of decision-making and responsibility; and an effective pattern of incentives – to work, to save and to invest – and a regulatory framework to supervise and maintain the market infrastructure, and to decide delicate and complex distributional issues.

The importance of firm macro-economic policies is no longer questioned. The South Commission has made the case quite strongly in its Report:

No country can make economic progress without reasonably stable macro-economic conditions. Fiscal, monetary, and exchange rate policies must be used to achieve a high level of savings and investment while avoiding excessive balance-of-payments deficits and controlling inflationary pressures. Such a macro-economic setting is essential to provide a reasonably predictable basis for making economic decisions, particularly those relating to investments in new industrial and commercial undertakings, and therefore for continuing economic growth.[2]

I would add that sound policies at the macro level, especially in fiscal and monetary policies, must persevere and be complemented by effective financial discipline at lower levels – local government, the financial sector and especially at the level of the individual firm – if economic reforms are to succeed. This probably means giving up some long-held habits – for example, the tendency to subsidize or protect inefficient or ailing companies. In some countries, the banking system effectively became an arm of the central government, extending credit to mostly inefficient public sector enterprises. The lack of effective credit control, and the inability of the banks to refuse requests for credit even when it was obvious that it would never be repaid, contributed in no small way to a rapid increase in the money supply and in inflation. It is therefore essential, when implementing a far-reaching reform programme, to maintain financial discipline because high inflation makes nonsense of price signals. It distorts savings and investment, and has arbitrary effects on social equity.

The need for structural reform is also widely acknowledged by the international community, although the timing and extent of reform often generate controversy. The South Commission reinforces the case for structural reforms in developing countries "to strengthen the performance of the public sector and its resource-generating capacity, improve tax systems, and create a stable environment in which the private sector can play its role in line with national priorities". The Commission adds that "reforms are required to promote exports, the earnings from which could be used to pay for imports and thus to contribute to the efficient management of the balance of payments".[3] Elsewhere in its Report the Commission identifies harmful effects arising from restrictive pricing policies, noting that "policies on tariffs, exchange rates, and domestic prices have often discriminated against agricultural producers, including peasant farmers",[4] and that policies preventing public enterprises from charging realistic product prices have limited earnings and thereby limited reinvestment, thus lowering efficiency and keeping costs high. Private industry has also suffered from indiscriminate tax incentives, subsidized credit, or protection against imports: "In many cases these concessions have been granted as giveaways and not made conditional on satisfactory performance; the results have been to bestow unfair benefits on a favoured few at the taxpayer's expense, to place an additional burden on public finances, and to retard advances in technology and learning processes within the private sector."

A first important element of reform must be a decisive move toward price liberalization: prices in the broadest sense of the word, that is, including the price of money, the interest rate and the price of foreign exchange, the exchange rate. Restoring market signals is the first crucial step in the transition towards a growth-oriented economy, because it clearly exposes the costs and benefits of different policy measures and allows both the governments and enterprises and households to make fully informed, economically efficient choices.

A second essential element of reform is the restructuring of economic institutions. Parastatals need to be transformed from recipients of government subsidies into profitable entities, and loss-making state enterprises privatized. The banking system should be reorganized to better serve the community's financial needs and to facilitate the channelling of savings to the productive sectors of the economy. The tax system needs to be reformed and government expenditure reoriented to raise savings and to promote investment, thus fostering economic growth.

A third major element of reform is a policy giving a more outward-looking orientation to the economy. Many economies now beginning their transition have suffered long years of isolation, frequently behind high walls of tariff protection and a multitude of quantitative restrictions. A more outward orientation can bring several benefits. In addition to the well-known gains from international trade, an open orientation imposes on domestic producers the valuable discipline of international competition, providing them with the incentive to produce higher-quality goods at reasonable prices. It offers opportunities for new exports and can attract much-needed capital and expertise into an economy. In addition to an exchange-rate system that is more responsive to market signals, the increased outward orientation of the reforming economies is characterized by the elimination of red tape surrounding external trade, such as the simplification of licensing and other administrative procedures, which have frequently impeded private sector development in the past. The liberalization of external trade also implies that importation of luxury consumer goods will be subject to appropriate tariffs. New investment codes, encouraging productive investment by both domestic and foreign investors, and the seeking of joint venture partners in all areas of the economy can also help to attract much-needed technical expertise. Outward-looking polices do not mean, of course, that production for domestic markets should be neglected. Particularly in food production, it will be important to ensure that a sound and efficient domestic production base is maintained, as the South Commission has stressed in its Report.

The Report contains a particularly useful discussion of possible initiatives to promote regional co-operation among developing countries. Among its many recommendations, the Commission advises that "controls on trade and foreign exchange should be rolled back, product coverage extended, and non-tariff barriers removed".[5] Expanding regional co-operation by reducing trade barriers and promoting freer exchange of investment and technology can make an important contribution to economic development, provided an outward orientation is maintained at the regional level as well as the national level. This is as essential for the regional arrangements established by industrialized countries as it is for those linking developing countries, as the South Commission recognizes. Otherwise the gains from international trade could begin to shrink as preferential regional trade barriers arise. This would be especially damaging to the economic prospects of the developing countries.

A fourth key element of reform must be closer attention by governments to the linkages between economic and social objectives. Laying the foundation for sustainable economic growth is certainly essential to the provision of income-enhancing opportunities for the poor, as well as to the financing of social services, but major economic changes have a significant effect on income distribution and, to be successful, reform efforts must address the impact of certain measures, especially on the most vulnerable or disadvantaged groups in society. Contrary to what is stated in the South Commission Report, I can certainly attest to the efforts the International Monetary Fund has been making in recent years to encourage and assist governments to incorporate equity considerations into their economic reform packages, including both ways to alleviate poverty and ways to protect poor and vulnerable groups during adjustment. Existing information on poverty in member countries is increasingly being gathered and analysed. Discussions are held with the authorities on how economic policies affect poor and vulnerable groups and ways to improve those policies so as to strengthen their positive effects and minimize any adverse effects on the poor. Among the means considered are: the mix as well as the specific nature of revenue and expenditure measures that can be designed to help, or at least not to have undue adverse effects on, the poor; the efficiency of the actual administration of taxes and expenditure; the possible need for targeted subsidies and other social expenditures to shelter the poor; and the introduction of various forms of "social safety nets" to supplement existing formal and informal arrangements. The Fund also helps to mobilize external financial support for economic programmes, including well-designed measures to mitigate any short-run adverse effects of such programmes on the poor.

A basic principle underlying, and to a degree constraining, the Fund's work in support of the incorporation of equity considerations or other factors into the adjustment process is respect for a country's prerogative to make its own social and distributional choices in its adjustment, growth and development processes. I note that the South Commission proposes no change in this regard in the fundamental relationship between the international community and the state. In fact, the Commission's Report rightly emphasizes throughout the primary responsibility of the state for fostering economic and social development.

The South Commission envisages economic development which is largely self-reliant and necessarily country-specific. There can be no disagreement with its view that "to be workable, a policy package must be country-specific, that is, suited to a country's particular circumstances, and free of ideological bias".[6] Certainly this is true of the Fund's economic policy advice and Fund-supported reform programmes. The great variety of policy measures included in such programmes and the considerable variation in the mix of major components are well documented, and do not justify the old references to the so-called single rigid model, which does not do justice to the Fund's persistent efforts to help countries design policy packages appropriate to their specific situation, including their administrative and financial resources.

Mobilizing Resources for Adjustment and Investment

The South Commission Report devotes much attention to the problem of securing financial resources to finance adjustment and investment in developing countries. The IMF is concerned with many facets of this problem. We have highlighted the growing global demand for savings and our concern that the projected supply of savings may well be insufficient at unchanged real interest rates. This presents an important challenge to the system of international economic co-operation and reflects an immediate and pressing need for each and every country to raise savings in order to avoid an increase in real interest rates – which would aggravate the debt-servicing burden of developing countries and probably lead to a crowding out of investment – especially in the poorer developing countries – and lower economic growth.

The industrial countries will have to make the largest effort, in view of their size and their importance in global financial flows. In essence, they need to improve their own fiscal performance, and so raise their own national savings. There is ample scope for the industrial countries to make this effort, especially by reducing unproductive spending; money wasted in prestige projects, protectionism, maintenance of unviable public enterprises, and very frequently excessive military expenditures. In a world characterized by reduced global tensions and the settlement of several regional conflicts, there is significant scope for reductions in military spending. For example, if countries had reduced their military spending by 20 per cent from the average level of 1972-1988, the global annual savings would have amounted to roughly 180 billion US dollars in the 1988 world economy.

Open international markets and a multilateral trading system based on clear and enforceable rules are essential if developing countries are to reap the full benefits of their economic reforms, including strengthening their export performance, which would lessen their need to import capital. The slow progress of the Uruguay Round is therefore very disappointing. A successful and timely conclusion of these negotiations is the most important item on the international agenda; and by successful, I mean an outcome that includes a removal of barriers to trade in such sectors as agriculture, textiles and clothing, as well as impediments to export diversification.

More balanced fiscal and monetary policies and more open trade policies in the North would help enormously, but official development assistance (ODA) is also indispensable. I am concerned, as is the South Commission, by predictions that ODA will not grow substantially in the near future. We cannot resign ourselves to this. I do not see any convinc-ing reasons for the industrial countries at the beginning of the last decade of this century to find any less binding the United Nations objective of devoting to ODA 0.7 per cent of their GDP, as they are only halfway towards its achievement. But in any case, even if, to my regret, the provision of ODA is not expected to grow substantially, there are several ways in which the industrial countries are actively seeking to enhance the usefulness of their assistance, focusing it better on truly productive investment, particularly in human resources, while streamlining their procedures for the approval and disbursement of such assistance.

The South Commission has underscored the problem of the external debt of developing countries. Some progress has already been achieved in debt relief, particularly in the co-operative framework of the Paris Club, and there have been several useful initiatives on the debt problems of the low-income countries – including that proposed by the British Prime Minister, John Major, when he was Chancellor of the Exchequer, for substantial reductions in the burden of official bilateral debt. At the London Summit in July 1991, the Heads of State or Government of the Group of Seven agreed that additional debt relief was needed, on a case-by-case basis, for the poorest and most indebted countries. Since December 1991, enhanced concessions are being offered in the Paris Club to low-income countries undertaking adjustment, including options in most cases for reduction of consolidated debt-service payments by 50 per cent. Official creditors also agree to consider reducing the stock of debt after three to five years of successful adjustment. I welcome this commitment to more far-reaching debt relief, and I am hopeful that the Paris Club will also soon recognize the special situation of some highly indebted lower-middle-income countries on a case-by-case basis. These more concessional debt restructurings are, in my view, indispensable for many countries, where the magnitude of debt overhang remains a major obstacle to sustainable growth and external viability.

The South Commission advises developing countries to press the North to do all I have just mentioned and more, but the Commission also prudently advises the South not to count upon significant improvement in the international economic environment in the decade of the 1990s. The Commission concludes that: "the development of the South will therefore need to be fuelled by its own resources to a much greater degree than in the past".[7] These resources can be mobilized by the developing countries – by cutting unproductive spending, promoting domestic savings and improving the efficiency of their economies. To the extent they succeed in implementing such policies they are also likely to find external financing more readily available from both official and private sources. Stronger economic programmes can both attract more external finance and accomplish more with a given amount of finance. The lesson, therefore, with which the South Commission would agree, is that bolder, more comprehensive adjustment is needed, not half-measures timidly adopted.

Participation and the Pace of Economic Reform

The South Commission, under the heading of "people-centred develop-ment", gives high priority to the "democratization of political structures and the modernization of the state".[8] This is not only morally correct, but also economically sound advice. The introduction of better management of the economy, greater transparency in policies, the elimination of complex regulatory procedures, the increased accountability of public institutions, and the dissemination to the public of adequate information about the economic situation: all these interconnected reforms would greatly facilitate the task of national consensus-building that is essential if effective economic strategies are to be implemented successfully. It is important to note here that the experience of many countries suggests that the population prefers to be told the truth, and to participate in serious efforts to correct the economy's weaknesses. In practice the people recognize that this is the only way to achieve genuine economic progress, and so establish the basis for improving their living standards.

Conclusion

The South Commission has proclaimed an ambitious set of goals for the developing countries, and its recommendations to industrial and developing countries, and to international organizations, are far-reaching. Many would require decision at the highest political level; many raise complex technical issues. All are constructive, however, and deserve to be studied and discussed more widely in the North as well as in the South. I am very glad, therefore, that the South Centre has been established as the follow-up office of the South Commission and will ensure that the Commission's Report is disseminated to all corners of the world, in several languages, and that it receives the serious consideration it deserves.

I have addressed just three themes within the rich panoply provided by the Commission: (a) the importance and, indeed, urgency of redefining the role of the state in the economy – one which gives greater scope to market forces but is certainly no less strategic than the role the state has played heretofore; (b) the challenge to the North as well as to the South to release additional resources for productive investment in developing countries; and (c) the merit of widening participation – and thereby understanding – by the public in the economic policy reform process, without compromising on the vigour, alacrity and thoroughness of reform. These are, to my mind, the critical items on the agenda for action. But they must be subordinate to a higher criterion, as the South Commission so eloquently reminds us:

> All economic processes are ultimately meant to serve the interest of human beings. Hence an abiding concern with social justice must go hand in hand with the pursuit of economic efficiency. It is only through a commitment to social justice that the call to dedicated collective effort for development can be sustained, its objectives given a high moral purpose, and the spirit of human solidarity kept alive.[9]

Notes

1. South Commission, 1990, p.83.
2. Ibid., p.118.
3. Ibid., p.67.
4. Ibid., p.90.
5. Ibid., pp.209-210.
6. Ibid., p.240.
7. Ibid., p.79.
8. Ibid., p.80.
9. Ibid., pp.275-276.

Bibliography

South Commission
The Challenge to the South: The Report of the South Commission, Oxford University Press, Oxford and New York, 1990.

22. SOUTH CO-OPERATION: NATIONAL DETERMINANTS

Bernard Chidzero

In its comprehensive and epoch-making Report, *The Challenge to the South*, the South Commission has placed great emphasis on what it has termed "The National Dimension". By this expression it wants to refer not only to "self-reliant and people-oriented development", but also to the wide range of state policy measures dealing with monetary and financial, trade and other issues.

National policies are the foundations for the successful pursuit of development objectives, at the national as well as the regional or inter-country level. What obtains or happens in one country not only determines the course of development or the political stability of that country; it also impacts directly or indirectly, favourably or unfavourably, on the form or modality or speed of regional co-operation. The reason is that nations are sovereign entities in themselves, as well as being the building blocks of regional co-operation or integration.

The range of issues is wide and complex. In the comments that follow, the term "national determinants" refers to a variety of matters covered in varying measure in the South Commission's Report, selected here to emphasize their critical importance to the very concept of the challenge to the South.

Not of Our Making

It is evident that there are "national determinants" which are physical or inherited yet bear on the fortune or course of events in forging regional or South-South co-operation. The size of nations (in area and population, for instance) and physical location (coastal or landlocked), natural resource base, inherited stage of physical and social infrastructure, and linkage with erstwhile "metropolitan" or former colonial powers – to say nothing of the vicissitudes or hazards of nature – all these are national determinants which directly influence development objectives and policy measures, inward-looking or outward-looking, narrowly self-reliant or collectively self-reliant.

Too often regional integration draws strength from the theory of comparative advantage and from the concept of collective self-reliance but tends to underplay the importance of determinants, like those cited above, which necessitate specific or preferential measures to address or assist to address those national factors which influence national perceptions, attitudes, and policy objectives or measures.

Deliberate Policy Determinants

Whether based on comprehensive national planning, indicative planning or simply on pragmatism in the approach to national socio-economic development, very often development objectives and their related policy measures are determined by national governements much more with respect to the national situation and the general international or world situation than with respect to the requirements for regional or South co-operation. How otherwise explain the fact – taking the African case for instance – that for a long time and at least in the majority of cases, the Lagos Plan of Action was seldom if ever incorporated in national development plans and policy instruments. Yet the Plan had been conceived and agreed as the framework for regional co-operation and development.

Furthermore, fiscal and monetary policies are adopted by individual countries in response to domestic conditions – inflation, unemployment, inadequate investment and growth, national or public debt and so on. In doing so, countries seldom if ever really take account of the possible impact on the economies of regional partners or on the process of forging and strengthening integration.

It was in realization of this state of affairs, again to take an African example, that in 1990 the Preferential Trade Area for Eastern and Southern Africa (PTA) established a regional Monetary and Financial Co- operation Committee, consisting of experts from central banks and ministries of finance, which reports to a Standing Committee of Governors of Central Banks, the latter reporting to a Committee of Finance Ministers. The objective was precisely to minimize the risk of conflicting fiscal and monetary policies and to give substance to monetary and financial harmonization within the framework of a broader treaty arrangement already agreed, and purposively to foster the habit of thinking and acting regionally.

Whereas the objective of South-South co-operation, regional or otherwise, is to promote in time the freer movement of goods and services, capital and labour, co-operating countries not infrequently take measures which have the opposite effect because of national considerations. Hence the national paraphernalia of exchange controls, import and export licensing, customs regulations of varying range and character, immigration controls and so on, treaty obligations notwithstanding.

Adjustment with National and Regional Growth

Virtually every developing country has carried out or is carrying out, in one form or another, a structural adjustment programme. What is most striking about these programmes, particularly those inspired by the Bretton Woods institutions, is that the macro-economic frameworks are individual country-centred or country-specific. Growth rates, inflation rates, exchange rates, fiscal deficits and current account deficits are all country-specific. So are the remedial measures. It is not certain, to say the least, that if one put together all these programmes, which in fact do not take account of regional dimensions, one would come up with mutually supporting programmes promotive of regional South co-operation. Furthermore, the programmes all tend to seek to promote trade liberalization and export-driven development. Regional requirements are not always clear or for that matter taken duly into account. In any case, how can we all be exporters without being importers at the same time!

The external financing of these programmes also tends to foster inward-looking policies, in so far as both the structural adjustment lending (SAL) or policy lending is country-specific and necessarily reinforces a measure of economic nationalism. More regional efforts by the World Bank and the International Monetary Fund are required in this field than is evident at present.

A particular point concerns tied aid in the financing of adjustment programmes. This form of aid is in practice not promotive of regional trade and development.

Would the situation not be different if national structural adjustment programmes were conceived and formulated within the framework of regional or multi-country programmes and financed accordingly?

It does appear that the predominant concepts and programmes of structural adjustment pose yet another challenge to the South.

Facing Challenges in a New World Order

The Challenge to the South rightly and forcefully deals with the issues of poverty, environment and sustainable development, as well as those which bear on human resources development and people's participation (including in particular human rights and the rule of law), technology transfer, transformation of the agricultural sector and food security. Yet for the most part national perceptions of these vital issues have tended to be narrowly confined within national frontiers. Admittedly, national policies and measures are called for, but the challenges transcend individual countries, the more so in a divided world, at a time when the North-South dialogue is increasingly subordinated to the acceleration of East-West co-operation and to the formation of regional economic blocs which could, say in the case of sub-Saharan Africa, lead to even greater marginalization.

The Challenge to the South has to do in this context with both the conceptualization and formulation of appropriate national policies, that is, policies consistent with or promotive of regional or South-South co-operation and drawing on the strength of collective efforts. But the challenge goes beyond that, especially given the policies or practices of industrialized countries in such matters as interest rates and exchange rate changes or adjustments regardless of their impact on the economies of developing countries, or in the matter of agricultural, industrial and trade policies that are by no means always promotive of interests of the Third World. In the face of all this, the challenge is how to strengthen the leverage of the South and collective bargaining to effect changes in the world system which for too long has been ethnocentric or Western-oriented in values, institutions and practices, especially in the domains of money, trade and technology control. But it must be underlined that the unity of the South is not a negation of North-South co-operation or a form of inward-looking "trade-unionism" of the Third World; rather, it is a necessary strengthening of the Third World with a view to rendering interdependence more meaningful, even if the co-operating units are of unequal strengths. This unity engenders self-respect as well as respect by others and contributes positively to the totality of world co-operation in a new world order in which multilateralism is the handmaid.

It is the primary responsibility of every developing country to eradicate poverty, to combat environmental degradation, to develop its own human resources and acquire technology, to institute human-oriented development and feed its people and improve their standard of living. But on no account should national efforts complicate or frustrate regional co-operation or lead to regional conflicts (for example on population movements and border issues). Indeed, the tasks are easier if tackled collectively.

There is also a broader imperative – and that is that the external or world environment must be favourable and helpful, materially as well as morally supportive in a whole range of tasks: to eradicate poverty, to prevent or control environmental degradation, to control the spread of such evils as AIDS and drug addiction, and to achieve sustainable development. Here it is not only the flow of resources (assistance and investment) that one has in mind; it is also changes or adjustment in the trade, monetary and industrial policies of the North – changes in favour of a more united world, for greater multilateralism, justice and equity. Here again, success is largely dependent on co-operative efforts and concerted policies. What is required is good national governance and good international governance.

A Concluding Thought

Perhaps the most deep-seated challenge to the South has to do with new ideas and institutions which would respond to the real problems and needs of the South, albeit relying on different models of development. Human-centred yes; sustainable development, yes; environment consciousness, yes. But can poverty, which is the biggest bane and challenge, be eradicated in the South on the basis of market forces, with the nation state providing only the legal and institutional framework? Is the nation state an adequate framework? I fear not.

National sovereignty should not be incompatible with a limitation of sovereign rights in co-operative entities such as are currently being created in the North as well as in the South. But the world environment and its institutions have to be favourable as well. And all this requires vision of a new order and sustained political will at the national as well as at the international level.

23. POLICIES FOR SUSTAINED GROWTH AND POVERTY REDUCTION

Barber Conable

The Challenge to the South is a singularly important document. The Report's emphasis on the national dimensions of development is a welcome change. It recognizes the policy and institutional shortcomings of many developing countries as a factor contributing to inadequate performance. At the same time, the Report correctly notes the importance of a wide range of external factors in conditioning the success or failure of developing countries' own efforts. This balanced discussion is a major contribution of the Report.

Sustained Growth and Poverty Reduction: Development Goals for the 1990s

The international development community has set two great goals for itself for the final decade of this century: the achievement of sustainable economic growth, and a significant reduction in poverty in developing countries. While some countries in the developing world managed to maintain (and even accelerate) growth during the 1980s, many among them – especially in sub-Saharan Africa and Latin America – contracted and fell further behind in providing for the essential needs of the poor. It is crucial that the current decade witness the resumption of accelerated growth throughout the developing world. This is essential to attaining all other development objectives. Moreover, the pattern of growth will be a key determinant of poverty reduction. The developing world is home to over 1.1 billion poor. Widespread poverty in developing countries is both a drag on economic growth and an affront to elementary notions of human decency. Reducing poverty deserves the highest priority.

The Importance of Domestic Reforms

Of course, attaining sustained growth and reducing poverty are difficult tasks. But they are realizable. As amply discussed by the Report, they will require greater attention to the mobilization of domestic resources and far-reaching policy reforms. Recent years have seen a growing consensus on the nature of the necessary measures, and the Report is another example of the widespread agreement characterizing current views on development. Notable, for example, is its discussion of the respective roles of the private and public sectors, which reflects a pragmatic realization that both have essential functions to perform. The private sector is crucial for stimulating growth and creating employment. The public sector needs to foster an enabling environment for private enterprise and to reduce poverty through the efficient provision of social services for human resource development, the installation of basic infrastructure in both rural and urban areas, and protection of the physical environment. For me, the heightened awareness of the complementarities of the private and public sectors in the pursuit of sustainable growth and poverty reduction is a distinguished feature of the Report.

Other aspects of the Report's discussion of the national dimension of development are noteworthy. I will refer to only a few here. One is the recognition of the need for substantially increased attention to the environmental aspects of development. Growth that despoils the environment will not be sustainable. Measures to reduce poverty can also reduce the poor's necessity for recourse to environmentally threatening activities. There are, however, difficult trade-offs, and developing countries will need considerable policy advice and adequate financial resources to ensure that their growth is compatible with environmental protection.

Human resource development is essential to poverty reduction. The provision of education, health and family planning services is fundamentally the responsibility of governments. Some have met the challenge and provided for human resource development in a cost-effective manner – even at relatively low levels of per capita GNP. Others, however, have largely failed to achieve human capital formation – even at relatively high levels of per capita GNP. Many lessons have been learned about the successful provision of social services, their financing and delivery, and the many synergies among them. It is vital that successful experiences be replicated elsewhere if the developing world's greatest resource – its people – is to be developed. Increased support for family planning services and more general measures for enhancing the economic role of women in development will be central aspects of ensuring human resource development in many countries.

Resource-constrained developing countries need to make tough choices about the allocation and reallocation of their public expenditures. Increasing such expenditures for environmental protection and human resource development is a case in point. Where are the domestic resources for these and other key activities to come from? As the Report notes, increased efforts at mobilizing necessary domestic resources will be essential. In some cases this may call for tax reform, likely to be difficult to engineer both technically and politically. Increased public savings through reduced budget deficits will be called for. It is also crucially important to increase domestic savings in the private sector and to adopt policies toward that end. Greater efficiency in the use of all resources will clearly be required.

A dramatic example of the need to reallocate resources is military expenditures. Such spending is excessive in many developing countries; in a number of them defence spending as a proportion of total government expenditure is above 20 per cent. In recent years, developing countries have spent almost as much on arms imports as on all their health programmes. Expenditures by developing countries on their armed forces are about five times the amount they receive from abroad in concessional assistance. Much of these expenditures are of course facilitated by the intense competition among arms exporters and, hence, easy access to subsidized finance. While there is no simple criterion for identifying an appropriate level of military expenditures, I am firmly of the belief that developing countries need to scrutinize such expenditures rigorously to determine the scope for promoting development more effectively.

Another aspect of the national dimension of development I would like to stress is what the Report calls "modernizing the state". There is increasing recognition that development in many countries is impeded by the low level of institutional capacity, the lack of accountability and transparency in government activities, absence of the rule of law, lack of popular participation in decision-making and outright corruption. Progress in improving these aspects of governmental performance will be essential to meeting the goals of sustained growth and poverty reduction. This is not a matter of imposing a "neo-colonial" agenda on developing countries. It is a simple statement of fact.

Co-operation among Developing Countries

Progress with these and other far-reaching domestic policy and institutional reforms is a necessary but by no means sufficient requirement for attaining the goals sought by the development community. That is why the South Commission Report rightly stresses the supportive role that can be played by two additional factors: greater co-operation among developing countries themselves, and needed improvements in aspects of the relations between developing and developed countries.

So far as co-operation among developing countries is concerned, the Report is undoubtedly correct in arguing that "there has been a wide gap between ... the rhetoric of solidarity ... and the action that has ensued".[1] While further actions are required to strengthen financial, trade and other linkages among developing countries, it is important to recognize that these cannot simply be legislated into existence or brought about in an excessively voluntaristic fashion. Rather, greater South-South co-operation will only occur in a positive way as the logical result of a more integrated and better functioning global system of trade and financial relations – not through carving out artificial networks among selected countries of the developing world.

For this reason, I am not persuaded of the "compelling necessity" of setting up a South Bank along the lines discussed in the Report. In my view, the existing set of institutional arrangements, including the World Bank and the regional development banks as well as the assistance agencies of the United Nations system, serves developing countries well. This is not to say that there is no room for improvement. It is apparent, for example, that the scope for improving co-operation and co-ordination among these various bodies – and for ensuring that the interests of developing countries are systematically taken into account in all their activities – is abundant. They will, however, be successful supporters of developing countries' own efforts precisely to the extent that they do not pose the false antinomy of North versus South.

Relations between Developed and Developing Countries

Looking at the third pillar of the Report's analytical framework – the nature of relations between developing and developed countries – it is clear that a number of initiatives are required to create a more favourable international environment for development. Three areas are particularly crucial: trade, aid and debt.

The Report correctly stresses the vital importance of export growth and diversification to the development efforts of developing countries. Both are threatened by increased developed-country protectionism. Indeed, 20 of 24 OECD economies are, on balance, more protectionist now than they were 10 years ago. The Uruguay Round's slow progress shows how vulnerable the principle of open trade remains. There can be no sustained adjustment and economic growth – and thus no lasting poverty reduction – without a more liberalized and dynamic international trading system, one that takes the trade interests of developing countries fully into account, particularly in agriculture and clothing textiles.

Similarly, the mobilization of substantial external resources – to complement the increased domestic resource mobilization efforts of the developing countries – will be crucial for attaining development objectives. Concessional assistance will be particularly important for low-income countries. The prognosis is poor. Flows of official development assistance (ODA) are projected to grow by only about 2 per cent a year in real terms for the foreseeable future – or less than the projected rate of growth in GNP in the principal donor countries. Donors should strive to do better. While there is a clear need for the more effective use of concessional resources by recipients, such increased effectiveness must be complemented by more assistance. A number of changes are also required in the effectiveness with which concessional resources are supplied by donors -- including less "tying" of assistance and reallocation of scarce aid resources toward low-income countries.

Other sources of external capital, including private direct investment, are also taking on added importance. However, a number of factors affecting both the supply and demand of capital imply a relative shortage of global savings in the years ahead. This in turn implies that real interest rates will remain at high levels during the medium term unless developed countries adopt appropriate macro-economic policies. Even if such policies are implemented, however, investors – heedful of the risks they have incurred in the past – are likely to be increasingly selective in the destination of their funds. Accordingly, it will be ever more important that developing countries create conditions which will attract foreign capital. Stimulating effective demand for foreign capital will be a major challenge for many countries – perhaps an even greater challenge than increasing the global supply of savings.

Debt remains, as before, a critical item on the international development agenda. While considerable progress has been made in relieving the debt and debt-servicing burden of many countries, there is ample scope for more far-reaching actions. For severely indebted low-income countries, mainly but not exclusively in sub-Saharan Africa, this means further concessional debt relief going well beyond "Toronto terms". I am pleased that this necessity was explicitly recognized by the Heads of State of the Group of Seven meeting in London in July 1991. While actions taken on behalf of the exceptional cases of Egypt and Poland are of historic significance, further efforts are required to deal with the debt burdens of other lower-middle-income countries with high levels of debt to official creditors. Severely indebted middle-income countries persisting with their adjustment efforts also deserve additional external support from creditors.

In short, the developed countries and international assistance agencies have the responsibility of ensuring that international conditions better support the wide-ranging reforms many developing countries are undertaking. Actions taken (or not taken) by the developed world could tip the balance toward success or failure for reforming countries.

The World Bank and World Development

Looking back on my years at the World Bank, I was struck by the congruence between many of the recommendations for domestic policy initiatives in *The Challenge to the South* and the recent work of the Bank — in its policy dialogues with borrowers, in its country assistance strategies, and in its lending operations. As a new President takes up the challenge of development, I am confident that the World Bank is well poised to assist developing countries in meeting their objectives of sustained growth and poverty reduction. Working in concert with other members of the development community over the course of this decade, the Bank can help to ensure that developing countries enter the 21st century as rapidly growing and full-fledged participants in the global economy. Toward that end, *The Challenge to the South* has charted a prudent and wise course.

Notes

1. South Commission, 1990, p.149.

Bibliography

South Commission
   The Challenge to the South: The Report of the South Commission, Oxford University Press, Oxford and New York, 1990.

24. NATIONAL AND INTERNATIONAL POLICIES FOR DEVELOPMENT

K.K.S. Dadzie

The Report of the South Commission is a political statement of great significance. Characterized by courage, realism and farsightedness, it cogently sets forth the premises for reinvigorating the development dialogue, a dialogue without which the considerable potential benefits of interdependence, for the South as for the North, cannot be realized. It brings to the notice of the international community a fresh vision from the South regarding the historical process of international co-operation for development and new ideas for breaking through the limitations which have plagued the development process in the South. It is unquestionably a valuable contribution to the efforts of the international community to bridge the gap between the haves and the have-nots.

The first of three main themes of the Report, referred to as the national dimension, emphasizes self-reliant, people-centred development and gives high priority to satisfying basic needs. There is a clear recognition that the countries of the South will have to rely increasingly on their own exertions, both individual and collective, and to reorient their development strategies towards the cultivation of a participatory culture in which development takes place from the bottom up, rather than the top down.

The Report rightly considers that high rates of economic growth are indispensable in order to generate the resources needed to satisfy basic needs and to support a progressive improvement in living standards. It accordingly stresses the importance of generating and mobilizing large increases in domestic savings to finance productive investment and, therefore, growth and development.

Giving effect to these broad policy prescriptions raises a number of questions which require continuing exploration in the dialogue on international economic co-operation for development. Achieving the required high rates of growth, for example, depends to a considerable extent on the implementation of effective adjustment programmes. How for instance should such programmes be designed and implemented so as to deliver effective adjustment with growth, equity and a human face? What are the policy measures most likely to raise levels of domestic savings and to ensure the most efficient use of financial resources? And what are the policy and institutional requirements for establishing the stable and predictable environment necessary to encourage savings and investment including foreign direct investment?

The issue of more effective development strategies and policies, which the Report also addresses in the context of the national dimension, is particularly important in the light of the experience of crisis management in the 1980s. This experience, it is recalled, entailed in many countries of the South drastic reductions in expenditures on social services, cuts in investment and the neglect of a number of other important development objectives. If development is to fulfil its long-term objective of improving the human condition, then it should entail a fuller participation of all sections of the population in the process and a fairer distribution of the benefits of economic growth. The recommendations of the Report of the South Commission in this area are a timely reminder of this important dimension of development. They also challenge us to approach development from a social perspective and to devise ways of translating such a perspective into workable policies.

National development policy is not, of course, amenable to the universal application of a single model. Yet there is no substitute for sustained national policies directed at liberating and mobilizing all the latent energies and impulses for development within developing countries, at promoting efficiency in the allocation and use of resources, and at taking advantage of the opportunities for trade, investment and technological progress provided by the changing global economic environment. Developing countries need to persist with or step up their efforts, in accordance with their national plans and priorities, to modernize their economies, keep control over inflationary tendencies, promote domestic savings, foster entrepreneurship, achieve favourable conditions for domestic and foreign investment, and increase their international competitiveness.

As well as macro-economic policy, the Report addresses the cluster of questions relating to the reform of the apparatus of government which, described as "good governance", have now become a major focus of concern in the development co-operation policies of developed countries. The need is for accountability to the public, transparency of government activities and an independent and honest judiciary, enforcement of the rule of law, and independent systems for public evaluation of government conduct. The South must indeed pay greater attention to these imperatives, not because of pressures from the North, but in its own self-interest in the cause of real development. Among other considerations, a predictable framework is essential for private sector activity, not least in order to reduce the uncertainties affecting investment decisions, which are at the centre of growth. This purpose requires legal frameworks defining with reasonable clarity what is and is not allowable, together with transparent processes for rule-setting and efficient institutions for sound public administration. These mechanisms must not be subject to ad hoc or arbitrary intervention by the politically powerful or offer scope for improper practices by economic agents and their interlocutors in public office.

Beyond considerations of good governance, development can be revitalized only within supportive frameworks of broad economic policy, international no less than national. Development efforts will not gather momentum if the global economy lacks dynamism and stability, and is beset with uncertainties. Likewise they will be severely handicapped if existing constraints such as external indebtedness, inadequate development finance, high trade barriers, and depressed commodity prices continue to prevail.

This set of issues is explored in the second basic message of the South Commission Report, pertaining to North-South relations and the management of the international system. Without detracting from the necessity for sound national policies and good domestic economic management, the Report stresses that the development performance of the South would be enhanced by, and is indeed dependent on, a more favourable international economic environment. To that end, reforms and adaptations are required in the structures, systems and arrangements underpinning international economic relations, particularly in the areas of trade, money and finance. There is a running emphasis on the centrality of adequate resources becoming available to developing countries to accelerate their economic and social development. This theme underlies the South Commission's proposals for the reduction of debt and debt servicing, increased financial flows, a resumption of SDR allocations, greater market access, improving the terms of trade for commodity exporters, and creating international régimes for science and technology and for the management of the environment. It also pervades the "Six-point Programme for Immediate Action". At a time when the North continues to receive net financial transfers from the South and is increasingly concerned with supporting the economic transformation under way in Central and Eastern Europe and the CIS, this emphasis on securing adequate amounts of external finance for development in the South is not misplaced.

If there are to be reforms in the international economic system and an improved management of interdependence which takes full account of the development dimension, developing countries need to be given a greater voice in international economic decision-making. Under current arrangements, they lack influence on international policy in several areas crucial to the welfare of their peoples – a condition which they share in some respects with smaller industrial countries. So far as the management of interdependence is concerned, the experience of the 1980s has shown that the tightening and diversification of the linkages between economies and between issues in the major areas of economic policy do not result spontaneously in outcomes that maximize the benefits for all, particularly where major countries pursue disconnected policies and independent courses of action. The proper management of interdependence accordingly requires that the national policies of countries having great weight in the world economy should be effectively co-ordinated.

Such co-ordination is needed to avoid inconsistencies among these policies and to ensure that they accord with global as well as national objectives, while taking fully into account the interests of other countries, particularly the developing countries. Enhancing the effectiveness of multilateral surveillance now commands wide support. But its scope should be extended to encompass policies affecting trade, capital flows and external adjustment. The common goal should be to provide firmer support, in particular for the development process, but also a more favourable setting for the vigorous policy reforms being carried out in most developing and other countries, as well as an improved climate for the efforts of developed countries to achieve better macro-economic management and structural adjustment.

The international trading system must become more open, secure and non-discriminatory and the new rules dealing with services, technology and investment issues should adequately reflect the requirements of developing countries. There is an urgent need, too, for a more coherent and effective commodity policy which would, among other things, promote a better functioning of commodity markets, stable and more predictable conditions in commodity trade, and a better contribution by the commodity sector to the development process.

The necessity for far-reaching adaptation and improvements in the existing international monetary and financial systems has been the subject of discussion for several years. An effective and durable solution of the debt crisis and an adequate level of long-term financial flows to developing countries are prime. Efforts should also be directed at securing greater influence for the international community over the creation of international liquidity so as to ensure a better response to global demand and the needs of developing countries; major improvements in the existing facilities for helping developing countries to cope with their immediate and longer-term balance-of-payments difficulties; greater stability and predictability of exchange rates and interest rates, the latter at levels consistent with high rates of growth and investment in the world economy and especially in the developing countries. The international community must also evolve policies which would allow the new more welcoming approach apparent in developing countries towards direct foreign investment actually to result in an expansion of such investment which would strengthen its impact on development.

UNCTAD has over the years strongly supported the call for these and other changes in the international economic system so as to make it more supportive of growth and development. The interactions between domestic economic management and the external environment have been the subject of considerable work in UNCTAD, which has helped to create a better understanding of the nature of the dependence of the former on the latter and reinforced the case for a supportive external environment in which the domestic policies of developing countries can be successfully implemented.

The third important theme of the South Commission Report relates to the strategic role which South-South co-operation – long a subject of study and action in UNCTAD – can play in promoting growth and development. The Report stresses two aspects: one is the need for closer and more diversified economic linkages among countries in the South; the other is the need for a more organized South which could better contribute to the process of reform in the mechanisms and institutions of the world economy so as to make them more responsive to development needs. It puts forward a wide range of proposals to further South-South co-operation in both of these areas.

The view that South-South co-operation should constitute an essential element of a global policy for development deserves firm support. Indeed, the economic rationale for strengthening such linkages is stronger than ever before. The success of economic reforms in developing countries is heavily dependent on increased export earnings. Slower economic growth and protectionist pressures in developed countries in the period ahead, together with the consequences of the economic reform processes in Central and Eastern Europe, may tend to limit the rate at which developing-country exports to developed countries can expand. Efforts to overcome these constraints call for a new emphasis on increased trade among developing countries. Advantage must be taken of the expanding complementarities in the economies of developing countries, both within and among regions, in production, financial resources, technological development and the service sector. In addition to the mechanisms already incorporated in existing regional integration arrangements, the Global System of Trade Preferences among developing countries, which has been evolved under the auspices of UNCTAD for the expansion of interregional trade among these countries, needs to be widened and improved.

At the same time, South-South co-operation needs to be adapted to present realities. For example, co-operation should not be pursued exclusively through inward-looking arrangements, but as a means of improving the overall efficiency and competitiveness of productive sectors in individual countries with a view to an increase in exports to all destinations. It should be integrally linked to broader development strategies and accordingly framed in the context of achieving closer integration into the world market. Also, more attention could be given to fostering investment flows among developing countries, as experience shows that such flows are often the key to production and to trade expansion and integration. Furthermore, greater emphasis should be given to promoting co-operation among economic operators in developing countries – industrial, business and trading enterprises and commercial banks. Some of these approaches are indeed already reflected in current initiatives under way at a bilateral level and among groups of like-minded developing countries as well as in the wider context of subregional, regional and interregional co-operation.

There is wider appreciation too that effective economic co-operation among developing countries requires a degree of harmonization among national structural adjustment policies and regional and subregional integration policies, including the design and implementation of trade, monetary and industrial policies. In addition to the steady elimination of trade restrictions, preferential schemes, on which several developing country groupings have relied for promoting growth in intra-group trade, would have to be complemented by a range of other measures involving co-operation for instance in the areas of production and transport. The evolution of such groupings would also benefit from stronger interactions between member governments and the private sector, particularly as regards investment promotion and joint ventures.

Even where market access is assured, trade cannot take root without the right kind of financial and monetary structures. In particular, trade financing on competitive and affordable terms is essential for trade expansion. Adequate longer-term credit facilities to fill this need are lacking in many developing countries, and foreign banks often do not have established customer relationships on both sides of trade exchanges among these countries. As demonstrated in recent UNCTAD studies, priority must be given to expanding existing trade financing schemes and, where appropriate, establishing new facilities for that purpose. Developing inter-country banking networks would also help mobilize market funds and improve credit access.

In addition to trade financing, monetary arrangements for settlement, for clearing multilateral claims and for securing convertibility as well as realistic cross-currency rates can be crucial to trade among developing countries. The strengthening of multilateral clearing and payments arrangements requires among other things the establishment of adequate credit facilities; the channelling of a substantial proportion of intraregional trade through clearing arrangements; a wider coverage of goods and services allowed into the clearing system; and measures to eliminate chronic intraregional indebtedness through supportive policies to develop the productive capacities of debtor countries.

Finally, arrangements for co-operation among developing countries need to address the problem of uneven distribution of benefits and costs among participants. Since the benefits of such arrangements tend, in the short to medium term, to gravitate towards the more advanced participant countries, it is reasonable for other participants to expect a measure of compensation. One possibility lies in compensatory mechanisms (which are readily applicable) against loss of tariff revenue or production, and preferential industrial measures to develop the productive capacity of the disadvantaged countries.

The South Commission Report emphasizes that strengthening South-South exchanges is first and foremost a responsibility of the South. It also stresses the need for stronger institutional support for South-South co-operation and proposes the establishment of a secretariat of the South. High-level intellectual, technical and organizational support is indeed widely recognized as essential if decision-makers in the South are to succeed in devising and implementing the measures necessary to transform their development aspirations into reality. Such institutional arrangements must be able to draw on the co-operation of the various organizations of the United Nations system, including the multilateral financial institutions. Support from developed countries would also be essential for specific South-South co-operative endeavours which would enhance the tempo of activity in developing countries and thereby contribute positively to the global economy.

These observations touch on only a few principal themes of the remarkable vision set forth in the Report. It is a vision of a rational and development-oriented international system in which the world community can secure its future through ever-widening co-operation on an equitable basis, and where the people of the South, who most urgently need change in the present world order, must take the initiative towards its realization.

25. THE CHALLENGE TO THE SOUTH: SEVEN BASIC PRINCIPLES

John Kenneth Galbraith

It is some 40 years since I first interested myself in the economic problems of the poor lands of the planet, called in more neutral fashion the South. There was then almost no literature on the subject. The erstwhile colonial powers accepted the poverty of their subject people as normal. A concern for the problems of the developing lands came with the end of the colonial era.

Teaching those early courses in economic development, I would have greatly welcomed *The Challenge to the South*. This splendid piece of work, the product of informed study and discussion and a remarkable will to find agreement, would have been a basic and nearly unique text. It would also have saved both my students and myself from a number of positions since shown by experience to be in error.

There is, perhaps, one flaw in this document. Although it covers much ground, there is some tendency, I believe, for the essentials to be lost in the merely good. And, on occasion, on particularly difficult matters, the role of the state in development being one, there is a slight sacrifice of emphasis to tact. Accordingly, I have thought in this comment to isolate in the shortest form what I believe to be the basic principles governing the economics and politics of development. There are times, I venture to think, when the errors of hard, short statement are less than what is lost in longer, more cautious prose.

The first need is to recognize the primary role in early economic life of agriculture – the peasant. Without food there is nothing, not life itself. One of the gravest of past errors has been in associating development with industry, notably primary industry. And farm prices, in frequent cases, have been deliberately kept low as a favour to the urban population. This has been a disastrous error, redeemed too often only in later hunger. It is noteworthy that the developed states, all of them in the past, strongly favoured their farmers and still do.

Second, and closely associated with agricultural development, is land reform. No country in recent times has flourished under an economic and political régime of great landlords or even small ones. Both economic progress and political democracy require that economic independence be accorded to the men and women who till the land.

Next, and third, is the central role of universal education. This the developed lands strongly emphasized in their emergent years – nothing was deemed so important as compulsory schooling for all. Progress has been made on this in the Third World, but there is far yet to go. Let it be remembered that there is no literate population on this planet that is poor, no illiterate population that is otherwise than poor. In the decades past too many physically impressive industrial plants have been located amidst ignorant people.

Next is the role of the state. This role is important, but it must be kept within the limits of the scarcest resource in the poor lands – that is the supply of honest and effective administrative talent. It is in the nature of planning, regulation and public developmental action that they early exhaust this scarce administrative resource. Socialism – the extensive public ownership of enterprise – especially exhausts this scarce resource and with strongly adverse consequences.

Next, and also central to the role of the state, is a firm fiscal context. There must be effective tax collection which bears firmly on ability to pay. No escape may be allowed through favouritism, corruption or incompetent administration. Expenditure must then be within the available revenues, well-considered longer-range investment apart. There must be no drainage of resources because of badly managed enterprises.

Next is the role of the military. This must be minimal and under strict civilian control. Military expenditure and the consequent claim on scarce resources in the poor countries is the greatest and most cruel scandal of our time. It is also one in which the developed countries, including notably the United States, happily participate. Military power is the major modern threat, directly or indirectly, to the democratic process.

Next, a closely related matter, is the devastating effect of international or internal conflict between or within the countries of the South. Nothing so ensures poverty leading on to starvation and death. In the direct Cold War confrontation between the Soviet Union and the United States extending over nearly half a century, no one got killed, a few espionage agents and escaping refugees excepted. Under American and Soviet auspices hundreds of thousands were killed and many more were further impoverished in Afghanistan and Indochina. (The issue was whether these lands should be capitalist or communist, both systems being irrelevant.) And elsewhere in the Third World millions were destroyed in national, ethnic or religious conflict and many, many more were reduced to impoverishment and starvation. Tolerance and peace must be a prime goal in all of the South. Nothing else should be so emphasized.

Finally, there is the role of the rich countries – the North. Here I strongly emphasize the writing down and writing off of debt unwisely incurred in the past. In earlier times Britain, Canada, France and the United States resorted to abrupt default when they could not pay. Now when foolish banks have made foolish loans to then-foolish governments, repayment should not be expected. An economically depressing share of the external earnings of Latin America and some other areas now go for service of redundant debt. Beyond this, I would like to see a continuing flow of help from the international agencies and directly from the rich countries. This is an elementary manifestation of civilized values.

There is much more in this admirable treatise. Here, I would argue, are the seven absolute essentials – the seven commandments. There is merit in the more complete discussion. There is also merit, I would urge, in identifying what cannot and must not be escaped.

26. THE "LEAP-FROGGING" APPROACH TO NATIONAL DEVELOPMENT

José Goldemberg

The Challenge to the South is an eloquent and stark manifesto describing the present status of developing countries and their expectations. It is not unduly pessimistic, but naive in the statement of the problem and too vague on the possible solutions of such problems.

The definition of development adopted indicates clearly that:

> Development is a process of self-reliant growth, achieved through the participation of the people acting in their own interests as they see them, and under their own control. Its first objective must be to end poverty, provide productive employment, and satisfy the basic needs of all the people, any surplus being fairly shared. This implies that basic goods and services such as food and shelter, basic education and health facilities, and clean water must be accessible to all. In addition, development presupposes a democratic structure of government, together with its supporting individual freedoms of speech, organization, and publication, as well as a system of justice which protects all the people from actions inconsistent with just laws that are known and publicly accepted.[1]

Such goals have been pursued for many centuries in many countries but only a few have been able to attain them. They are deeply in- grained in the teachings of many religions, and lip service is paid to them by almost all rulers. The reasons for that are complex but there is no question that colonial exploitation is not the only reason for the failure to attain them, as is often hinted.

Even *The Challenge to the South* recognizes that, for it emphasizes that "placing too much confidence in the theory that growth would trickle down, they [the developing countries] took little direct action to improve the productivity and raise the incomes of the poor or to ensure a less unequal distribution of the benefits of growth through such programmes as land reform".[2]

On the contrary, "in Africa and Asia the sense of collective purpose and shared objectives that had marked the liberation struggles gave way in many cases to division and to social unrest".[3]

In my view, the description of the disease is correct but the identification of its causes is not: it blames "scientific and technological dependence on the North".[4] Then the Report goes on to say that "some advances in science and technology led to production processes that were more knowledge-intensive, with considerable savings in the use of raw materials, energy, and unskilled labour-factors of production abundant in the majority of countries in the South. This trend tended to erode the South's traditional comparative advantages on the world market and weakened its economies".[5]

To believe that abundant unskilled labour was one of the main assets of developing countries is, in my opinion, the basic flaw of *The Challenge to the South*. What has been shown not only by a number of analysts but by the facts of life is that technology is the answer to development and not labour, inexpensive and abundant as it might be.

The emphasis on technological dependence is completely mistaken since there is no possibility – nor reason – to develop indigenous technologies when abundant and well-proven technologies exist. The fact that they were first developed in the North is irrelevant; what is relevant is to have access and learn how to use them.

The very fact that "advances in medicine led to a dramatic fall in the death rate – and to longer life expectancy – in many developing countries well before the birth rate declined in response to higher living standards"[6] proves that it is not necessary to reinvent antibiotics in the South before using them. The "green revolution" is another example of a technology developed in the North which – when applied properly in the South – was successful enough in many countries to eradicate hunger which had been due to the loss of crops or to low productivity related to unfavourable rainy seasons.

The emphasis on the importance of basic sciences is therefore somewhat misdirected. Even in countries where basic sciences were given priority attention, universities and research centres became fairly isolated from the rest of the country in a sort of "ivory tower" much more connected to research centres in England or the United States than to their own centres.

This fundamental point is touched upon in *The Challenge to the South* when it states that "policies on science and technology were usually not integrated into the national development plan, but were an isolated adjunct to it".[7]

In some cases, countries tried to correct that by encouraging "the use of local resources and the development of local technology. But very often the procedures were complex, rigid, and cumbersome, and led to long delays and escalating costs."[8]

Summing up, one can say that the idea that there is a science and technology adequate to the South is flawed.

The successful experience of the "Asian tigers" shows that international economic integration is proceeding rapidly, and developing countries can play a very significant role in this process using whatever technology and production processes are available and putting them to work.

Autarchy just does not seem to be the way to go, as is clearly shown by the crumbling of Eastern European régimes.

What seems to be required to make development a reality is a dynamic entrepreneurial class backed up by enough science and technology to allow it to make the correct technological choices and leap to the frontiers of productivity innovation to gain comparative advantages – "leap-frogging" the path followed in the past by today's industrialized countries.

The Challenge to the South comes very close to recognizing this when it states that:

> For the foreseeable future, most countries of the South will have mixed economies in which the state and market mechanisms will have to complement each other in a creative way if their development potential is to be realized. For this to happen, reforms are required in the machinery of government in addition to the reorientation of policies. The aim should be to modernize the state apparatus, as well as to create a stable and development-oriented macro-economic framework, encourage entrepreneurship, initiative, and innovation, and make the public sector more efficient.[9]

What seems to be implied in this statement is that the state should not do everything but should facilitate, guide and finance private enterprise as the Japanese, Koreans and other "Asian tigers" have done so well. This of course is only possible when a well-trained workforce of good quality exists, that is, an indigenous educational capacity that can be incorporated in the development process.

To proceed otherwise leads to the creation of heavy governmental bureaucracies and public universities which are organized on a "supply side mode" cultivating whatever science and technology is fashionable in the North, waiting forever in "ivory towers" for the time when such competence would trigger development.

This is the reason why science and technology budgets are almost entirely covered by the national treasury in developing countries and not by the productive sector. By contrast, in the dynamic economies of the South, such as South Korea, the support for universities shifted from a "supply side mode" to a "demand side mode" in the short span of 20 years.

In 1965, 90 per cent of the expenditures on science and technology (S&T) in South Korea was covered by the government and 10 per cent by the private sector. By 1985 the situation had been almost reversed: 80 per cent was covered by the private sector and 20 per cent by the government.

In terms of the share of the gross domestic product (GDP) applied to S&T in South Korea the numbers are also interesting: total expenditure on S&T amounted to approximately 2 per cent of GDP – quite similar to the share applied to S&T in the North – of which 20 per cent, 0.4 per cent of GDP, was covered by the government. The situation in a country such as Brazil is also quite telling: 0.7 per cent of the GDP was spent on S&T in 1990, of which 90 per cent was contributed by the government and only 10 per cent by the private sector.

In the words of the South Commission "very few countries of the South devote more than a meagre 0.5 per cent of their national income to research and development; by contrast developed countries allocate 2 to 3 per cent. The yawning gap in knowledge between the North and the South will grow even wider unless the South greatly expands its allocations for research and development."[10] However, this plea has to be qualified.

This is the reason why the present Brazilian government decided to try to invert the situation in the five years 1990-1994, encouraging the "demand side mode" through loans to industry.

Turning to the problems of environmental degradation, one has to consider the national and global dimensions which pose not only a challenge to the South but also present a great opportunity.

National environmental problems in the South are intimately connected to poverty, of which they are both a cause and consequence. There is very uneven treatment of such problems by local governments. There are instances in which cities (and whole regions) have been "cleaned", such as the heavily polluted industrial city of Cubatao, near So Paulo, and others such as Mexico City, which is literally choking under heavy atmospheric pollution. This is a matter of local regulations, and a judicious application of the "polluter pays" principle can work admirably well. No significant international help can be expected for such actions because this is a problem remote from the populations and governments of the North, which are usually more impressed by great natural disasters resulting from the monsoons in Bangladesh, earthquakes in Armenia or periodic famines in Ethiopia.

There is, however, a new problem related to pollution in the South which is global in nature and which therefore affects seriously the North: the "greenhouse effect". Gaseous emissions from the burning of forests or fossil fuel consumption in the South are very significant contributors to net emissions of CO_2 (and other greenhouse gases).

CO_2 emissions from fossil fuel burning have levelled off over the years in the industrialized countries but are growing in a linear fashion in the developing countries. In 1985 emissions from the South represented 27 per cent of the total, not including emissions from deforestation. If one includes deforestation, the South is already contributing more than 40 per cent to total emissions. This poses an important opportunity for joint action by North and South.

The reduction of emissions from deforestation is quite easy and has to do with the creation of other opportunities for employment and invest-ment in forested areas. To reduce emissions from fossil fuel burning (in energy generation, transportation and industrial uses) the same technologies and production methods can be used which were used in the last decade or so in the industrialized countries. In fact, these countries succeeded in continuing to grow in economic terms while keeping energy consumption at the levels of the 1970s. For example, GDP in the OECD countries grew 37 per cent in the period 1973-1987 while energy consumption remained constant.

This implies that developing countries have to incorporate in their process of development the new technologies tested and available in the North, that is, to leap-frog stages of development which do not necessarily have to be retraced.

Countries of the South offer much better opportunities for such a strategy than countries of the North, since there is so much growth ahead which is surely needed by the growing population.

This strategy is of interest not only to the South but also to the North, because it will remove an important component of the global threat to the environment. The countries of the North have a direct self-interest in helping the South to pursue this path, and resources for that purpose should not fall within the usual "official development aid" (ODA) category. They should be regarded as an extension of national programmes of the countries of the North which are really more cost-effective than many domestic programmes geared to reduce emissions inside their own borders.

Actions under the Montreal Protocol which are intended to reduce emissions of chlorofluorocarbons (CFCs) in developing countries are following that route and are being paid for by a special fund set up by the industrial nations; this is, in my view, the road to be followed in tackling the problem of emissions of CO_2 (and other greenhouse gases).

This challenge to the South and the opportunity it provides the South are rather unique. Relying not on good will but on the self-interest of the North, the venture can succeed!

Notes

1. South Commission, 1990, pp.13-14.
2. Ibid., p.37.
3. Ibid., p.38.
4. Ibid., p.39.
5. Ibid., p.41.
6. Ibid., pp.36-37.
7. Ibid., p.43.
8. Ibid.
9. Ibid., p.81.
10. Ibid., p.110.

Bibliography

South Commission
    The Challenge to the South: The Report of the South Commission, Oxford University Press, Oxford and New York, 1990.

27. THIRD WORLD IN AN UNDIVIDED WORLD

Godfrey Gunatilleke

Reconstructing the Development Dialogue

Covering as it does the entire range of the major development issues of the time, the Report of the South Commission is a truly impressive achievement for a document of its size. It can be read at several levels. Even apart from the agenda it outlines, it demands attention as an appraisal of the challenges facing the world community as a whole, presented from the point of view of the South. On national strategies, the Report provides policy-makers with a concise evaluation of the various prescriptions for development that have been applied at different times, illustrating the need to use them selectively and adapt the mix of policies to the great diversity of the development situations in the South. The Report is a valuable digest of the "state of the art" of South-South and North-South relations. It provides a comprehensive overview of the institutional and other changes that have been proposed in the effort to restructure international economic relations. Above all, it underscores the integral connection between three scenarios of development: the transformations at national level; co-operation among countries of the South; and North-South relations.

For all these reasons, the Report is a substantial contribution. But when this has been acknowledged, the real worth of an effort of this nature is most often judged on its capacity to add dimensions which are significantly new to the subjects with which it deals. Initially it has to be stated that the expectation of newness from a report on development issues such as those considered by the Commission is often based on a faulty conception of what is possible or necessary. These issues have been analysed, time and time again; various initiatives and strategies have been proposed on innumerable occasions. The development recipes, the policy responses and the institutional innovations that are possible at the national, regional and global levels to deal with the problems have been explored almost to their furthest limit. In such a situation there is little scope for offering solutions that are dramatically.new. What is possible is at best a mix which is different from what has been offered before – a reordering of priorities which alters basic perceptions of the development problem as it manifests itself at the national, regional and global levels; a rearrangement of known elements which provides the framework for a new engagement with the problem, on the part of all concerned. It is on criteria of this type that the work of the Commission has to be assessed.

The sequence in which the issues are presented in the Report defines the order of priorities as well. The core of the message in the Report is that the primary responsibility for the economic and socio-political transformation of their societies lies with the developing nations themselves. The international system can only create the enabling environment for that process. That system is critically important for the transformation, but the way in which the enabling environment is created will itself depend on the capacity of the developing societies to manage their own transformation. By itself, this is not a startlingly new message; it has become part of the conventional wisdom about development. The importance of the message, however, lies in the way in which the Report uses it in an attempt to reconstruct the development dialogue on a more rational and objective foundation.

Sharing Responsibility for Development

The debate concerning who should assume primary responsibility for creating the conditions for development has been for the most part a futile and frustrating exercise.

By their very nature, the arguments that have been used for defining that responsibility, fraught as they are with conflicting historical interpretations and ideological preconceptions, are incapable of producing any conclusive or meaningful outcome. On the one hand, the developed countries have emphasized the need for the developing countries to create the preconditions for development within their own societies. On the other, the developing countries have argued that the reform of the international economic system has its own independent rationale and should not be linked to the national preconditions. These two approaches have often tended to stall the movement towards an open dialogue which could have reached consensus on the preconditions for development at both levels – the national as well as the global. In the absence of such a consensus, introducing "conditionalities" for development becomes a process which has to be imposed almost unilaterally on developing countries by the multilateral agencies that provide financial support and assistance. It has been more or less delinked from the responsibility of the world community to provide the enabling framework. The approach taken by the South Commission creates a unique opportunity to reverse the unilateral process of conditionality which has grown in one part of the system, to link it to the global responsibilities and to resume the North-South dialogue on a new basis.

A New Paradigm?

The South Commission attempts to provide a conceptual framework which takes the dialogue on development, and particularly the North-South dialogue, out of the traditional ideological mould. At a more ambitious level, without explicitly saying so, it attempts to replace the paradigm of the New International Economic Order of the 1970s with a new paradigm in which the changes within the developing societies, in relations among the countries of the South and in those between the North and the South are integral parts of a global transformation. The Report would probably have been more persuasive and its message more powerful if this paradigm had been spelt out more clearly and more prominence had been given to the qualitative difference between the language of discourse on development in the past and what is now proposed. There are of course inherent problems and dangers in such a restatement. The development "militants" would regard such a restatement as an abandonment of the cherished battle cries and a capitulation to the pressures of the industrialized countries. But irrespective of these misgivings, the substantive positions taken in the past by the Group of 77 on many specific issues continue to be relevant partly or wholly in the changes that are needed in the global order.

The problem is, however, one of placing all these elements in a new configuration and providing them with a more powerful rationale than in the past. In one sense, the dialogue on world development must make an entirely new beginning without the overhang of the past dialogue which was a failure. A new language of discourse, new conceptual approaches and above all a new global value system have to be discovered for the purpose. In another sense there is need for a process of renewal, a rediscovery of what was left undone, a reintegration of the old elements in a new design. The Report attempts to steer between these two; there are both gains as well as losses in this process. The loss is manifested in the way in which the new directions charted in the Report tend to get subsumed in an agenda which carries a great deal of the past agendas. The old language of conflict and self-assertion of the Third World is not fully aligned to the idiom of the shared vision of One World.

Despite this limitation, the plea for a new development consensus comes through strongly. The agenda for each level, the national, the South-South and the North-South, is presented in considerable detail and specificity. Most of the elements of each agenda are of course familiar. They have figured in the numerous reports and conferences on the same development issues that are covered in the Report. The Brandt Commission covered much the same ground, proposed similar remedies, emphasized "the responsibilities of the South to complement measures of international justice with domestic ones", argued that "all the lessons of reform within national societies confirm the gains for all in a process of change that makes the world a less unequal and a more just and habitable place" and proposed remedial measures of a similar type and an emergency programme for the first half of the 1980s.[1]

The South Commission updates the Brandt Commission agenda. It develops the three scenarios – that of national development, South-South co-operation and North-South relations – in much greater detail. It elaborates on the theme of global interdependence. What is perhaps important is that this time it is a voice that is unmistakably speaking for the South. It signifies that outside the intergovernmental encounters in the formal international fora, there is a process which is moving towards common ground and which is attempting to define the major development issues within a paradigm of "an undivided world".

The South Commission describes it as the "vision of the South" and states "that it has to embrace the whole world, for it is part of that world ... the South seeks an undivided world ... the South's goal is a world of equal opportunities in which ... nations in their variety would work together in pursuit of jointly agreed goals".[3] It goes on to argue that "this vision of the world can be made real only through a very long series of steps in a consistent and deliberate movement".[3] But before it can be made real the vision has to be shared without reservation by both the North and the South. There has to be a strong constituency for an undivided world among the people in both the North and the South, and more and more voices from both sides have to join together to communicate that vision. The International Brandt Commission and the South Commission have initiated the movement in that direction.

A Strategy of Implementation – The National Analogy

But the goal of a world of equal opportunities in an unequal global order is attractive enough for the South. In the South Commission's words "it is the people of the South who most urgently need change in the present world order".[4] While no one would dispute the argument that the South must therefore take "the initiative to make this vision of the world a reality",[5] the countries of the South cannot do this by themselves. The countries of the North must share the vision; they have the major part to play in making it real. But the crucial question is what is there in it to motivate the North? The South Commission recommends a mix of strategies in which two processes must complement and mutually reinforce each other. One process involves co-operation among the countries of the South which would enhance their economic power and political effectiveness in the international system. The order involves the recognition on the part of the North that a more equitable global order is needed to sustain stable orderly societies in the world as a whole, that this is essential to manage the growing interdependence of the North and the South and is therefore in the long-term interests of the developed countries themselves. The former is concerned with the existing distribution of power in the world system and aims for a better balance; the latter invokes both enlightened self-interest and, in the key word "equitable", introduces a moral dimension and a value system that should guide international economic relations.

Both the Brandt Commission and the South Commission draw an analogy between the social responsibility assumed by a national entity and what ought to be assumed by the world community. The Brandt Commission refers to the national processes of reform during the evolution of the industrialized societies which have lessons for the world community. The South Commission describes how the world with its North-South divide would be perceived for what it is – "an unviable semi-feudal entity ... divided within itself ... inherently unstable" if one thinks of "all humanity as a single nation state".[6] During their industrial transition, the democratic societies of the developed world were able to evolve systems which, by and large, succeeded in eradicating absolute poverty, mitigating income inequalities and pursuing the social and economic objectives of raising the standard of living for their populations as a whole.

Enlightened élites responded to the social needs. The state intervened with systems of social welfare and social security in areas where the market was ineffective in protecting the poor and disadvantaged. Macro-economic policies were designed to correct the imbalances and aberrations of the market in order to move towards full employment, increase effective demand for the whole population as a whole, and sustain a high rate of economic growth.

What is envisaged is an analogous process for the global order. The question then arises: what was the historical process which made this possible for the nation states? To what extent can such a process be emulated on a global scale within the limits imposed by a collectivity of sovereign states? And are there now developments within the international system which contain the main elements of that historical process which took place within national entities?

Answers to these questions may be found by considering, in the light of what happened in the North, the two complementary efforts needed to make the South's vision real. First, in the North, the national processes were the outcome of a long struggle which required mass organization of collective interests, the growth of countervailing power and the slow evolution of a new distribution and balance of political and economic strength. Second, there was broad acceptance of an overarching system of human values which themselves were derived from deep-rooted religious and moral traditions. These provided the humanitarian motivations and the ideological drives which helped to promote equality of opportunity, democratic participation and the welfare state. They were also a significant factor in producing enlightened élites who established the institutions that enabled the first process to take place in an orderly manner.

At the global level, the equivalent of the first would be South-South co-operation. The nearest equivalent of the second would be the evolution of the UN system and similar international institutions. If these are the two processes which are critical for realizing the desired global order, then the ineluctable reality is that both are as yet in a rudimentary state of evolution, they are progressing very slowly and have a long way to go before they can become truly effective.

Implementing the Agenda for South-South Co-operation

The agenda for South-South co-operation presented by the South Commission assembles a wide range of proposals covering all the important areas. Many of these, such as those concerning a South Secretariat, a debtors' forum, joint supply management of primary commodities exported mainly by the developing countries, a programme of technological co-operation, the speedy implementation of the GSTP have been discussed and considered by the South for a long period. Therefore the issue is not even one of collectively adopting an agenda of this type. Similar ideas have received the collective approval of developing countries in various fora, such as conferences of the Group of 77, conferences of the Non-Aligned Movement and UNCTAD. The crucial issue is whether proposals of this kind are capable of motivating the developing countries sufficiently to translate them into action. Developing countries must be able to identify clearly their major national interests in the programmes of South-South co-operation that are proposed, and thereby find a compelling incentive and motivation to implement the programmes. Up to now a global programme encompassing the whole of the South has not been able to provide such a motivation. The progress on the GSTP, which is the only scheme on this scale that has been adopted, has been painfully slow and on the South Commission's own evaluation has had "only a symbolic value".

This state of affairs raises questions about the entire strategy of implementing a programme of South-South co-operation. While the Commission has not specifically elaborated a strategy of implementation, the Report contains most of the elements of such a strategy.

As has been often pointed out, the South is a vast and heterogeneous collectivity of countries at very diverse levels of development. It is almost impossible to find one unifying common interest which can bring them together. Hence, the strategy of South-South co-operation has to be built around clusters of common interests. For example, supply management of primary commodities exported by developing countries would be of priority interest to one group of countries, a programme for promoting investment flows within the South would be crucial for yet another group. The global programme of South-South co-operation would have to be constructed from components for each of which a group of countries would take the lead in response to a compelling need arising from their own national interests in the programme. The comprehensive agenda presented by the South Commission lends itself to such a structure.

More work, however, would have to be done in identifying the special interest groups for each component and in designing the institutional frame-work through which it may be possible to implement such a programme of co-operation through "leader groups" of developing countries.

There are two recommendations in the Report which need to be implemented right at the outset to inaugurate a programme of South-South co-operation. One is the proposal for a summit meeting of heads of state in the South which would take the decision to activate a programme of South-South co-operation and identify the first set of priorities for action. The second is the establishment of the South Secretariat to undertake the essential technical work and the servicing of the programme on a regular basis. The South Commission envisages a secretariat which would service several Third World institutions – the Group of 77, the Non-Aligned Movement and the Summit-Level Group. It is not clear who would take the initiative in establishing the secretariat. It would need not only an advisory body but a governing body. Could such a body be appointed jointly by the institutions that the secretariat would serve? These organizational aspects need to be worked out in greater detail so that the Summit meeting could be presented with a blueprint of an operationally viable institution.

Strategic Changes in Approach

The Commission's agenda for South-South co-operation includes several initiatives each of which has important implications for the strategy itself. One example is the involvement of the business sector. In the current context in which economic reforms for structural adjustment and macro-economic policies are giving an increasing role to the private sector and the market, the main thrust of economic co-operation among countries in the South would have to be market-driven, with the state playing an enabling role. This would lead to a qualitative change in the processes and mechanisms that are needed. There has to be much greater reliance on South-South contacts outside the government sector, on regular flows of information between private sector groups of the developing countries, on an institutional framework which would facilitate interaction between such groups for purposes of identifying opportunities for co-operation.

Regional and subregional groupings raise another set of issues which concern the overall strategy of co-operation. Undoubtedly, the potential of co-operation among developing countries would be highest for a group of countries in relatively close proximity to each other. Such co-operation would generally encompass common political, economic and socio-cultural interests. Against this proposition, it might be argued that such co-operation also poses the greatest problems as contiguous states are also often centres of conflict in the South. However, the conflicts and the potential for conflict by themselves generate the compelling need to find a resolution through forms of regional and subregional co-operation. Such co-operation therefore plays a major role in creating the peace and stability which are the preconditions for economic growth and South-South co-operation.

Although the performance of the regional groupings in the South has been very varied and although those groupings have illustrated the limited potential for co-operation among resource-poor countries, they are natural groupings of common interests and have the potential to develop programmes of co-operation in most of the areas identified in the South Commission's agenda, including common positions on global issues. The Commission recommends a systematic effort to promote co-operation among these groupings where subregional and regional groups move in a progressively widening network of South-South co-operation. Therefore, revitalizing regional and subregional co-operation would be more than one element in the agenda. It would in fact provide the basic structure for South-South co-operation in which the co-operation in what the Commission describes as functional areas is closely linked to and emerges from perceived regional interests and needs.

Finally, South-South co-operation will need to contend with and accommodate another process which seems to be inevitable. Regional groupings in the South will develop special relationships with regional groupings of the North. Initially, the reaction of the protagonists of South-South co-operation to such South-North groupings is likely to be adverse. These groupings, however, need not have negative outcomes for the South nor need they weaken South-South links. A great deal would depend on the way in which the framework of North-South co-operation is negotiated and on the nature of the interdependence that develops. The experience of one such grouping could be of value to another such grouping. These regional groupings would have to be approached as forms of North-South interdependence and should be negotiated and developed to strengthen global interdependence. This would require a new flexibility in developing South-South co-operation and the capacity to respond to and absorb the new forms of North-South linkage in ways maximizing the benefits to the South.

Creating a Global Value System

The Commission's Report concludes with a message which reaffirms the values which should inspire global transformation. It calls for "the formulation of a vision of a more democratic international structure capable of steering social, political, and economic change in the interests of humanity as a whole".[7] But while it states that the vision has to be "adopted through international agreement", the emphasis is on the process that must take place within the South, "the difficult and prolonged struggle", on acquiring "the maximum countervailing power", on relying increasingly on the sources of growth within the South itself and generating "the locomotive power ... within the economies of the South".[8] This is the global equivalent of the process of struggle and countervailing power which helped in transforming national societies, making them more equitable and democratic. But the Commission simultaneously uses the language of "consensus". In doing so it is referring to the second process which helped to transform these societies – that is, the profound transformation that took place in other parts of these societies, the ethos and value systems that evolved and inspired the transformation, and the self-transformation of the élites who made space for and managed the changes.

There has to be an analogous process at the global level if the vision of the South is to be made real. Consensus implies a shared vision accepted together by the North and the South. The growth of countervailing power of the South and its incorporation in the global system have to be seen and accepted as a necessary and positive element for a stable world order with a more equitable sharing of power. A world in which inequality has been reduced to acceptable levels and in which poverty and hunger are eradicated must be perceived as providing a better quality of life for the developed societies as well.

It has been often argued that a decisive factor in creating a more equitable world order is the enlightened self-interest of the developed part of the world. There has been a considerable volume of analytical work which has tried to demonstrate that, under conditions of increasing global interdependence, the reform of the international system is in the long-term interest of the developed countries themselves. The Commission's Report makes this point repeatedly. However, the degree to which self-interest becomes enlightened and the extent to which societies are prepared to forgo readily perceived short-term interests for the sake of long-term ones – which may seem distant and uncertain – are problematic. As international negotiations have demonstrated, it is difficult to find the technical solutions which are beyond challenge and will be universally accepted. The enlightenment of self-interest would be determined ultimately by the moral and ethical foundations of a society, the restraints which the élites are ready to accept and the value system which shapes the social and political will. The global consensus on an equitable world order will depend on such a value system, its strength and capacity to shape the will of the world community, particularly that of the developed societies. A major challenge to the proponents of a new equitable world order is that of developing, strengthening and activitating such a value system.

There has been some movement towards such a value system, however faltering and hesitant it might be. It is manifested in the covenants, agreements and international norms which have been adopted in the United Nations system and other international agencies. The impact they have had in many fields such as human rights, development assistance, poverty alleviation, global responsibility for refugees, aid in times of famine, disarmament, has not been negligible. In these initiatives the world has witnessed the slow growth of a global conscience, the evolution of a core of values and concepts which can provide the moral and intellectual foundation of a new global order. It is important to identify, nurture and develop the nuclei of this process, both through international institutions and through non-governmental movements in the North and in the South. Among other things, the process needs a North-South intellectual partnership which would promote the concepts and values of an undivided world. Therefore the line of argument in the Commission's Report which relates to building up international consensus, mobilizing wider sections of the public in Northern societies and "linking all forces that believe in the shared destiny of humankind" needs to be given sharper visibility. Along with the growth of Third World self-reliance it becomes central to the realization of the global vision which is presented in the Report.

Notes

1. Brandt Commission, 1980.
2. South Commission, 1990, pp.9-10.
3. Ibid., p.10.
4. Ibid.
5. Ibid.
6. Ibid., p.2.
7. Ibid., p.285.
8. Ibid., pp.285-286.

Bibliography

Brandt Commission (Independent Commission on International Development Issues)
   North-South: A Programme for Survival, Pan Books, London, 1980.
South Commission
   The Challenge to the South: The Report of the South Commission, Oxford University Press, Oxford and New York, 1990.

28. NATIONAL DIMENSIONS OF DEVELOPMENT STRATEGIES FOR THE SOUTH

Nurul Islam

The South Commission in its Report *The Challenge to the South* has highlighted – to a much larger extent than did similar reports in the past – the crucial role to be played by domestic policies and programmes in the achievement of a self-reliant and broad-based development in the years to come.

The deliberations and recommendations of the Report cover a large number of policy issues ranging over a broad spectrum of themes. These include traditional development issues, such as domestic resource mobilization and investment, macro-economic management, import substituting industrialization, food security and rural development, but also such specific but hitherto neglected aspects as the integration of women's role and environmental considerations in development and the dynamics of cultural change.

An overarching theme cutting across the various aspects of develop-ment strategy is the role of the state and of markets. The debate on this theme in the development community in recent years has been greatly influenced, on the one hand, by the collapse of the political and economic command system of the communist states and, on the other hand, by recent trends in the Western industrialized countries towards the disengagement of the state from direct interventions in economic life. The South Commission examines the role of the state in the development of the Third World countries, distinguishing them by the different stages of development, and provides important insights which are based on pragmatic grounds rather than on ideological considerations.

The Path To Efficient Industrialization

The Commission recognizes the shortcomings of the high-cost, and often capital-intensive, import-substituting industrialization policies pursued by most developing countries in the post-Second World War period. Industrialization started in most of these countries by way of substituting, for imports of industrial goods, mostly domestically produced consumer goods, for which there was not only a ready domestic market but also frequently a supply of raw materials for their production. What went wrong with this rather logical first step was the choice of instruments such as high import barriers and complex methods of discretionary industrial licensing which were used to promote specific industries with scant regard to their comparative cost advantage. The consequent high costs and inefficiencies were the result of limitations imposed by the small size of domestic markets, the capital-intensity of the industrial processes or techniques and the complexity of the requisite organizational structure.

The Report recognizes the adverse effects which a high-cost, industrial import substitution strategy imposes on agriculture as well as on all exports, both agricultural and non-agricultural. An over-valued exchange rate, coupled with high levels of import restrictions, not only creates rents and windfall profits for the importers and the high-cost domestic industries but also depresses the returns to the export and agricultural sectors. Compensatory measures are indeed undertaken in various countries, including direct and indirect export subsidies and subsidized credit. The adverse effects on the agricultural sector are often offset by subsidies on inputs such as fertilizers, water, pesticides and credit.

Both analysis and experience now confirm that import substitution, if it is to be carried out efficiently, must be based upon (a) a lower level of protectionism, preferably through tariffs rather than quotas; (b) a much lower range or degree of dispersion in the rates of protection provided to specific industries; and (c) a sustained implementation of supportive policy measures such as technological research, training and education, and development of infrastructure. The need for "learning by doing" does require "infant industry" protection, but the sooner it is removed or reduced, the better. In a highly discriminatory system of import restrictions the least-cost industry often ends up getting the highest level of protection. Recent experience indicates that with proper public education, including that of consumers and other interest groups such as importers, traders, export industries or industries using high-cost protected products, it is possible to generate the necessary pressure to reduce protectionism over time. The lessons of the experience of the successful industrializing countries in East Asia, such as Taiwan and Korea, confirm those conclusions.

The industries which started as import-substituting industries gained efficiency and competitive strength over time and became successful exporters. As import-substituting industries in Korea faced the limitation of a narrow domestic market, and were thwarted from reaping the economies of scale, they started producing for the export market, with the benefit of a variety of export incentives and specially subsidized credit. Export markets offered opportunities for the realization of economies of scale but also exposed them to the forces of competition, in response to which they improved efficiency and reduced costs. The import substitution or export promotion strategy was also sufficiently flexible to adjust to changing conditions of technology and export demands. Whenever either a specific import-substituting or export industry proved to be high-cost and inefficient or uncompetitive in the export market, the government let it decline and switched its support to new activities or industries, which proved more promising in the light of changed circumstances. What was important was the flexibility of policy combined with the ability and the willingness to reverse past policies, if they proved unsuccessful. While the government's policy measures were directed towards picking the "winners" for a concentrated application of various support measures to enable them to compete in export markets, there was considerable flexibility in order to change course, abandon the failed enterprises or activities and pick new prospective winners.

The Commission's Report seems to convey the impression that export promotion strategies rather than import substitution strategies are suitable only for small countries with narrow domestic markets, on the grounds that their domestic markets would be too small to benefit from economies of scale. This should not imply, however, that export markets can or should be neglected in large economies. In countries with large populations the domestic market size for technologically advanced industries may still be small because of the low level of per capita income. Moreover, a small domestic market leaves room for only a few enterprises in a particular industry, thus inhibiting the evolution of a competitive market structure.

Competition is essential for ensuring efficiency and for improved productivity; this can only be provided under the circumstances through the competition of imports and/or participation in export markets. Whatever the size of the domestic market, an efficient pattern of industrialization is best promoted through reliance on comparative costs and competition. To achieve optimal resource allocation, the real effective exchange rate, including all direct and indirect taxes and subsidies, should be the same for exports and imports. Given the neutrality of the incentive structure for exports and imports, in small countries successful industries will most probably be those based predominantly on export markets. In large countries, on the other hand, there will be industries able to benefit from economies of scale on the basis of the domestic market; none the less, depending on the way in which costs vary in relation to size, there will be many industries serving both domestic and export markets in varying degrees.

In recent years many developing countries have liberalized trade and exchange rate policies, often as part of agreements with the international financial and monetary institutions. The discrimination against agriculture and exports has been reduced in many countries. In several middle-income developing countries, especially the newly industrializing countries, as well as in low-income countries like India where an organized class of prosperous medium and large-scale farmers has grown up in recent years, the agricultural sector has lately been receiving increasing govern- ment support, sometimes at price levels above the world market. As technological progress brings substantial gains to large and medium-scale farmers, they acquire the organizational and economic strength to act as pressure groups and to wield political power for extracting concessions and subsidies from the government. This results in an increase in the overall level of protectionism across the board, in all sectors.

The Role of Agriculture in Food Security and Overall Development

Agricultural growth stimulates overall growth through intersectoral production and consumption linkages; it stimulates the demand for consumption goods and for inputs originating in the non-agricultural sector; it provides output for processing, marketing and distribution, which in turn stimulates trade, services and industries. An agricultural develop-ment strategy which is labour-intensive and employment-oriented is also often associated with labour-intensive industrialization. This contributes to the alleviation of poverty, since in many developing countries the most abundant resource at the disposal of the poor is labour. The impact on the non-agricultural sector through consumption linkages can be maximized only if growth in the agricultural sector is broadly based, that is, if small and medium farmers account for a major share in the rise in agricultural productivity, since an increase in their income is most likely to lead to increased demand for mass-produced, labour-intensive consumer goods. In general, whatever the nature of intersectoral linkages, in order that the supply in the non-agricultural sector should respond to the demand stimulus from the agricultural sector, there must be the necessary infrastructure facilities, namely roads, transportation, communications, as well as a marketing and distribution network. At the same time, education and training, especially at primary and secondary levels, needs to be widely spread so as to encourage the growth of an entrepreneurial class who can exploit these new opportunities in the non-agricultural sector.

Undoubtedly, equitable broadly based agricultural growth, in countries where land is very unequally distributed, is facilitated by land redistribution. This is especially true in Latin America, the Near East and in some countries in Africa where communal property rights are being legally or semi-legally transformed into large private ownership holdings. Land reform contributes to employment and income generation for the rural poor, if supported by the supply of credit, inputs and marketing and distribution infrastructure. By redistributing economic and political power in the rural areas, land reform promotes the development of self-governing local government institutions – so essential for rural socio-economic development. This will make possible a more equitable distribution of resources, including inputs and credits, among the farmers. However, in many countries substantial land reform encounters political obstacles. In such cases, measures such as improved security of tenants or sharecroppers, accompanied by an expansion of non-farm rural employment, tend to raise the income of the rural poor. At the same time, extension of educational facilities and improved organization of agricultural workers and landless labourers will greatly strengthen the bargaining power of the rural poor. No less important is the role of rural non-governmental organizations in providing services and organizational inputs for the rural poor.

The South Commission lists the various measures which are needed to improve agricultural productivity, especially of the small farmers. They range from technological advances through agricultural research, education, extension and training of the farmers to the provision of inputs, such as irrigation, fertilizers, pesticides, and credit and equipment. The South Commission stresses that "a policy framework that offers farmers adequate incentives to increased production is essential for agricultural progress and moving towards food security".[1]

However, there are several interrelated issues pertaining to food security which the Report has mentioned but not dealt with adequately. They relate to (a) the pursuit of self-sufficiency in food; (b) stabilization of food prices; and (c) assurance of access to food on the part of the poor.

Memories of the 1973-1974 world food crisis and periodic food shortages and famines since then, in several poor countries especially in Africa, led many developing countries to place the objective of food self-sufficiency high on their agenda for action.

There is a perception of uncertainty regarding exclusive reliance on international trade to meet food needs in the poor countries, especially where the per capita food consumption level is so low that a drop in that level due to food shortages causes immediate distress and sometimes starvation. It is widely feared or apprehended that imports can be subject to interruptions if there is a policy of exporting, mostly to developed countries, and if there are disruptions in shipping and transportation, compounded by civil strife and/or wars.

The important policy question here is: what is the excess cost or price of domestic output over the cost of imports that developing countries are willing to pay in order to accommodate or allow for their perception of uncertainty and risks? This perception varies greatly among developing countries. In this context, whether and to what extent food should be produced domestically depends on a comparison of domestic costs in relation to the import prices, estimated on the basis of the shadow price of foreign exchange, allowing for an excess of domestic cost to compensate for the risks and uncertainties of world trade. The extent of the allowance to be made for risks and uncertainties is a matter of value judgement. The lower the premium paid for this uncertainty, the greater will be the efficiency gains for the economy as a whole, from which both the consumers and the producers will benefit.

Ideally, developing countries should aim at self-reliance rather than self-sufficiency such that a developing country should be able to procure the basic food it needs either by domestic production if it is a low-cost, efficient producer, or through imports in exchange for exports, either non-food or non-agricultural exports, in which it has a comparative cost advantage.

The pursuit of self-reliance in food is often linked with the desire to reduce reliance on food aid. In many poor countries, especially among the low-income, food-deficit developing countries, most food imports are supplied by food aid, which accounts sometimes for 20 to 30 per cent of total cereal consumption. Food aid, especially bilateral food aid, is very uncertain; only a few countries provide such aid, which, in addition, fluctuates from year to year often in response to available food surpluses. Intra-country allocation of food aid is influenced by non-economic, that is, political and strategic considerations. Developing countries that depend on food aid, especially if heavily dependent on such aid, not only face uncertainty, but also lose a certain independence of action internally and internationally. Heavy reliance on food aid is a more sensitive issue because food is, by its nature, a basic need. A shortfall in food supply resulting from a reduction in food aid has much graver social and political consequences than does a shortfall in other forms of aid. However, to reduce dependence on food aid to a level which is socially and politically tolerable is not to eschew commercial food imports financed by export earnings. It does not necessarily lead to self-sufficiency in food.

The sharp year-to-year fluctuations in food prices, caused by variations either in domestic food production or in import prices, lead to deprivation and distress among the poor when prices rise; conversely, low prices discourage production and long-term investments. A policy of stabilization of food prices within a reasonable margin requires either domestic food stocks or a compensating variation in imports. The domestic prices of food imports can be regulated by means of taxes and subsidies on imports. If import prices rise above the domestic "ceiling" price, subsidies are needed; if they fall below that level, taxes should be charged on imports.

The optimal combination of domestic stocks and reliance on food imports, financed either by an accumulation of foreign exchange reserves or by means of guaranteed access to international financing facilities, depends on the particular circumstances of the country concerned. The following criteria determine the appropriate size of domestic food stocks: the degree of fluctuations which are politically tolerable and economically efficient – this will determine the price band, that is, the gap between ceiling and floor prices – within which stabilization of prices is to be sought; the cost of food stocks, including the required amount of investment in stocks and costs of storage (in developing countries both spoilage in storage and storage costs tend to be higher, the latter because of higher interest rates); the time interval between the procurement of supplies from abroad and their distribution at home – which determines the amount of food supplies to be released from stocks at times of shortage.

The third important issue relating to food security is the assurance of access for the poor. The South Commission deals with the question of food subsidy for the poor but stresses the high costs, in the sense that resources devoted to the subsidies could be used alternatively in raising employment and income opportunities for the poor; in addition, there is the possibility of leakages of the benefits of the subsidy to the non-poor. The Commission gives qualified support to food subsidy schemes which could be used for the improvement of the nutritional status of vulnerable groups.

There is no way but to opt for a second-best solution, trying to avoid as many inefficiencies and high costs as possible. Experience indicates that one such measure which tends to ensure self-targeting is the introduction of public employment schemes such as labour-intensive public works projects, including food-for-work projects. Wages may be paid in cash or in food. Provided that employment is offered at less than the going wage rate, that is, less than what is available in alternative private employment opportunities or self-employment, such schemes are not likely to compete with existing employment opportunities and are most likely to attract those who are otherwise unable to find employment. The second measure is some kind of specifically targeted subsidized food distribution scheme. Feeding programmes for particular vulnerable groups among the poor, for example the landless poor or female-headed households, are unlikely to involve any considerable risk of leakages to the non-poor. Both the public employment schemes and targeted food distribution programmes can be integrated with development programmes, that is, provision of physical infrastructure such as roads, irrigation and drainage schemes or training and education of the poorest groups for income-earning activities in both self-employment and wage employment.

Admittedly the administration of such poverty-oriented schemes is costly. By now a considerable body of experience has accumulated; this can provide guidance for successful and cost-effective replication and can be adjusted to the special circumstances of the country concerned. Several requirements seem to be clear. First, such schemes should be decentralized to the local government level for both their implementation and the mobilization of resources. Second, transparency and accountability in the administration of such schemes must be assured, in order that the beneficiaries and local populations at large are kept informed not only about the criteria for the selection of the beneficiaries but also about the nature of projects undertaken and the way in which resources are spent on these projects. Third, explicit linking as far as possible of the poverty- alleviating schemes to development projects, that is, to investment in physical and social infrastructure, will ensure that they are less like welfare schemes and more in the nature of development projects contributing to the formation of either physical or human capital.

Investment in Human Capital

The South Commission appropriately points out that investment in human capital formation is no less important than that in physical capital formation in its contribution to growth and development. The analyses and recommendations of the South Commission in respect of human capital formation are very similar to those of the UNDP Human Development Reports published subsequently in 1990 and 1991.[2] The main conclusions are as follows. First, expenditures on social sectors, that is, on health and education, etcetera in developing countries are inadequate in relation to the needs of development. Second, the disparity between urban and rural areas, where most of the poor reside, is considerable. Third, rural services are roughly 40 to 60 per cent of what is available in the urban areas. Fourth, there is also a bias towards curative health services, catering to the needs of the affluent classes and taking resources away from rural-based, primary health care services oriented towards the poor; in respect of education, as well, the bias is towards urban areas and towards higher education, such as university education, from which the urban rich benefit most.

There is now an increasing convergence of opinion that expenditure on human capital formation, that is, on health and education services, has to be expanded in developing countries, with a greater emphasis than in the past on primary and preventive health care services as well as on primary education and adult literacy programmes, with greater access for women to both education and health services. Obviously, the appropriate balance between primary and higher levels of education and health services depends on the stage of development of the country concerned as well as on the current availability of these services.

There are a number of policy issues in respect of social expenditures in developing countries. First, what is the best way to finance a large increase in such expenditures? Such an increase necessitates a revision of the order of priorities of public expenditures in developing countries, away from unproductive expenditures, especially military and security expenditures, toward social expenditures. Military expenditures in developing countries accounted for 5.5 per cent of GNP in 1986, whereas those on health accounted for barely 1.4 per cent. Second, there is a need for a more efficient and cost-effective use of resources in social sectors. Both these aspects are related to the way these services are organized and managed. Accountability and transparency in the provision of such services, their closer supervision, as well as the mobilization of resources for their financing, are enhanced if the provision of such services is delegated to the local governments. Third, an enhanced role for the private sector in providing (a) expensive, specialized and curative health services, and (b) higher levels of both general and technical education deserves serious examination. Fourth, the possibility that beneficiaries might pay at least a part of the cost of such services, even when they are provided by the public sector, deserves to be considered.

The Role of the Market, Prices and the State in Development

What role, if any, should the state play in promoting economic development? The South Commission attempts to deal with this question in a pragmatic and straightforward manner which is quite refreshing. The period of the 1980s had seen an extreme reaction against the interventionist role of government in development. "Getting prices right and letting the markets free" summed up the dominant philosophy. The possibility that publicly owned and managed enterprises engaged in trade, services and production could respond to price signals and act competitively was ruled out. It was emphasized that independence of action and autonomy of decision-making, untrammelled by political interference, which is necessary for efficient public enterprises, were unlikely to be realized in practice. Furthermore, public enterprises are likely to be entrusted with a multiplicity of objectives, such as regional development, or employment creation/guaranteeing, or high wages for labourers, which might not be consistent with maximizing profits or minimizing costs.

The Report seeks to take a balanced view of the role of government in economic development and steers clear of the extreme positions of relying exclusively on the "invisible hand" of the market, on the one hand, and, on the other, on the "oppressive and all-embracing hand" of the government. The Commission advocates a role for government which is more in the nature of a "helping hand" to compensate for market failures, wherever necessary, and to enable the market mechanisms to function efficiently. The Commission recognizes three different types of functions of government: macro-economic management, such as ensuring non-inflationary growth without large fiscal deficits and external payments disequilibrium; a planning and regulatory role to influence the allocation of resources; and government's role as an entrepreneur. There does not seem to be much controversy regarding the first set of functions. It is in respect of the second and third set of functions that controversy exists.

To compensate for market failures or to enable efficient functioning of the market, in cases where social and private costs diverge, external economies prevail or monopolistic trends persist, the government can either resort to physical controls or rely more on indirect tools such as taxes and subsidies. However, the Report of the South Commission does not rule out the possibility of direct control in certain circumstances, especially in the short run, where supply and demand elasticities are too low for taxes and subsidies to work through changes in relative prices.

The government's pre-eminent role in providing public goods such as roads, communications, transport, research, education, training, health, nutrition and family planning services is now more or less universally agreed, whatever the political philosophy of the governments in develop-ing countries.

It is in respect of the entrepreneurial function of the government in directly productive activities in agriculture, industry and trade that major disagreements exist. In cases where private enterprise does not exist or function, the government can either seek to promote private enterprise or directly undertake the required activity. The Report confirms that "whatever may have been the compulsions at an earlier stage in nation building, and whatever the social and political philosophies that bear on development strategies in the future, we believe that the role of the state as entrepreneur should now, for most developing countries, be more selective and discriminating as well as more efficient. These two objectives converge, for if the state's role becomes selective it has a better chance of becoming more efficient."[3]

The Commission emphasizes the role of government in strengthening the entrepreneurial business sector in a number of ways, first through training for entrepreneurs; promoting interactions between business leaders, politicians and public officials; provision of basic service buildings, power supplies and technical and business advice and information on market prospects, etc. Second, since the long-term success of the business sector depends on the stability and predictability of the economic policy environment, it is necessary to ensure that laws and regulations are consistently applied and that the macro-economic framework is such as to make it possible for economic calculations to be made with a reasonable degree of certainty. Third, the laws and regulations governing economic activities that inhibit the efficient performance of business need to be eliminated, with a view to encouraging competition and modernization.

The administrative and managerial ability at the disposal of the governments of developing countries is very scarce. Extending the state's responsibility to those activities which the private sector can perform as well or moderately better or worse usually incurs the cost of inefficiency – sometimes serious – in the performance of the essential functions of the government which the private sector cannot perform! An efficient public sector which establishes the regulatory framework and is responsible for macro-economic management and infrastructure is a necessary supplement to the efficiency of the market and the private sector.

Governance and Economic Development

Lately, much has been said about governance in developing countries, that is, honest government engaged in promoting economic development. An inefficient and corrupt government cannot play an effective promotional role in economic development. The Report calls for the modernization of the state, which includes transparency, accountability and participation. Within the concept of modernization the South Commission includes not only efficiency and motivation of the bureaucracy but also political institutions which ensure accountability, transparency, participation and the possibility of a peaceful change in government. There is the need for a political process which will generate a national consensus on development objectives as well as broad agreement on the sharing of the costs and benefits of development. Whatever the appropriate form of political institutions, certain principles must, however, be recognized. A broad consensus is essential in order that the various interest groups and segments of society should accept the objectives and results of the development process. The legitimacy of the government needs to be assured at least to the extent that those who do not agree with the actions and policies of the government none the less acquiesce in them and do not feel strongly enough to resist and subvert the government's policies and actions.

The South Commission notes that "participation in the political process means much more than the opportunity to exercise the vote. It means as well having a political climate that not merely tolerates dissent but welcomes it ... Accountability requires not only enforcement of the rule of law but the existence of independent systems for public evaluation of government conduct ... There is also a need, we believe, for more open discussion of the extent of corruption and its detrimental effects on development and on society. This must be the basis for vigorous efforts to curb this growing evil."[4]

It should be emphasized, however, that democracy and political pluralism are desirable objectives or ends in themselves and should be pursued on their own merits. Moreover, there is enough evidence to suggest that, in most cases, political democracy does promote the achievement of other aspects of human welfare, such as wider access to health and education services.

Experience shows that economic development and economic liberalism after a period lead to a demand for political pluralism. Participation in markets, involving enterprise, initiative and innovations, leads to a desire for participation in decision-making in the political process.

Environment and Development

The Report recognizes that in an interdependent world, global and environmental problems such as global warming and depletion of the ozone layer affect the prospects of future growth of developing countries, including the rate and the pattern of utilization of their natural resources. With the modernization of their economies and with rapid industrialization and agricultural intensification, the contribution of developing countries to global environmental degradation will go on increasing. Therefore, in common with the industrialized countries, they have a responsibility in devising a global rgime consistent with the requirements of their growth and development in the future.

Aside from the international arrangements in which developing countries should be able to participate fully, there are a variety of ways in which they are obliged to integrate environmental concerns in their domestic development policies and programmes. Given the pressure of their current poverty and the demands of an increasing population and rising incomes on natural resources, strategies need to be devised which will minimize damage to the environment. Resources which are being degraded or depleted now should be subject to renewal and regeneration in the future; forests need to be replenished; fisheries should be restocked; soil fertility should be restored and soil erosion should be contained and reversed. An environmentally sustainable development strategy requires an appropriate set of policies, technology and institutions. In this respect it is essential not only that the awareness of environmental concerns is strengthened among the researchers and policy-makers in developing countries but also that national capacities are built up to enable them to analyse the impact of current policies and programmes on their environment as well as to devise alternative options.

Unequal distribution of land, in consequence of which the poor are often left with fragile and marginal land, leads to overexploitation of land either for crop cultivation or for cattle grazing or other uses. On the other hand, large tracts of land owned by the rich remain unutilized, either because of a shortage of labour or because of a lack of interest on the part of the landowners, who are often absentee landlords living in urban areas. In many developing countries the management of common property resources in the rural communities has broken down, and as a result there is excessive and indiscriminate use of such resources, which in turn leads to soil erosion and deforestation.

Taxes, subsidies and price policies in many countries have led to an excessive or inordinate use of chemical inputs such as fertilizers and pesticides that cause soil degradation; in some others, incentive schemes, including subsidized credit and tax incentives, have been used to encourage human settlements in forests which are frequently on marginal and fragile soils. There is a vicious circle of interaction between poverty and environmental degradation. Environmental degradation reduces the productivity of the land and the incomes of the poor dependent on degraded land; the poor, with low incomes and large numbers of dependants, are then obliged to exploit resources even more intensively, especially since they have neither the means to restore the fertility of the soil nor access to productivity-enhancing inputs. This obliges them to move on to fragile or marginal lands, as the yield from existing land resources becomes inadequate to provide them with sustenance.

For the purpose of ensuring an environmentally sustainable growth pattern, both agricultural and industrial, it is necessary to encourage suitable technological innovations. In the foreseeable future, an alternative to the continued use of chemical inputs will have to be sought. For example, how to combine organic or inorganic inputs, that is, fertilizers or pesticides; how to use biological methods for controlling pests or enhancing crop yields; how to combat waterlogging and salinity – these are some of the questions which an environmentally oriented research agenda must address. Lands in various agro-ecological régimes differ widely in terms of their potential yield and susceptibility to environmental degradation. Consequently, the appropriate technology is likely to vary according to type of soil and according to the potential of the land. If high-potential areas are not exploited with the use of modern inputs, some of which are at the present time not environmentally safe, there are risks – in many cases a certainty – that the populations will move on to low-potential regions in search of their livelihoods, owing to the declining productivity of high-potential regions. The result would be the degradation of the low-potential areas; in a vicious circle poverty is further aggravated.

Conclusion

In their search for a better future, developing countries are at a crossroads in the early 1990s. As they emerge from the shocks, dislocations and turmoil of the 1980s -- which resulted for many of them in slow growth or stagnation or even a decline in per capita income -- they face the uphill task of trying to achieve a high rate of growth with equity and sustainability during the 1990s and beyond. The Report of the South Commission has done yeoman service in analysing the challenges which the developing countries face on the domestic front. The members of the Commission have been candid and forceful in their recommendations, the application of many of which would require a significant break from past policies and practices. In some respects, the developing countries will confront new uncertainties; the consequences of several suggested policy reforms cannot yet be predicted fully. Meeting future challenges and managing the unpredictable are not easy tasks, particularly for developing countries with inadequate capacity for analysis, policy formulation, and implementation. The South Commission Report is outstandingly forceful in outlining the political and other preconditions for such a redesigned development strategy for growth, equity and sustainability in developing countries.

Notes

1. South Commission, 1990, p.90.
2. UNDP, 1990 and 1991.
3. South Commission, 1990, p.115.
4. Ibid., pp.116-117.

Bibliography

South Commission

   The Challenge to the South: The Report of the South Commission, Oxford University
   Press, Oxford and New York, 1990.

UNDP (United Nations Development Programme)

   Human Development Report 1990, Oxford University Press, New York, 1990.
   Human Development Report 1991, Oxford University Press, New York, 1991.

29. MANY PATHS TO DEVELOPMENT

Saburo Okita

Japan is a country that has moved from being an impoverished country right after the Second World War to being a highly advanced industrial economy today, and I have frequently hoped there might be some way the Japanese experience could prove instructive for other countries on the same road. In fact, I found myself in agreement with many of this Report's analyses and recommendations, and I would like to focus this commentary on those areas where our interests overlap.

As numerous other people have pointed out, the global economy is becoming increasingly interdependent and integrated with the amazing advances in transportation and telecommunications. This is true not only economically but also politically, as symbolized by the collapse of the Berlin Wall and the transformation that is under way in the former Soviet Union and in Eastern Europe. Although there will still be considerable uncertainty until some new international order can be structured after the end of the Cold War, it seems clear already that the world must focus on North-South issues now as never before – not only because the decade of the 1980s was a "lost decade" for many of the countries of the developing South but also because of the overriding importance of global environmental and other issues with worldwide ramifications. The collapse of the Berlin Wall symbolized the end of East-West confrontation, and I hope that it will also mark the start of a new era of North-South co-operation. At the same time, some parts of the old "East" are now beginning to be thought of as "South", including several of the former Soviet republics.

Once thought of as uniform, the developing countries today have vastly different interests and are at very different stages of development. For this reason, it is impossible to devise any one single development strategy that will be equally effective for all developing countries. While political solidarity among the developing countries is important, it is even more important to realize that different economic strategies are needed for the newly industrializing economies, the middle-income developing economies, and the very poor developing economies. This realization of the differences in their stages of development then raises the question of the government's and the market's roles in development.

This is an important point of reference for this Report, and this was also important for Japan as a later-developing industrialized country in a number of respects. First, while it is important to liberalize micro-economic areas, it is essential to establish broad guidelines governing the formulation and establishment of macro-economic policies. Second, it appears that those countries which are attempting to catch up with more industrialized countries need stronger government leadership than the front-running industrial countries do. Third, planners have to read the market signals carefully and incorporate them in their planning. This means planning *with* market forces rather than planning *against* market forces.

What these first and second points imply is that, depending upon their stage of development and their development process, the developing countries may adopt very different patterns of behaviour even within the capitalist paradigm. While it is generally to the better that the world economy is gradually formulating new rules of behaviour and standardizing economic norms, it is crucial that this process should not be one of any one country's demanding that the other countries "do the same as I do", or "do as I say" and that, instead, this should be a give-and-take process with all countries borrowing the best that the other countries have to offer. Japan and the United States, for example, have different ways of looking at things. This is only natural, given their different histories and present situations. Yet neither is completely right or completely wrong. There are many rooms in capitalism's house. What Chalmers Johnson has called a "capitalist developmental state" could just as well be called "catch-up capitalism" or "the capitalism of the late-comer".

In a developing country where the private sector is still immature, the role of the government is to forge an effective alliance between planning and market mechanisms, and there are a number of countries in East and South-East Asia where the governments have emphasized this role and which have done very well with export-oriented development strategies. This then relates to the third point mentioned earlier. Export-oriented development strategies are thought to be preferable to import-substitution strategies because, by imposing an unforgiving cost-consciousness, they expedite the most efficient allocation of management and production resources and, as a result, enhance the entire country's economic efficiency. Costs must be considered even when economic plans are drawn up, and it is essential that plans be drawn up so as to take maximum advantage of market forces.

At the same time, the very same export-oriented development strategies that have made it possible for the countries of East and South-East Asia to achieve their flying-geese pattern of development are now encountering increasingly strong protectionism from the industrial countries. What does this mean for South-South co-operation?

Faced with import barriers in the North, the countries of the South are increasingly trading with each other. This would not, of course, be possible if they all wanted to export the same products, but because of the vast diversity within the South and because of the increasing differentiation among the developing countries South-South trade is increasingly viable. This viability would be enhanced and their economies made even more productive if the developing countries were to adopt more liberal trade policies, and South-South trade were to be liberalized as an integral part of the global effort to liberalize the trading environment.

Another area where the developing countries have been weak and where they could benefit from greater South-South co-operation is the area of policy formulation. It is essential that the individual developing countries should strengthen their capacity for policy formulation and implementation. Indeed, indications are that there is a very strong correlation between the quality of government and the quality of development. Capital, raw materials and other material considerations are not themselves the determining factors in development. Rather, it is the capacity of government to organize the available resources for productive purposes that is the most crucial factor.

There are two ways to strengthen the government's capacity in this respect. The first approach is the rather traditional one of technical assistance from the industrial countries, and the second is to devise some mechanism through which the developing countries can learn from each other's experiences. The developing countries' own experiences over the past several decades – both the successes and the failures – are arguably their richest source of information and ideas.

It is important that this resource should be tapped, perhaps by establishing a forum where the developing countries could learn from each other.

The self-help efforts by the developing countries and stepped-up South-South co-operation need to be supplemented by greater bilateral and multilateral support from the international community. South-South co-operation may also be extended to triangular co-operation among South-North-South countries. For example, a Korean institution and a Japanese aid agency may be able to contribute jointly to training Vietnamese business managers. Similar activities may offer significant opportunities for enhanced development co-operation.

It is worth looking back here at the recent history of development assistance. At the time when the Pearson Commission wrote its report *Partners in Development*,[1] most thinking on development assistance leaned toward placing the priority on assistance to countries that were making a strong policy effort for bootstrap development – countries that were working to raise their savings rates, to promote exports and thus to accelerate their growth rates – in the hope that this assistance would enable these countries to graduate from the aid-receiving side of the table and eventually to move to the aid-giving side of the table. Development assistance was to be based upon the principle of concentrating on the countries with the best prospects and trying to reduce the number of impoverished countries as quickly as possible.

However, enervated by their everyday destitution and at the mercy of international commodity markets and economic trends in the industrialized countries, many developing countries found they were not able either to raise their savings rates or to expand their exports as much as they wanted to. At the same time, concern was expressed that concentrating on the countries with the best graduation prospects might lead to writing off the more impoverished countries. As a result, it was argued that development assistance policies should also include the provision of such basic human needs as food, sanitation and elementary schooling – that the efficiency principle should be tempered with what might be called the welfare principle.

Since then, political considerations have been added to this tug of war between the efficiency principle and the welfare principle, and the priorities have shifted back and forth depending upon the times and even the situation of individual countries. In fact, there is now no single principle underlying development assistance on a global basis. The equation has been further complicated by the need to consider the demands of sustainable development as expounded by the Brundtland Commission's report *Our Common Future*.[2] No country – industrial, developing, or destitute – can afford to ignore the impact of development on the global environment.

Looking at development assistance, the South Commission Report calls upon the industrial North to double its official development assistance (ODA) to the least developed countries by the year 1995 and to raise the level of ODA to these countries to 0.2 per cent of the donor countries' GNPs by the end of this decade. In addition, the Report calls for a global programme of immediate action to double the volume of concessional transfers of resources to the developing countries through the multilateral institutions by 1995.

Similarly, the Stockholm Initiative on Global Security and Govern-ance, promoted by such statesmen as former West German Chancellor Willy Brandt and Swedish Prime Minister Ingvar Carlsson, produced a report, *Common Responsibility in the 1990s*, in April 1991, proposing that all industrial countries set public date-targets to provide 1 per cent of GNP for international development co-operation.[3] There is clearly widespread agreement that more needs to be done. How, for example, has Japan responded?

In 1988, Japan adopted its Fourth Medium-term Target for ODA calling for total ODA over the half-decade through 1992 to be double that for the previous half-decade and to total at least 50 billion US dollars. At the same time, the Cabinet called for raising the ratio of ODA to GNP, currently 0.31 per cent. Personally, I feel the industrial countries should work to raise their ratios of ODA to GNP to 0.7-1.0 per cent by the end of the century.

Qualitative enhancements have been under way in Japanese ODA, and the grant element, for example, has been gradually raised from 77.7 per cent in 1979 to 81 per cent of total ODA as of 1989. More important than the grant element percentage, however, is the question of whether or not Japanese assistance has been responsive to the real needs of each beneficiary developing country at its particular stage of development. In fact, the successful developing countries of East and South-East Asia received over 90 per cent of Japanese bilateral assistance in the 1960s and early 1970s and about 70 per cent of the total in the late 1970s and 1980s, and the bulk of this assistance was structured to encourage bootstrap development efforts. While observers had complained about the low grant element percentage in Japanese assistance, the fact that this region has achieved such dramatic advances and dynamic growth would seem to vindicate the concept of assistance based on the efficiency principle.

Referring to the international monetary system, the South Commission Report states that both the countries running surpluses in their balance of payments current accounts and the countries running deficits should have symmetrical obligations for adjustment in the reformed monetary system. A surplus-running country itself, Japan has steadfastly implemented a programme to recycle no less than 65 billion US dollars in financial resources to the developing countries over the five years beginning in 1987. This is about the same amount, in real terms, as was transferred from the United States to Europe under the Marshall Plan shortly after the end of the Second World War.

It is imperative that Japan should continue to funnel capital to the developing countries, especially since there is a net outflow of capital from the developing countries to the industrial countries and since most forecasters expect a global capital crunch over the next few years. This is particularly urgent now that the United States – formerly a capital supplier – has become the world's largest debtor country and is pulling in over 100 billion US dollars every year. As C. Fred Bergsten, Director of the Institute for International Economics, has written:

Elimination of the overall budget deficit, however, remains crucial for foreign policy as well as economic reasons. The budget deficit is the chief cause of the trade deficit, which in turn requires the United States to borrow huge sums abroad and thus adds greatly to its external dependence and its insecurity. In addition, as long as the United States drains resources from the rest of the world, it cannot be a net financial contributor to other countries. Indeed the United States competes with others for scarce world savings. Hence America's greatest contribution to recovery in Eastern Europe or the Third World would be correction of its own fiscal position.[4]

Although the end of the Cold War should produce a "peace dividend" through the reduction of military expenditures, the massive demand for capital and the limited supply of surplus savings may result in a general shortage of financial resources and higher international interest rates. At the same time, the high risks and low financial return may tend to discourage the flow of private capital to the developing countries if there is strong competition for scarce funds. Hence the official and semi-official flows on concessional terms will have to be expanded. It is also absolutely necessary to raise domestic savings rates in both the developing and the industrial countries and to make more efficient use of available financial resources.

Given the grave importance of the debt problem, it is imperative that the debtor governments, the creditor governments, the creditor commercial banks and the multilateral financial institutions agree to share the burden of making any solution work. Looking just at the debtor developing countries, it is important that they formulate policy and manage their economies to facilitate the most efficient possible use of all available resources. Here the South Commission Report calls for scaling down debt service to levels which would allow growth to be sustained at a rate that would yield annual increases in per capita income of at least 2-3 per cent, and this may well be needed to maintain the developing countries' economic and political sustainability. At the same time, it is essential that the developing countries use every possible means to stem effectively the flight of indigenous capital.

Yet this call for growth by the developing countries does not mean that they should aspire to become carbon copies of today's industrial countries. In fact, the Commission's Report specifically rejects the industrial countries' commercialist models and argues that the South's development strategies should be oriented towards meeting basic human needs better, priority being given to eliminating poverty and hunger and narrowing the North-South gap. At the

conclusion of the Tokyo Conference on the Global Environment and
Human Response toward Sustainable Development (September
1989), I drew up a Chairman's Summary that included the following
passage:

> Designing for a sustainable future beyond the 20th century will
> require a new commitment to Environmental Ethics by all nations,
> upon which actions can be taken by integrating a variety of socio-
> economic policies, enabling people in developing countries to meet
> their basic needs, and modifying socio-economic activities including
> the lifestyle in developed countries. Broad-based participation and
> contribution of concerned groups and the public are needed and inten-
> sive public information and awareness activities should be fostered.[5]

The imperatives of the global environment will demand new initiatives
– technological, financial and otherwise – from the industrial countries.
Japan (for example) is currently in the process of disbursing a total of
300 billion yen (approximately 2.25 billion US dollars) in bilateral and
multilateral environmental assistance in the three years from 1989 through
1991. While there is considerable debate about what can be accomplished
given the political and economic conditions in the developing countries,
there is no doubt about the urgency of environmental issues.

It is important that international negotiations on environmental
conservation should seek to devise measures that take account of both
the global environment and economic conditions in the developing
countries. The protection of the tropical forests is an illustrative case:
most of these forests are in the developing countries, yet the great
biological diversity that exists in these forests is a reservoir of
potential for developments in biotechnology benefiting all
humankind. Surely arrangements can be negotiated for trading
financial and technological co-operation from the industrial countries
for wiser economic and environmental policies in the developing
countries. In this connection, it would be most desirable to establish
a body that might be called the United Nations Environmental
Security Council to deal with these issues comprehensively. When
the diversity of interests makes it difficult to reach global agreement,
it may be necessary to deal with these issues in regional and subregional
frame-works on an interim basis.

Likewise, it is imperative that the industrial countries should do
more to develop the technologies for preventing acid rain and global
warming, for conserving energy and developing low-cost alternative
energies, and for meeting other environmental needs, as well as to
transfer these technologies to the developing countries. In addition, the
international community should make every effort to work out methods

for assessing the environmental impact of development assistance in order to ensure that this assistance is not counter-productive in the long term.

While everyone acknowledges that technology transfer is important to the developing countries' economies and that this technology should be appropriate to the recipient economy's stage of development, people sometimes tend to forget that providing these countries with environmentally sound technology is in everyone's best interests.

Instead of sitting back and waiting for these technologies, the developing countries must make a concurrent effort to develop their own human resources and to enhance their own technological capabilities. Happily, the South Commission Report is forthright on the social and economic importance of education in all countries.

Japan offers a useful example in this respect. Japanese educators tended to argue that education is important in its own right and should not be seen in economic terms. When the issue is considered dispassionately, however, it is clear that there must be some connection between society's needs, the abilities the economy requires and the educational process that gives people these abilities. Otherwise our schools will end up turning out large numbers of highly educated, overqualified and unemployed people. As I emphasized in the early 1960s, the education and economic planning realms, while not concentric, do overlap to a considerable degree.

The same is true of nutrition, sanitation, and health care as they relate to economic development. All too often, the developing countries suffer from a vicious circle of malnutrition and poverty. Food is to humankind what fuel is to an engine. No engine will perform well unless it has enough good-quality fuel, and no one can work efficiently without a sufficiency of good-quality food. Not only does malnutrition in the formative years have serious effects on health, but malnutrition at any stage aggravates the individual susceptibility to disease and saps the community's overall effectiveness.

As the Commission on Health Research for Development noted in 1990:

> The proposed expansion of research on health problems of developing countries will require substantial increases in funding. We recommend, therefore, that developing countries, bilateral and multilateral development agencies, industrialized-country research agencies, foundations, NGOs, and the pharmaceutical industry all raise funding levels for health research. Specifically:
>
> developing countries should invest at least 2 per cent of national

health expenditures in research and research capacity strengthening, and at least 5 per cent of project and programme aid for the health sector from development aid agencies should be earmarked for research and research capacity strengthening.[6]

Population is another crucial issue, and the South Commission Report provides a very practical approach to this highly political and extremely sensitive issue. It is imperative that the industrial countries and the international institutions concerned should provide financial and technological co-operation and that international efforts should be aimed at braking world population growth and stabilizing the global population as soon as possible.

Finally, while it is important that we strengthen our international institutions lest they be completely overwhelmed by the enormity of the issues, it must be noted that they have been weakened by the drift away from multilateralism. Frustrated by the unwieldiness of the global approach, countries have increasingly turned to regional or bilateral arrangements. It is, however, essential to differentiate between deliberative organizations and executive organizations at all levels (national, subregional, regional, interregional and global).

The major objective of deliberative organizations such as UNCTAD is to build consensus and to enhance legitimacy in the international community. Understandings reached in such multilateral fora are the basis and authority for pursuing shared goals, and this legitimacy is essential if anarchy is to be avoided and progress made.

By contrast, the major objective of executive organizations such as the World Bank is to de-politicize issues and actions by taking them out of the unilateral realm. For instance, aid policy can be highly political in the bilateral context but is less so in the UNDP and the World Bank.

While the distinction between deliberative and executive organizations is important, in both types of organization the tendency away from multilateralism means eroded legitimacy and heightened politicization. In effect, the shortcuts of bilateralism and regionalism complicate the quest for long-term solutions to global issues.

The revival of protectionism and regionalism notwithstanding, the increasingly global nature of the world economy and the accelerating advances in transportation and telecommunications technologies are powerful forces pushing us to multilateralism. As the South Commission Report notes, the fault lies not in the stars but in the lack of effective public opinion leadership in the industrial countries. If North-South co-operation is gaining a better understanding of the problems facing the developing countries and the industrial countries alike and could be expanded from the governmental level to the NGO level, this broad-based discussion would contribute immeasurably to understanding in the industrial countries. In turn, increased public concern in the industrial countries would spark new debate on development issues and stimulate the formulation of more effective assistance policies.

At the same time, it should be possible to avoid the politicization of aid policies by identifying those areas where the interests of the industrial countries and the developing countries converge to create a positive-sum game. These convergences of interests and areas of agreement not only help to facilitate effective assistance, they are also essential to enhanced multilateralism and for ensuring that the emerging regionalism does not end in the creation of rigid economic blocs but is a step on the way to global multilateralism. Happily, there are individuals and governments in the North who understand these issues, and their efforts are gradually starting to pay off. What we need now is an international climate more conducive to the growth of such efforts for sustainable development by both North and South. If the Report of the South Commission can help to achieve that objective, the time and effort that its authors have put into its writing will have been more than worthwhile.

Notes

1. Pearson Commission, 1969.
2. Brundtland Commission, 1987.
3. Stockholm Initiative on Global Security and Governance, 1991.
4. C. Fred Bergsten, 1990, p.105.
5. Saburo Okita, 1989.
6. Commission on Health Research for Development, 1990, p.89.

Bibliography

Bergsten, C. Fred
  "The world economy after the Cold War", *Foreign Affairs*, Summer 1990.
Brundtland Commission
  Our Common Future, Oxford University Press, Oxford, 1987.
Commission on Health Research for Development
  Health Research: Essential Link to Equity in Development, Oxford University Press, Oxford, 1990.
Okita, Saburo
  Chairman's Summary, Tokyo Conference on the Global Environment and Human Response toward Sustainable Development, September 1989.
Pearson Commission
  Partners in Development: Report of the Commission on International Development, Praeger Publishers, New York, 1969.
Stockholm Initiative on Global Security and Governance
  Common Responsibility in the 1990s, Prime Minister's Office, Stockholm, 1991.

30. NEW CHALLENGES FOR DEVELOPING COUNTRIES

Alicia Puyana

Since the publication of the South Commission Report the world has undergone radical changes in the political sphere: the disintegration of the Soviet Union and the socialist bloc and, with this, the so-called "collapse of socialism" and the end of the Cold War. At the same time, a process of democratization has been taking place from Africa to Latin America, marked by the retreat of the odious apartheid system and the overthrow of military dictatorships. The immediate effect of these political trans-formations has been to consolidate capitalism as the only viable model of social organization. This article wishes to draw attention to some of the consequences of this assumption and to illustrate, from Latin America's experiences, the dangers for the future of democracy and the socio-economic development of the Third World countries.

Although the ideal of democracy has been alive in Latin America since the very beginnings of its republican existence (national political constitutions were inspired both by the principles of the French Revolution and those of the Constitution of the American Union), "up to the Second World War democracy was primarily an idea with no empirical content. Later, democracy was an experiment that failed in nearly every country."[1] The oscillation between authoritarian or dictatorial régimes and democratic governments has led to deep scepticism or, at least, immense caution in predicting the political future of Latin America.

On the threshold of the 1990s the region entered an exceptional period: for the first time since independence, all but one of the countries of the region are ruled by elected governments and have managed to consolidate democratic régimes. The fact that this process of transition to democracy took place just at the time of the debt crisis at the end of the "lost decade" is surprising, and raises doubts as to whether the pendulum may not swing back again to its starting point,[2] while it also set a number of restrictions on the real political possibilities of the new régimes.

The process of democratization that Latin America is living through today covers all countries and all types of government in the region, since it does not simply mean the overthrow of military régimes but also involves the modernizing processes of institutional change taking place in countries that are relatively stable democracies such as Venezuela and also Colombia. Latin America, like other regions of the South, has two gigantic tasks before it: first, to create democratic institutions and a democratic political culture and solve the problems created by the economic crisis, and, second, to execute the familiar economic adjustment and liberalization programmes and remedy the ravages of extreme social inequality. These are tasks that appear contradictory or impossible to carry out simultaneously.

The political climate in the region and the world at large seems to have tilted the balance in favour of a hierarchical system that gives priority to consolidating the tasks implied by democracy while deferring those of social justice that inspired the political plans and programmes of numerous governments in the 1960s and 1970s, when even military governments, such as that of Velasco Alvarado in Peru, pursued radical social reforms. In this sense, it would seem that democracy may be becoming an end in itself and be essentially defined as the choice of leaders through competitive elections in which theoretically every adult citizen is eligible to stand for election and has the right to vote.[3] This concept, which springs from the experiences of modern societies in the developed countries, is limited[4] and, in Meyer's view, insufficient[5] under the conditions prevailing in Latin America and nearly all other developing countries.

What are these conditions? In the first place, economic underdevelopment which, combined with the regional economic crisis and world recession, has created new situations of ungovernability. The regression of the economy as a result of the external debt and world trade problems in the past decade led to a shrinkage of Latin America's presence in the world markets for capital and goods as well as in its share within the group of developing countries as a whole. There has been a weakening of these countries' export capacity which, unless it is reversed, will lead to lower rates of investment and widen the gap separating these countries from the developed economies. Second, in Latin America in the 1990s, the figures for poverty are higher than at the beginning of the 1980s, and not only has per capita output declined, but employment itself has declined, levels of health, education and housing have deteriorated, productive investment has become stagnant while capital has been exported through external debt servicing or illegal transfers abroad. Lastly, the number of people living in dire poverty has risen from 120 million to 160 million.

The international economic climate indicates that, even if a serious effort at "economic adjustment" is made, it is doubtful whether the financial resources are ample enough. The developed countries have not overcome the crisis, and will continue to attract external savings to offset the lack of domestic savings since, in order to assure higher economic growth rates, the investment coefficient has to be raised. Then, too, Eastern Europe, the former Soviet Union and the Middle East are all clamouring for external financing on a bigger scale.

As a result of the poverty levels referred to above, large social groups are on the verge of malnutrition, have no housing or essential services, and of course no access to a basic education that would equip them to become citizens in the full sense of the term, with the ability to exercise their rights and carry out their duties rationally. Unlike the developed countries where want and extreme poverty affect only a small proportion of the population, in Latin America, as in other developing countries, at least a quarter of the inhabitants suffer from these ills. While the richest 10 per cent of society account for nearly 50 per cent of total income, the poorest 20 per cent have only 2.3 per cent. Can a democracy become firmly established without seriously intending to correct this imbalance? It is not a question of achieving an egalitarian society but simply of giving each citizen the possibility of living in dignity. However, external and domestic factors suggest that concern with redistribution and the relevant programmes are by no means a priority on the agendas of the ruling parties or governments.

First, the same internal political conditions that favoured the movement towards democracy in Latin America indicate that, at best, democracy signifies conservatism without stagnation and reform without revolution.[6] In a situation of economic liberalism and a decline in the redistributive capacity of the state, this implies the preservation of the economic *status quo*, that is, the maintenance of the present levels of poverty and continued failure to meet the basic needs of broad sectors of the population.

Second, at the very heart of the process of transition towards democracy is the need for greater guarantees of stability and general consensus. It was the self-same authoritarian governments, in fact, that drew up the agenda for the nature and tempo of transition, which involved establishing areas that would be left untouched by the changes – "social reforms and the military rgime were taboo"[7] – and succeeded in enlisting the very sectors that had in their time supported those governments.[8] It is understandable, therefore, why the new Colombian Constitution, in force since 5 July 1991, did not modify the former military régime in any way and why measures to reduce the present level of unemployment are not mentioned in the new development plans.

This desire for "continuity" and consensus could lead to the exclusion of the sectors that press for change. Moreover, political theory offers arguments in support of this "insufficient" concept of democracy by suggesting that there is no direct relation between efficiency in economic management, the ability or inability to provide public goods such as employment or income redistribution, and polities.[9]

Public goods – political factors, civil liberties and opportunities for public debate – are therefore the most important elements of political legitimacy, and are virtually exclusive to it. The Latin American political left also agrees with this, and the decision taken by the new Chilean government not to modify the economic model inherited from the military government also seems to endorse this point of view. Latin America is moving towards the preservation of these conditions, which shore up and reproduce "social apartheid"[10], which makes it impossible to speak of "democratic consolidation".

The capitalist ideology which, upon the collapse of the socialist model, assumed a triumphant and hegemonic role presents the market as a synonym for democracy, whereas in fact the market is also a political category and a power relationship and, under the conditions prevailing in Latin America, the free play of market forces can hardly mitigate the outward signs of the extreme concentration of wealth. Moreover, in purely economic terms, it is clear that, with keener competition, the concentration effects due to growth will be stronger than the dispersion effects, since a highly stratified economy with pronounced income concentration tends to reproduce the concentration model in distributing the benefits of growth.

The politico-economic proposition implicit in the neo-liberal model assumes that economic growth alone will suffice to eliminate, or reduce, extreme poverty. But, as the Latin American experience indicates, there is no connection between economic expansion and redistribution. During the period of fast growth in the 1960s and up to 1977, when the product increased by 161 per cent, poverty was reduced by only 18 per cent.[11] Moreover, in emphasizing and giving priority to the increase of capital accumulation in the private sector, the rate of profit became sacrosanct,[12] and any redistributive policy, such as the preservation of the real purchasing power of wages, has to be discredited.

What must be done in Latin America to ensure that democracy ceases to be a utopia and acquires a social content?

First, all citizens must be guaranteed the minimum conditions that constitute the basis of social life: education, health, nutrition. The guarantee of education is vital since, without it, no one will be free or equal, nor will there be the possibility of genuine free participation in democratic political life.

This line of action implies, in practice, guaranteeing equality of opportunity and not the provision of minimum living conditions. In education, for instance, it is necessary to go beyond primary schooling and to make modern technical knowledge available in accordance with the needs of the real world and the trends and requirements of specialization and labour flexibility.

This line of action also implies general and stable employment that is stimulating and remunerative, and that will generate sufficient income for the social groups that are now indigent to have access to the goods and services of modern society. Anti-poverty programmes would then cease to have "welfare" overtones and would become economic development programmes and catalysts of productive expansion.

Second, genuine processes of modernization should be promoted that would imply, among other things, political secularization, the strengthening of political parties to enable them to act effectively as mediators between civil society and the state, popular participation in the management of the state, and the affirmation of public interests and republican principles. The cornerstone of the essential political changes will be the assurance of the effective working of institutions that "guarantee the enforcement of human rights ... and the equality of all citizens in the eyes of the law".

Third, as the struggle for democracy is centred on access to state power to manage economic resources and influence the allocation of the economic surplus, democracy must guarantee that, in the event of a possible political ascent of the sectors that seek for change and social justice, it would not be restrained by *de facto* measures as was the case after the elections in 1992 in Algeria. The violent repression of popular protests against adjustment policies and the two failed attempts at military coups d'tat which have destabilized the social-democratic government in Venezuela – "the most stable democracy of Latin America" as it has usually been called – appear to bear out the misgivings implicit in this article. No developing country can afford to ignore the social demands of the mass of the people or build up the nation on fragile foundations of the kind postulated in exclusive economic models. The failure of the military coup in Venezuela should lead to a broad social agreement for the preparation of macro-economic policies designed to raise the income levels of the social groups hit by adjustment.

Notes

1. L. Meyer, 1989, p.30.
2. E. Huber, 1990, p.16.
3. S. Huntington, 1989, p.16.,
4. Huber, 1990, p.160.
5. Meyer, 1989, p.31, suggests that this type of democracy can be a desirable end for

enlightened conservatives, the military or civilians, since it prevents extreme positions, maintains stability and pre-empts military confrontation with neighbouring countries.

6. Huntington, 1989, p.24.
7. C. Gillespie, 1986.
8. L. Whitehead, 1989.
9. R. Kaufman, 1989, pp.217-222.
10. J.A. Moises, 1991.
11. V.E. Tokman, 1991.
12. Ibid.

Bibliography

Gillespie, C.
"From authoritarian crises to democratic transition in Latin America", *Latin Ameri-can Research Review*, Vol. XXII, No. 13, 1986.

Huber, E.
"Democracy in Latin America", *Latin American Research Review*, Vol. XXV, No. 2, 1990.

Huntington, S.
"The modest meaning of democracy", in R.A. Pastor (ed.), *Democracy in the Americas: Stopping the Pendulum ...*, Holmes and Meier, New York, 1989.

Kaufman, R.
"Debt and democracies in the 80s", in B. Stallings and R. Kaufman (eds.), *Debt and Democracy in Latin America*, Westview Press, Boulder, Colorado, 1989.

Meyer, L.
"Democracy from three Latin American perspectives", in R.A. Pastor (ed.), *Democracy in the Americas: Stopping the Pendulum ...*, Holmes and Meier, New York, 1989.

Moises, J.A.
"Democracy Threatened: The Latin American Paradox" (mimeo), Sao Paulo, 1991.

Tokman, V.E.
"Pobreza y homogenizacin social: tareas para los 90", *Pensamiento Iberoamericano*, No. 19, 1991.

Whitehead, L.
"The consolidation of fragile democracies", in R.A. Pastor (ed.), *Democracy in the Americas: Stopping the Pendulum ...*, Holmes and Meier, New York, 1989.

31. NATIONAL DEVELOPMENT AND SOUTH-SOUTH CO-OPERATION: MOVING FORWARD[1]

Delphin G. Rwegasira

Introduction

The Report of the South Commission has been and should be broadly welcomed by the peoples of both South and North. For the peoples of the South, this Report is a "home-grown" product of deep and multi-disciplinary analysis and reflection relating to the problems, development strategies and aspirations of the South. For this reason, the Report also offers a comprehensive framework for analysts and international negotiators, particularly from the South, in dealing with the complex problems facing the developing world. For the peoples in the North, the Report presents a unique opportunity for better understanding the South -- its plight, its aspirations and its interpretation of the place it occupies in the global politico-economic setting.

As the Chairman of the Commission, Mwalimu Nyerere stressed when introducing the Report at the Ministerial Meeting of the United Nations Economic and Social Council, in July 1991, that the Report is addressed in the first place to the peoples and governments of the developing countries. "For neither people nor their nations can be developed from outside."[2] But for the obvious reasons of interdependence, the Report is also addressed to the North in the context of the constraints and opportunities the industrial economies present for the development prospects of the South. The primary responsibility for development in the countries of the South, however, lies in the South. As a result, national development policies and measures and similar instruments applied to promote greater co-operation among developing countries assume critical importance.

These remarks focus, therefore, on national development policies, in particular, with some reference also to related issues in South-South co-operation. The remarks are organized around the objective of advancing toward the principal development goals indicated in the Report at both the national and the South levels.

Some Strategic Considerations

The development strategies and agenda discussed and recommended for individual countries of the South and for collective efforts by those countries are wide-ranging. It may be tempting to comment analytically on the issues covered in terms of breadth and depth, to determine whether the Report addresses satisfactorily the questions facing the developing countries. That approach would certainly have some advantages. However, given the space available for these remarks, the approach preferred is to indicate some strategic considerations which may be useful in discussions about ways of advancing towards the key goals mentioned in the Report.

Continued search for agents of change

In order to approach many of the indicated development goals within a meaningful time-frame, the Report correctly stresses the imperative of fast and sustained growth – in food and agricultural production, in appropriate industrialization, in the development of the service sector and in international trading. Higher growth would in turn increase the ability of countries to do more in key areas like human resource development and the protection and improvement of the environment. Central to all this is a healthy and efficient saving-investment process. With respect to who does what in order to make progress on these fronts, the Report takes up the various developmental roles of the state, the planning process and the market. It is rightly argued that the state, apart from its traditional responsibility for macro-economic management, should now be more selective and discriminating in its function as an entrepreneur – according a greater role to the private sector. It should also be modernized by, above all, cultivating a democratic ethic that "allows all ideas to contend". The role of the business sector – public enterprises, private firms, co-operatives, micro-businesses, etcetera – is also discussed.

The broad division between the state and the market in promoting socio-economic change – in directly productive areas and in other areas like human resource development and the environment – seems balanced. However, given the development experience in some developing countries, the level of generalization leaves one still in search of more specific agents of economic change. The discussion on the role of the business sector attempted to examine this topic but perhaps more ought to have been said. For instance, given the emphasis, throughout the Report, on popular participation in economic and political decisions, surely one could envisage more dynamic roles for local and regional co-operatives as well as for local governments in some developing countries. How about greater development possibilities through non-governmental organizations, the youth and voluntary movements? And what are the contributions that specialized local and national institutions could make to accelerate the expansion of domestic and foreign private investment (private initiative and the private sector)? With respect to enhancing the saving-investment process, what are the lessons of experience in regard to the mobilization of small rural and urban savings? Assuredly more imaginative actions are needed on the part of domestic financial intermediaries and other mechanisms – by, for example, extending the range of financial instruments and the geographical coverage in operating such institutions. Similarly, domestic stock exchanges and related institutions, if promoted, could assist in the same direction. All these examples point to one conclusion: faster national development would benefit from a continued identification of and support for agents of socio-economic change, aimed at promoting greater understanding of the dynamics of society and at mobilizing all possible energies for development. Academic and applied research could contribute useful ideas in this respect by relating the relevance of such factors to particular circumstances.

A similar conclusion could be reached with respect to greater co-operation among the countries of the South. Many suggestions are made in the Report on how this could be brought about. But the search for strategies and mechanisms should continue. As is well recognized in the Report, the major regional development banks, for instance, which are now quite strong in terms of financial resources and expertise, should find ways to do much more in the areas of financing multinational (integration) projects and promoting South-South trade and co-operation generally. Greater scientific and technical co-operation among the countries of the South calls for similar systematic research efforts.

Sharpening policy focal points

The achievement of the various national development goals indicated in the Report clearly requires, among other things, focused policy analysis and efficient policy-making. It also requires explicit recognition of the inter-relationships among the objectives and among the key economic and social activities and sectors within a national economy.

In practice, policy co-ordination and the management of the inter-sectoral linkages necessary for the pursuit of national socio-economic goals remain strikingly weak in some countries – at both the technical and policy levels as well as at the political decision-making level. And this weakness is often accompanied by low capacity in policy analysis. This combination of circumstances reduces the impact of individual and national development efforts. Indeed, in other cases, there are outright contradictions in policies partly because of weak policy frameworks, misguided political perceptions or bureaucratic rivalries. Poor countries can ill afford these kinds of avoidable waste. Every effort, therefore, ought to be made as part and parcel of the national development process to streamline and harmonize policies continually and to sharpen policy focal points. It may be helpful, within a national framework, for instance, to provide a few clear and strong fora or define a well-streamlined supervisory structure, at both the technical and political levels, to ensure that related developmental questions are rigorously and comprehensively addressed And such a structure ought to be supported by strong policy analysis and advice which in turn calls for strengthening technical capacity for such work. This whole process would also be aided by policy and research centres outside the usual framework of government business, which would provide more "independent" and possibly more detailed analysis and advice. To be sure, all these require financial and other resources to build the requisite skilled manpower and to support appropriate institutions. But available resources and institutions (universities, policy analysis units within government ministries, etcetera) could also be more efficiently used to meet part of the demand.

The South Commission Report well recognizes the wide-ranging developmental issues facing the South and the constraints and opportunities arising from its relations with the North. The Report, therefore, convincingly proposes the establishment of a strong focal point – the South Secretariat – to act as a pillar in the building of South-South co-operation and to assist in the negotiation and promotion of equitable global relationships. In the same spirit, the Report welcomes the establishment of a Summit Level Group for South-South Consultations and Co-operation. These two ideas are consistent with the general point being made -- that national development and South-South co-operation would be helped by providing focal points that could help to mobilize the necessary efforts. What should be emphasized for reasons of efficiency and economy is that these focal points should use, as much as possible, existing institutions – regional research and policy centres, financial institutions, subregional and regional political organizations, etcetera – as the Report also recognized. Also important is the more effective use of international organizations which were specifically established to strengthen development in the Third World (that is, UNCTAD).

Ensuring consistency between policy goals and instruments

Strong focal points for policy analysis and national decision-making would be helpful in furthering progress towards principal development goals. But additional efforts would be required, either by co-ordination among the few focal points themselves or by higher levels of national leadership, to ensure consistency between various policy objectives and the actual instruments of policy applied. The success of these efforts may at times require giving greater autonomy to selected national institutions or placing them higher in the political hierarchy in order to accord them sufficient authority.

The South Commission Report places great emphasis, for instance, on domestic resource mobilization, which is essential for raising the investment rate and for national self-reliance. It goes on to point out that fiscal, monetary and exchange rate policies must be used to promote macro-economic stability that significantly and positively influences investment. The Report also notes the past failure in many developing countries to maintain fiscal and monetary discipline – "which has not served the cause of long-term development". Beyond this, the Report addresses relevant and interesting issues situating the problems of financial instability, particularly in small developing countries, in the context of economic openness and external shocks.

One feels, however, that it might have been useful had the Report returned to the problem of fiscal and monetary indiscipline. For this problem demonstrates the point being made here – that extra effort is required at the national level to ensure consistency between policy goals (a healthy saving-investment process) and the applied instruments of day-to-day macro-economic management (monetary and fiscal practices). It is true that inflation and balance-of-payments problems in developing countries cannot be ascribed simply to expansion in domestic credit or the money supply. However, for inflation to be sustained it must be financed ultimately through the money-creation process. For this simple reason, the performance of central banks in developing countries must be related to the failure in monetary and fiscal discipline mentioned in the Report. But quite often, the central banks did not have sufficient authority to contain deficit financing by governments (basically through finance ministries which are the "bosses" of these banks). Central banks were at times also unable to control other forms of domestic credit partly because of reasons related to government practices of supporting major public-sector institutions through commercial bank lending.

It is certainly possible for governments in developing countries to give greater autonomy to central banks in the strategic national interest of ensuring consistency between the major goal of enhancing the saving-investment process and the use of macro-economic instruments (monetary and fiscal practices). There is nothing "monetarist" in saying this. The manner of extending greater autonomy to national central banks would inevitably vary from country to country, but what is of greater importance in the context of these remarks is the principle itself. Indeed, the broader and more fundamental question is not just that of central bank autonomy but the willingness of governments to heed well-grounded independent counsel and to adhere to established norms and restraints in the interests of sustained development. This issue is also quite separate from the principle of appropriate political accountability for all institutions, which is perfectly acceptable. And it may be said in passing that this principle of central bank autonomy is assuming considerable significance in the current discussions relating to the strengthening of European economies through greater integration envisaged in the 1990s.

Related to the desirability of greater autonomy of central banks for the purpose of ensuring better monetary discipline is the need for counter-cyclical macro-financial management. Developing country governments, for instance, have tended to increase expenditures very rapidly during export booms, but failed to contain the expenditures accordingly during downswings. The eventual outcomes have usually been rapid depletion of national foreign exchange reserves, import shortages and price inflation. These in turn adversely affect the saving-investment process. This broad area of counter-cyclical macro-economic management clearly requires close co-operation between national fiscal and monetary authorities, but strong and more autonomous central banks could help greatly in terms both of independent advice and of monetary control.

The need for greater consistency between goals and instruments is in practice also equally demonstrated in the areas of trade and industrialization. The case of dynamic export growth to permit adequate aggregate growth in the highly import-dependent developing economies, and to promote the benefits of competition and diversification, is well argued in the South Commission Report. Also well presented is the case of appropriate import-substitution. It should be said, however, that even in these well-argued cases development management would require greater specificity at the national level. Who, for example, should determine the industries to be protected, the level of protection and the timing of lifting the protection? Past experiences indicate that appropriate approaches to these kinds of issues are required to ensure a timely and smooth transition from protection to competitive industrialization and exporting.[3]

The objective of ensuring consistency is similarly to be pursued with respect to the promotion of South-South co-operation. There should be focal points – in the form of the South Secretariat and otherwise – not only to enhance the co-operation but also to find appropriate ways of constructively criticizing and advising developing country governments about their policies and practices as they affect South-South co-operation. Indeed, the South Secretariat could issue occasional or regular reports on these matters going beyond intra-South co-operation to addressing the

North on its positive or negative actions vis-à-vis South-South co-operation. The role of criticizing and advising the countries of the South by the voices of the South would be comparable to that of such organizations as the OECD which assess individual industrial country policies. The Report of the South Commission rightly proposes also the creation of focal points at the national level – a government ministry or department and a national committee – to ensure consistency of national actions with the objective of South-South co-operation.

Enhancing capacity for timely change

Beyond ensuring consistency between goals and policy instruments, greater efficiency with respect to national policy-making and implementation would also require enhanced capacity for timely change in many developing countries. Quite often, policies initially put in place to promote key objectives, as advocated in the Commission's Report, tend to be "sticky" (assuming lives of their own), to create vested interests and eventually to be even counter-productive. That way, policies that are otherwise inherently useful *ab initio*, gradually stand in the way of desirable change and progress. It is, therefore, important as one looks at the management of socio-economic change in the 1990s and beyond that governments adopt greater flexibility and pragmatism in policy-making. This aspect of development management has probably been underlined by the recent dramatic changes in the socialist or communist countries where rigid ideology and over-centralization of policy-making have clearly led to serious underperformance vis-à-vis national expectations on both the economic and socio-political fronts.

Timely change and a greater flexibility in policies would, of course, be greatly assisted by promoting a democratic ethic that, in the words of the Report, keeps the "process of political participation open at all levels". In order to accelerate socio-economic development, the governments of the South should move away decisively from positions of "natural" or acquired monopoly on political power. They should explicitly encourage pluralism and allow groups to openly compete for power in the market of political and economic ideas. Genuine concerns and constraints relating to societal peace in the transition must, of course, be appropriately addressed, but the way forward should be toward pluralism even if qualified with necessary political safeguards and other mechanisms.

Similarly, enhanced collective capacity is required in the South for timely analysis of issues affecting South-South co-operation and North-South relations – in order to prepare or press for requisite changes. Such changes may be strategic or simply tactical in nature. Two areas may be cited, as examples, to demonstrate this need for closely analysing evolving circumstances and deriving appropriate actions. One is the problem of external indebtedness. Although this has been a persistent problem for over a decade now and although the problem remains formidable, in recent years there have been significant tactical and, to some extent, philosophical changes on the part of the creditor community. It is necessary to follow these changes more closely and relate them to some of the proposals that have originated from the South. The debtors' forum proposed in the Commission's Report could, for instance, continually address the debt issue with more analytical support from the South.

The second area requiring a close analytical and dynamic follow-up is the evolution of East-West relations and their implications for South-South relations. The Non-Aligned Movement, for instance, will have to re-define its role and very likely redirect some of its energies to North-South issues. All this will require analytical support in order to make an impact both in mobilizing the South and in influencing opinion in the North. The areas of debt and the evolving East-West relations are only examples which would naturally call for a South Secretariat and other centres in the South to serve as focal points for facilitating timely change.

Advancing on foundations of long-term development
The Report of the South Commission and other reports on certain aspects of the South[4] agree that development in the long term will not be sustainable unless the process is clearly seen to go well beyond conventional projects and programmes to address critical issues like the environment, science and technology, population dynamics and so on. These matters, including the central issue of economic co-operation and integration and the importance of addressing the gender dimensions of development, are so extensively discussed in the Report that it is not easy to add much that is new by way of broad framework. Only three brief points will, therefore, be made relating to the road ahead.

First, it is important to recognize that considerable analytical and interdisciplinary work is required – both at the national and intra-South levels -- before meaningful practical policies and measures can be put in place in respect of the environment, population, science and technology, and similar issues. Co-operative approaches are, therefore, clearly called for as the ability to handle the issues satisfactorily will ordinarily lie beyond the capacity of any one given national or regional institution.

Second, many issues under this umbrella are cross-sectoral . It would, therefore, be necessary to address them within broad frameworks, extending across the main sectors and identifying the technical and policy linkages. Also, it would follow that specific focal points – national and intra-South – would be required with respect to both analysis and advice, on the one hand, and management, on the other, in order to address these foundations of long-term development adequately.

Third, by any reasonable indications, the resources required for reversing environmental degradation, financing population programmes, etc. are considerable. The importance of an efficient national saving-investment process underlined in the Commission's Report is, therefore, restated here. But, realistically, these aspects of development call for the wider financial and technical support of the international community.

Pragmatism in creating new structures

In implementing the development strategies and agenda for the countries of the South, there would naturally be a need for creating new structures and institutions, both national and collective. A minimum of these is indicated in the Report of the South Commission – the most obvious of which is the South Secretariat. Carefully assessed demands for new structures must, of course, be met as much as possible. But, in the light of past experience with the creation of new institutions in the South, it is necessary to caution against the pressure to create new structures, given further the serious financial constraints facing many of the countries. In Africa, for instance, there has been a proliferation of institutions both at the national level and in the context of subregional groupings. Many of these are underfunded and poorly co-ordinated, hence inefficient in resource use. And, in spite of the caution advanced under the Lagos Plan of Action[5] – that no new multinational institutions should be created unless their creation has been thoroughly examined – the pressure to hurriedly create new institutions in Africa is still on.

It is, therefore, important to point out that greater pragmatism is required in moving ahead to mobilize resources and create new institutions and structures for implementing the wide-ranging development agenda proposed in the Report of the South Commission. Whether in moving on the national dimension of development (Chapter 3 of the Report) or in addressing the key functional areas relating to South-South co-operation (Chapter 4), every care should be taken in first exploiting the strengths and potentialities of existing institutions. Financial and human resources are severely limited in many of our countries, and the South can ill afford the frustrations of institutional underperformance or failure resulting from poorly conceived structures.

North-South Interactions: Constraints and Opportunities

The foregoing remarks on the Report of the Commission have been deliberately restricted to concerns relating to national development and

South-South co-operation. Yet, it is difficult to conclude these thoughts without saying a few words on the constraints and opportunities posed by North-South interactions. This is partly because, as was put by the Commission's Chairman, "the North is the holder of real power, and its actions do affect the South, [therefore] it has an overriding duty to help and not to hinder the South in its development efforts".[6]

Given that power of the North and the extensive and complex relations between North and South (discussed at some length in the Report), only three brief points will be made – assuming some supportive role on the part of the North. First, the impact of the various adjustment programmes being undertaken in many countries of the South will remain minimal (and could even become negative in social terms) unless the North adequately addresses the pressing issue of resource transfers. The three central dimensions in this regard are debt relief, concessional resource transfers and, ultimately, commercial and non-debt creating (private) flows. To be sure, positive action on all these also require continued and deepened domestic policy reforms.

Second, the North could significantly help national development efforts in the South by strengthening existing and creating new mechanisms to cushion reliably and predictably the weak economies of the South against external shocks of various sorts. For instance, in the case of Africa, the United Nations Programme of Action for African Economic Recovery and Development, 1986-1990 (endorsed by the international community in 1986), was largely derailed by an unforeseen loss in export revenues of the order of 50 billion US dollars over the Programme period (apart from the decline in net real resource flows).[7]

Third, given that improved international trading (exporting) is an aspect of strengthening national self-reliance, the North should show much greater willingness to open up markets particularly for processed and manufactured products from the South – reforming trade and agricultural policies in the North as well as equitably addressing and resolving the relevant issues under the Uruguay Round of trade negotiations. A more open trading system is advantageous to both North and South.

Conclusion

As the Commission's Report rightly points out, the countries of the South can do much to bring about change individually and collectively. The Report has contributed greatly to meeting this challenge by proposing what should be done and in what manner -- while situating the efforts of the South in the context of global constraints and opportunities.

The global context remains difficult, but the countries of the South must press on not only to improve their economies through structural change and competitive production and trading but also to work collectively for change in world arrangements – in trade, finance, technology and related areas. In this context it is only reasonable to count on the support and goodwill of some elements of the population in the North and to work collectively for greater influence on opinions in the North. Very likely the results will be limited and slow in the medium term.

There remains room for debating, modifying and enriching the development agenda proposed by the South Commission, but there is no question that the Commission has proposed a very welcome framework. The remarks in this short paper have been made with this conviction. The countries of the South should be able to make timely advances to improve the lot of their people by, among other things, enriching and modifying their strategic approaches to development management – by continuing the search for agents of socio-economic change, sharpening policy focal points, ensuring greater consistency between policies and instruments, enhancing capacity for timely change, advancing significantly in addressing the foundations of long-term development, and adopting greater pragmatism in creating new structures and institutions.

Notes

1. The views expressed in this paper are personal and may not necessarily reflect those of the African Development Bank. I am grateful to my colleagues Mr. M.G. Woldu, Dr. Q. Din and Dr. G. Kariisa for helpful comments.
2. Speech by Mwalimu Julius K. Nyerere, Chairman of the South Commission, to the United Nations Economic and Social Council (Geneva, 3 July 1991).
3. Statement by Mr. Babacar Ndiaye, President of the African Development Bank at the ECOSOC Panel Discussion on the South Commission Report (Geneva, July 1991).
4. See, for instance, in the case of Africa, African Development Bank, 1989.
5. Organization of African Unity, 1981.
6. Speech by Mwalimu Julius K. Nyerere, see note 2.
7. See United Nations, 1991.

Bibliography

African Development Bank
> *Africa and the African Development Bank: Current and Future Challenges (Report of the Committee of Ten)*, Abidjan, 1989.

Organization of African Unity
> *Lagos Plan of Action for the Economic Development of Africa, 1980-2000*, International Institute of Labour Studies, Geneva, 1981.

United Nations
> *Report of the Secretary-General of the United Nations on the Final Review and Appraisal of the Implementation of the United Nations Programme of Action for African Economic Recovery and Development, 1986-1990*, New York, September 1991.

32. MULTILATERAL COMPACTS SUPPORTING ECONOMIC REFORM

Arjun K. Sengupta

The South Commission Report talks about building up a "development consensus". If one looks at the situation in the countries of the North, the political and military upheavals they have gone through and the demands on their economic resources by all the conflicting claims, one would think that the most important need of the hour is that "development consensus". Together with that there must be a universal desire to reform the system of global governance. The way the world economy is running today, without proper management or co-ordination, without any set of generally accepted rules established through universal negotiations, and with individual nations responding to specific challenges in an ad hoc, unsystematic manner considering only the national or, at best, regional interests and ignoring the broader interdependence, there does not seem to be much hope for that development consensus to be built up. And even if, with a good deal of effort, some rudiments of that consensus can materialize, there is little chance of that reflected in practice, if the system of global governance does not change. It is time to look into this aspect of North-South relations and consider mechanisms which would be regarded by both the North and the South as capable of redressing the present situation in their common interest.

The effectiveness of any system of global governance would depend very much upon devising appropriate rules of the game that national governments are expected to play in an interdependent world economy. Those rules must be perceived by all the participants as conducive to improving their welfare. If there was an effective authority to enforce these rules, armed with instruments to dispense penalties and rewards, they could take the form of contracts, binding the countries. In the absence of such an authority in a world of sovereign states, however, these rules could hardly be much more than compacts, supported by solemn pledges and promises by the participants, but without any formal sanction. In the final analysis, the sanction behind any law or rule is the perception of the sacrifice of benefits that would follow from the disregard of those rules. The idea of multilateral compacts described in the following paragraphs is based on a similar approach to acceptable rules of behaviour. They would have clearly discernible benefits for all parties, which could be large enough to persuade them to honour all the commitments.

There has been a major transformation in the economic thinking and policy-making of most developing countries during the last few years. A "silent revolution", in the words of Michel Camdessus, the IMF Managing Director, is spreading through them. The old insular, regulated and restrictive régimes are giving way to market-oriented, liberalized and outward-looking economies. Most of them are carrying out their economic reforms under adjustment programmes, supported by the IMF, the World Bank and other international agencies. About 30 African countries are applying programmes sponsored by the IMF, which is supporting 20 other countries in various regions and is also conducting "dialogues" with nearly another 20 countries with a view to formulating policy reforms. That means more than two thirds of all developing countries are coming under the "Fund discipline", adopting policy packages conforming to the Fund conditionalities.

If these adjustment efforts succeed and the developing countries manage to introduce the intended economic reforms, the world economy will be radically transformed. The expanding markets of the developing countries will provide enormous scope for increased trade and an improved division of labour in the industrial countries, a sustained improvement in the productivity of resources and higher rates of return on investments. The prosperity of the developing countries achieved in a framework of free market competitiveness and open trade will in turn add to the prosperity of the industrial countries. The old unequal and antagonistic relationships between the industrial, metropolitan countries of Europe and North America and the commodity-producing, low-technology underdeveloped former colonies of Asia, Africa and Latin America, which have continued to characterize, in some form or other, the North-South economic relations will be replaced by a new relationship of genuine interdependence. Both the industrial and the developing countries have therefore a substantial stake in the success of these efforts.

The history of adjustment efforts of the developing countries is, however, replete with examples of failure. In a few cases, the failures have undoubtedly been caused by policy lapses of the adjusting countries. But in most others the programmes had to be given up in mid-course, well after the authorities had started implementing them in earnest, taking unpopular decisions and making hard choices. Attributing the failures in these cases to lapses on the part of the authorities in implementing the policies would be begging the question: Why could they not do what they had set out to do? Why did the pursuit of the policies prove increasingly difficult in the process of carrying out the adjustment programmes? Why did the authorities risk total isolation from the world economy by not meeting their commitments rather than sticking to the programme by all means?

Sometimes unforeseen developments pushed the programmes of adjustment off track, for example if they were not sufficiently flexible to deal with certain contingencies, or possibly the resources provided for coping with these contingencies were inadequate. The design of the programmes themselves might have been faulty, based on mis-specified models with wrong sequencing of policies and with little accounting for inflationary expectations. However, in most cases the social costs of adjustment proved so severe that the authorities had little choice but to suspend the programme. Exports did not increase as projected, debts were not reduced as expected, unemployment increased, real wages fell, and assistance did not materialize in the form or in the amounts expected or promised. Hence, the authorities were unable to implement their policies. But their task would have been much easier if there were some multilateral mechanisms such as compacts to support them if they persevered with their efforts of adjustment.

The idea of such multilateral compacts that developing countries have long been advocating follows from the guiding principles of the Bretton Woods institutions: symmetry, reciprocity and balanced obligations. The elimination of payments deficits in some countries would require the reduction of surpluses in others; and the effectiveness of a country's monetary and fiscal policies crucially depends on policies of other major countries. The interdependence of the different economies is now much closer than it was at the time of the Bretton Woods conference, and the success of the policies of any one country has become even more dependent on the complementary measures taken by others. But the mutuality of obligations implicit in the Bretton Woods agreement went beyond the technical requirements of economic interdependence. It was an extension of the co-operative spirit which motivated all the operations of the Bretton Woods institutions and which assumed that all member nations were equal and all accepted obligations, often at the cost of narrow national interests, to help each other to achieve the desired policy outcome.

Accordingly, the developing countries have argued that when some of them adopt radical adjustment programmes in consultation with the international agencies, the major industrial countries should also accept the obligation to provide the required assistance in cash, credit and market access in tandem with the implementation of those programmes. The Norwegian Foreign Minister Stoltenberg, at a 1989 OECD conference, extended this idea to "a system of development contracts" for financing medium- and long-term development plans "binding the recipient government and donors, banks and international organizations". For stabilization and structural adjustment programmes, the scope of the multilateral compacts could be more modest, based on an understanding between the major industrial countries, international agencies and the country implementing the programme. If that country pursued all the policies in good faith, the other parties would support it with the necessary policy and financial assistance. There would be a mechanism of consultation between the parties, monitoring the implementation of the programme and assessing the requirements of assistance. If the programme implementation faltered, or circumstances changed, the quantum of assistance might have to change. Similarly, if the level of assistance was not adequate, or if supporting policies could not compensate for that inadequacy, the design of the programmes or the phasing of their implementation might have to be altered.

The IMF tried out this flexible approach of multilateral compacts for the debt-ridden countries which were in arrears with the Fund. Once these countries adopted IMF-monitored adjustment programmes, support groups of the Group of Seven and the concerned donor countries, with other multilateral agencies, were to be formed to assist them. These support groups were to assume voluntarily the obligations of responding to the needs of the adjusting countries, providing help either by themselves or by mobilizing others. These experiments, however, have been somewhat halting. The countries in arrears were at the end of their tethers, with limited capacity for implementing the reforms. There was also the complicating factor that, according to their constitutional instruments, the international agencies were unable to assist these countries so long as they had not cleared their arrears.

In the case of normal adjustment programmes, however, this support group approach, based on multilateral compacts, would be assured of the effective support of the international community if they carried on with their efforts. If the circumstances changed, the consultations with the support group would allow them to modify their programmes. The flow of finances and the complementing policies of other countries would also be accommodating. In other words, the multilateral support group could review the performance of the adjusting countries, case by case, help in their difficulties and, with their supportive assistance, guide their persevering efforts. The performing countries would have every incentive to perform, and the laggards would have every reason to rise to the challenge of reform. The developing countries must, of course, be fully responsible for implementing the adjustment programmes. But their task would be much easier if there were those multilateral compacts to support them.

There are at least three areas where such multilateral compacts could be important. First, a support group could effectively help an adjusting country to deal with its indebtedness. The chances of success of Paris Club initiatives proposed by the group in the light of a country's adjustment efforts would be much greater than the usual schemes of across-the-board relief for official debts. Similarly, the different market-oriented schemes for reducing a country's commercial debt overhang would be greatly helped if they benefited from some official, even if partial, backing, guarantee or burden-sharing, organized by the support group.

Secondly, the adjusting countries must be assured of export markets. There are IMF-World Bank studies to show that because of protectionism in the industrial countries developing countries have lost in export earnings in recent years twice as much as they have received in development assistance. While the global campaign against protectionism must continue, the support groups could ensure at least for the adjusting countries adequate market access, if necessary through some preferential arrangements. The Generalized Scheme of Preferences (GSP) has by now had a fairly long history, preferences being granted unilaterally by the industrial countries to developing countries, without much uniformity. The European Community recently granted to selected Latin American countries GSP similar to those accorded to the African, Caribbean and Pacific (ACP) countries. It would be more justifiable to grant preferential access on similar terms to countries following adjustment programmes, a larger duty-free access, a higher ceiling to the quotas, or more liberal treatment under the Multi-Fibre Arrangement. The greatest danger for multilateral trade today comes from numerous non-tariff barriers (NTBs). The support groups could organize arrangements for at least withholding the NTBs against the adjusting countries, pending a total overhaul of the whole system of non-tariff barriers.

Thirdly, the design of adjustment programmes, the period over which they are to be effected, the deflationary impact on employment and living standards and the possibility of growth in output and capacity, all depend upon the amount of finance available to the adjusting countries. If adequate finance does not materialize, the programmes have to become tighter, the countries have to make greater sacrifices of current consumption, and prospects of growth and investment are reduced. Under the multilateral compacts the support groups of donors could assure the countries under-taking adjustment that if they stuck to the policies agreed upon, they would not be deprived of the finance necessary to execute the programmes.

A major advantage of this system of multilateral compacts would be that it could take account of most of the concerns of the donor community about safeguarding human and social development programmes in a country undergoing balance-of-payments and structural adjustment. The record of most of the countries applying stabilization and macro-economic adjustment programmes shows that, in the short or medium term, as a consequence of the compression of demand and of the reduction of expenditure, which are almost always the necessary ingredients of the programmes, the budgets of human and social development programmes are seriously shrunk. Where these budgets are not very tight and have unnecessary "fat", a pruning may actually improve the efficiency of all the operations covered by them. But the motivation in pruning these expenditures is seldom the need for improving efficiency. These are usually the easiest items to cut because the groups affected by such pruning are the weakest in the society, without an influential lobby to press for their cause.

Although the result of these cuts in the social and human development expenditures may be very detrimental for the country, they can be overlooked in the name of short-run expediency and the need for stringency in the overall budget expenditure. The support groups under the multilateral compacts could prevent the potential harm by demanding the protection of these expenditures in any review of the implementation of the adjustment programmes. By siding with the weakest groups on these issues they can ensure that what is good for the long-term health of the country is not sacrificed to the short-term requirements of expenditure compression. In some cases the support groups may have to mobilize additional funds to protect the social programmes. But, in general, it would be sufficient if the support groups worked out a proper distribution of expenditure cuts among the alternative claims on the budget.

As a matter of fact, in most of the adjustment programmes, especially under the IMF, the design of policies does not integrate promotion of human and social development in the policy reforms. It is, however, not very difficult to do, provided that the support group of donors is willing to press for their integration and assure the country of additional assistance if required and complementary policies when needed. Once such integration is achieved, and social and human development programmes are carried out in the framework of a general macro-economic adjustment, the cost-effectiveness of all human development assistance would be enhanced.

33. ACHIEVING SUSTAINABLE GLOBAL DEVELOPMENT

Maurice F. Strong

Environment, Development and Security

The scholarship and practical suggestions of many of the international independent commissions that have addressed the issues of development, security and the dichotomies between developing and industrialized nations have done much to raise awareness of these important issues. They demonstrate that in a climate of international co-operation the objective of sustainable development is attainable.

In 1980, the North-South Commission, led by Willy Brandt, presented its proposals for improving relations between industrial and developing countries, based on mutual interests and peaceful solidarity.[1] In the same year, Olof Palme founded his Independent Commission on Disarmament and Security, which discussed confidence-building measures and disarmament, and considered the security needs of the South. When the World Commission on Environment and Development, chaired by Gro Harlem Brundtland, produced its landmark report *Our Common Future* in 1987,[2] its main theme was the relationship between economic development and the environment. The Brundtland Commission produced a series of recommendations for integration of the environment and the economy which provided the primary basis for the decision to hold the United Nations Conference on Environment and Development.

The Challenge to the South stressed the responsibility of developing countries to ensure a better future for themselves, while recognizing the importance of a favourable international economic climate for development, and greater co-operation between North and South. It echoes the views of the Brundtland Commission that environment and development are two sides of the same coin. The major contribution of the South Commission has been to provide an explicitly developing-country focus on development issues, to recognize that the South can ill afford to copy the consumption patterns and lifestyles of affluent societies, and to see our common salvation in a mixture of North-South co-operation and regional co-operation among developing countries.

A unifying theme of all these commissions is that growing global interdependence needs now, as never before, a high level of international co-operation. In particular, a higher degree of assistance from the North will be necessary to enable the South to satisfy its development needs without threatening its, and the global, environment. I believe that we can draw some encouragement from history, which tells us that people and nations have always been willing to give priority to action for dealing with threats to their own security and to find the resources needed to meet these threats. As we approach the 21st century, we face new and unprecedented risks to the security of our planet as a viable and hospitable home for our species and other forms of life. Massive redeployment of existing resources, including a reduction of military expenditure, must now be undertaken to invest in measures for averting a security threat of another kind. The growing awareness of the threat to environmental security opens up the prospect of a new global partnership based on common interest and common need. The necessity of securing the co-operation of developing countries to ensure our common environmental security adds a new and compelling dimension to the moral and political rationale for increasing the flow of resources to them.

Differing Points of View in Industrialized and Developing Countries

The unprecedented increase in human numbers and activities since the industrial revolution, and particularly in this century, has given rise to a deterioration of the environment and depletion of natural resources that threaten the future of the planet.

The gross imbalance that has been created by the concentration of economic growth in the industrialized countries and population growth in the developing countries is at the centre of the current dilemma. Redressing this imbalance will be the key to the future security of our planet in environmental and economic as well as traditional security terms. This will require fundamental changes in both economic behaviour and international relations. Effecting these changes peacefully and co-operatively is, without doubt, the principal challenge of our time.

In this important undertaking, co-operation can only be based on common interests and needs, and, given the disparities between them, it should be no cause for surprise that the views of developing countries on the issues differ substantially from those of industrialized countries. Developing countries point out that the industrialized countries are largely responsible for the environmental risks created to date, and have been the main beneficiaries of the wealth that has accumulated through the processes of economic growth. They insist that they cannot divert resources required to meet the most immediate and fundamental needs of the people, to pay the additional costs of incorporating into their development policies and practices the measures needed to reduce major global risks.

Meanwhile, the industrialized nations have faced environmental problems of their own; problems which are, ironically, the result of the same processes that have produced their unparalleled levels of wealth and prosperity.

The preoccupation of industrialized countries with issues such as air and water pollution, and with long-term sustainability, may seem far removed from the day-to-day worry about survival of the poor in the developing world. How are such different concerns to be reconciled and how is remedial action to be translated into the active co-operation between nations that will be crucial in the transition to sustainable development?

As the views of our planet from space make clear, nature does not respect boundaries. The trans-boundary and systemic nature of environmental issues and the globalization of the economy are making global interdependence increasingly apparent. As *The Challenge to the South* points out, this interdependence means that all nations have a common cause to work together in dealing with the shared problems of environment and development that threaten the future of our planet.

The interrelatedness of the environment and development issues was central to both the Stockholm Conference on the Human Environment and to the report of the Brundtland Commission. The main challenge for the 1992 United Nations Conference on Environment and Development has been how to translate the principles of sustainable development from concept to action. Recognizing that environmental impacts are the result of our economic behaviour and can only be addressed effectively by changes in that behaviour, the task of the Conference has been to attempt to move the environment issue into the centre of economic policy and decision-making.

The Changes Inherent in the Transition to Sustainable Development

The changes to be made in economic life and international relations in order to effect the transition to sustainable development are fundamental in nature and will be extremely difficult to achieve. For they will entail changes in economic, energy, transport, industrial and urban policies which will be fundamental in nature and will have major impacts on the economic interests and competitiveness of nations and of industry as well as on the lives of people. This will require the full engagement and co-operation of business and industry as the primary agents for the conduct of economic affairs.

Similarly, the transition will require the active involvement of people and of the non-governmental organizations through which they act from the grassroots to the national and international levels. The lifestyles of the rich are the source of the primary risks to our common future. They are simply not sustainable. Those who enjoy these lifestyles are all "security risks". Their patterns of production and consumption have brought the whole human community to the threshold of risks to survival and well-being which rich and poor alike must share. In order to reduce the impacts on these thresholds and to make room for the growth of developing countries a transition is required to lifestyles that are less wasteful and indulgent, more modest in their use of resources and the pressures they exert on the environment. The shifts in culture and values which must provide the basis for this transition will impose challenging responsibilities on the educational system, and on the religious leaders, communicators and public figures who are the primary agents of change.

This will involve significant changes in lifestyles for both North and South. More people in the industrialized world will opt for lives of sophisticated modesty, and people of developing countries will receive greater support in their attempts to achieve livelihoods which do not undermine or destroy the environment and resource base on which their future livelihoods depend.

In all countries, the fiscal system has provided incentives and subsidies designed to achieve a wide variety of political and public policy objectives usually unrelated to environmental considerations, many of which have become deeply entrenched and difficult to change. Agricultural subsidies are a prime example. It is now realized that many of these, in addition to their economic cost and the distortions they create in the market economy, also provide incentives for environmentally unsound economic practices. Governments of North and South alike must therefore undertake an extensive review and reorientation of the system of incentives and penalties that motivate the economic behaviour of corporations and individuals to ensure that they provide positive incentives for environmentally sound and sustainable behaviour.

Sustainable development cannot be imposed by external pressures; it must be rooted in the culture, the values, the interests and the priorities of the people concerned. While the transition of the developing world to sustainability will require support from the industrialized countries, this must not provide a basis for external imposition of new conditions or constraints on development. Developing countries cannot be denied their right to grow, nor the right to choose their own pathways to growth. Nor should that right be constrained by new conditions on financial flows or trade imposed in the name of the environment.

Africa comprises more than three quarters of the countries which are classified by the United Nations as least developed and it contains one of the world's largest desert regions. Today it is experiencing the disastrous degradation of its lands and endowment of renewable resources, which is jeopardizing future productivity and posing an imminent danger to the livelihoods of its millions of inhabitants. In most of the least developed countries, the result is a serious and accelerating deterioration of the carrying capacity of the principal resource and ecological systems on which development and survival depend. The ever larger numbers of poor who are driven from the land to seek refuge in the crowded cities and towns add to the pressures on these equally vulnerable urban systems. Most cannot keep up with the need to provide safe water supplies, health services and job opportunities. Thus, for fragile economies already heavily burdened by debt, unfavourable terms of trade, dependency on external supplies of food and energy, and with inadequate infrastructure, institutional and professional capacities, ecological deterioration translates quickly into economic decline and human suffering. The great African famine of 1984 and 1985 was as much a product of the interaction between ecological breakdown and economic recession as it was of the extended period of drought that afflicted much of sub-Saharan Africa. The pattern could easily repeat itself.

Africans themselves have the responsibility for their own future and that future will depend primarily on their own efforts. But the nations of Africa must clearly have substantially increased international support, on a sustained and dependable basis, to enable them to build the stronger and more diversified economies they require to meet the needs and aspirations of their people, to effect the transition to sustainable development and to reduce their vulnerability to changes in the international economy. The response of the international community has not been sufficient. Despite some helpful moves towards debt reduction and improvements in the prices of some commodities, most African nations continue to suffer disproportionately from intolerable levels of debt, inadequate export earnings and insufficient external resource flows. At a time when special support for Africa has never been more necessary or deserved, one can only view with dismay the fact that Africa seems to have receded to the margins of the world's attention.

A Supportive International Economic Climate for the Developing World

The Brundtland Commission made a compelling case that, for the purpose of ensuring global environmental security, a substantial and sustained increase is required in the flow of financial resources to support poor countries which, although they find themselves at a different stage in their development process from the industrialized world, have every right to develop. This notion was echoed by the South Commission and incorporated into the resolution that provided the mandate for UNCED, which recognized that new and additional financial resources will have to be channelled to developing countries in order to ensure their full participation in global efforts for environmental protection.

The prevailing global economic conditions are not favourable to developing nations, which have in many respects become the victims rather than the beneficiaries of the recent globalization of the world economy. Interdependence has made their fragile economies highly vulnerable to changes in world economic conditions over which they have no control. It compels them to compete in an international market-place in which the principal sources of added value and comparative advantage are technology, capital, management and marketing skills and scientific knowledge. In all of these areas the developing countries are seriously handicapped. They are often forced to overexploit the natural resources on which their future and their development depend.

The South Commission recognized that the primary responsibility for the future of developing countries rests, of course, with them, and their success will depend largely on their own efforts. But they deserve and require an international system that lends strong support to these efforts. This includes substantially increased financial assistance, and much better access to markets, private investment and technology to enable them to build stronger and more diversified economies, to effect the transition to sustainable development and to reduce their vulnerability to changes in the international economy. They must be helped to break the vicious circle of ecological deterioration and economic decline and to adopt environmentally sound patterns of natural resource use and agricultural production. Industrialized countries must help developing countries to move away from the low value-added, low-technology production and exports that continue to widen the division in economic power between North and South. This can be done by providing them with better access to the world's markets and to energy-efficient and environmentally sound technologies on terms that they can afford, thereby enabling them to add value to the natural resources and commodities on which they presently depend for the bulk of their export earnings.

Finance

Priority must be accorded to the need to reverse the outflow of resources that has stifled the economic growth of the developing countries and to ensure that these countries have access on a long-term basis to the substantial additional resource flows they will need to revitalize their economic life and make the transition to environmentally sustainable development. Of critical importance in this is action to deal more fundamentally with the debt issue. Debt-for-nature swaps may be useful in addressing particular needs, but are marginal in their overall effect. The principle behind them may, however, serve as a basis for the kind of reduction in debt servicing charges that is essential to the revitalization of development.

There have been several proposals for the establishment of new global funds to deal with environmental and related development needs. The South Commission favoured the creation of a United Nations-administered Planet Protection Fund. Another proposal calls for the creation of a general "sourcing" fund, which would not in itself be operational in the investment and expenditure of the funds it would receive, but would rather dispense these through existing mechanisms such as the World Bank, UNDP and other existing funding organizations.

Technology

It is essential that developing countries improve their technological capacity. Today, technology is an indispensable ingredient of economic growth, and without economic growth, developing countries have inadequate capital to support environmental protection. Developing countries thus need access to the best environmentally sound and appropriate technologies. The cost of these can be a major constraint on their availability, but even more constraining is the lack of adequate institutional and professional capacities to choose and use them. In the past, technology transfer has frequently been supply-led, often taking little account of local tech-nologies and knowledge. The emphasis should now be on co-operation by means of which externally developed technologies can be adapted to local conditions and needs and integrated with traditional technologies and experience.

The South Commission makes it clear that the inevitable development of the South will take place at the expense of the environment, unless the accompanying industrialization and domestic growth are energy efficient. The use of energy-efficient and environmentally safe technologies should be encouraged, and the North should be urged to transfer them at a cost that the South can afford. Access to, and the application of, environmentally sound technologies, can contribute significantly to raising the productivity and sustainability of resources in such areas as agricultural production, energy efficiency, renewable energy generation and pollution control. In addition to these evident environmental advantages, such measures promote development.

Self-reliant and People-centred Development

While calling for efforts to improve North-South co-operation, the South Commission recommends that developing countries should focus on self-reliant and people-centred development. It states correctly that a lack of emphasis on self-reliance inevitably leads to the ultimate unsustainability of the growth process. The Commission stresses the importance of the benefits of greater co-operation among developing countries. Collective strength is sometimes considerably greater than the sum of its parts, whether in the field of research, training and capacity building, or in creating networks of information on technology.

Capacity Building

The South Commission recognizes the pressing need for developing countries to build their own human skills and institutional capabilities so that the pace of absorption and diffusion of science and technology can be accelerated. The key to self-reliance is the creation of a pool of indigenous talent that can adapt and innovate, in a world where knowledge is the primary basis of competition.

A new thrust for capacity building would mark a major contribution towards mobilizing the South towards greater co-operation among developing countries, as the South Commission advocates. The UNDP's Sustainable Development Initiative offers a promising framework for co-operative arrangements of this nature at the regional level. There was a strong regional component in the UNCED preparatory process, and the United Nations regional commissions are collaborating with the regional development banks, UNDP, UNEP and other regional and international organizations to design a sustainable development and technology support system. Such a system should bring a major new impetus and support for the strengthening of institutions and human development programmes in all the regions of the developing world. There must be a special emphasis on the least developed countries, and particularly sub-Saharan Africa.

In the final chapter of its Report, the Commission sets out some priority tasks for the developing world. These embrace the kind of fundamental change in society that will be necessary to effect the transition to sustainability of the North as much as of the South, including the pursuit of an effective population policy and the long-term commitment to rational and prudent management of the environment and its natural resources. They also focus on the immediate and urgent challenge for the societies in the South: the removal of extreme poverty, provision of food security and the satisfaction of basic human needs.

Notes

1.Brandt Commission, 1980.
2.Brundtland Commission, 1987.

Bibliography

Brandt Commission (Independent Commission on International Development Issues)
    North-South: A Programme for Survival, Pan Books, London, 1980.
Brundtland Commission
    Our Common Future, Oxford University Press, Oxford, 1987.

Index